THE WILD WOMAN OF CINCINNATI

THE WILD WOMAN OF CINCINNATI

GENDER AND POLITICS ON THE EVE OF THE CIVIL WAR

MICHAEL D. PIERSON

LOUISIANA STATE UNIVERSITY PRESS | BATON ROUGE

Published by Louisiana State University Press
lsupress.org

Copyright © 2023 by Louisiana State University Press
All rights reserved. Except in the case of brief quotations used in articles
or reviews, no part of this publication may be reproduced or transmitted
in any format or by any means without written permission
of Louisiana State University Press.

Designer: Michelle A. Neustrom
Typeface: Sentinel

Cover image taken from *The Wild Woman; or, The Wrecked Heart*,
by Alice Galon (Cincinnati: Barclay, 1857). From the Collection
of the Cincinnati & Hamilton County Public Library.

Portions of chapter 3 first appeared, in somewhat different form,
in "The Politics of Gender: The Wild Woman of Cincinnati Exhibit and
Partisan Loyalties in 1856," *Ohio Valley History* 22, no. 2 (Summer 2022):
34–55, and in "Four Feral Women and the Rise of Sectionalism in the 1850s,"
American Nineteenth Century History 23, no. 2 (2022): 165–84.

Library of Congress Cataloging-in-Publication Data

Names: Pierson, Michael D., author.
Title: The wild woman of Cincinnati : gender and politics on the eve of the
 Civil War / Michael D. Pierson.
Description: Baton Rouge : Louisiana State University Press, [2023] |
 Includes bibliographical references and index.
Identifiers: LCCN 2022030986 (print) | LCCN 2022030987 (ebook) | ISBN
 978-0-8071-7872-0 (cloth) | ISBN 978-0-8071-7948-2 (pdf) | ISBN 978-0-
 8071-7947-5 (epub)
Subjects: LCSH: Women—United States—Social conditions—19th century.
 | Sex role—United States—History—19th century. | Women—Legal status,
 laws, etc.—United States. | Mentally ill women—Legal status, laws, etc.—
 United States. | Human zoos—Ohio—Cincinnati—History—19th century. |
 Cincinnati (Ohio)—History. | United States—History—1815–1861.
Classification: LCC HQ1418 .P43 2023 (print) | LCC HQ1418 (ebook) | DDC
 305.420973/09034—dc23/eng/20230110
LC record available at https://lccn.loc.gov/2022030986
LC ebook record available at https://lccn.loc.gov/2022030987

FOR
Flora, Rebeka,
AND
John Daniel

CONTENTS

ACKNOWLEDGMENTS • ix

Introduction • 1

1

The Capture and Exhibition
of a Woman • 7

2

Closing the Show and Trying
a Woman in Court • 47

3

Sex-tionalism and the Gender Ideologies
of the Political Parties • 77

4

Women and Power
in Antebellum America • 111

NOTES • 137

BIBLIOGRAPHY • 159

INDEX • 173

ACKNOWLEDGMENTS

Historians and other scholars often do their writing in a kind of isolation, and that has been particularly true for me while working on this book during a pandemic. Still, I have benefited enormously from the help of many smart people who have generously aided the project. It is a pleasure to acknowledge the kind support of Holly M. Kent, Joshua A. Lynn, and Kathrinne Duffy, who heard me through an early stage of this work and made up a collegial panel at a Society for Historians of the Early American Republic conference.

My colleagues at the University of Massachusetts, Lowell have offered kind words and useful suggestions. I am especially thankful to be able to talk over matters large and small with Lisa Edwards, Christoph Strobel, and Christopher Carlsmith. Melissa Pennell offered early encouragement to pursue this topic.

I have also been the beneficiary of astute, detailed, and kind reader reports for the entire manuscript. This work is done anonymously, and so it cannot be acknowledged by name, but the care and effort that has gone into this work is a tribute to the readers' professionalism, scholarship, and generosity. They will see their contributions reflected in many places, even if their names cannot appear here. Thank you!

It is my pleasure to thank the editors and anonymous readers who have shaped shorter versions of my work on the Wild Woman as they have guided it through to publication. Thanks especially for the enthusiasm and support of Matthew Mason and Natalie Zacek at *American Nineteenth Century History* and David Stradling and Patrick Lewis at *Ohio Valley History*. Thank you also to their journals for permission to reprint material that is included here in somewhat modified form in chapter 3.

This will be my second book published through Louisiana State University Press. In both instances, it has been a pleasure to work with Editor in

Chief Rand Dotson. I am grateful for his calm and professional demeanor. He has found especially thorough and astute readers for both of my manuscripts. His efforts have made my work better than it otherwise would have been, and I am grateful to be able to work with him.

Thank you to Katrina Marshall, digital services supervisor at the Cincinnati and Hamilton County Public Library, for friendly and speedy help securing the images from a rare book in their collections.

Laura Barefield deserves the most thanks. Her love and kindnesses over the past few years of quasi-isolation and loss have been essential. This project, and so much more, would have been impossible without her scholarly talents and emotional support. And lastly, thanks to my nieces and nephew, Flora and Rebeka and John Daniel, for their good cheer and excellent company. I can hardly wait to see what they do next!

THE WILD WOMAN OF CINCINNATI

INTRODUCTION

People looking for entertainment in Cincinnati in 1856 had many options. Choices ranged from high culture to shows barely above the level of the tawdry. You could attend *Macbeth* at the National Theatre or hear the opera *Lucrezia Borgia* performed by Mademoiselle Teresa Parodi at Smith and Nixon's Hall.[1] If those seemed too cultured, you could see the Empire Minstrels or the Campbell Minstrels play at the Melodeon.[2] Even after the People's Theatre burned down in June, there were still many venues vying for customers. As historian Steven Ross writes, Cincinnatians in these years "organized an unprecedented number and variety of activities to provide themselves with fun, relaxation, and, occasionally, knowledge."[3]

The Wild Woman of Cincinnati was put on display in the hope that a feral woman could win a share of the city's leisure market. Competition was formidable. The show, however, had many features that commanded public attention. The Wild Woman herself was attractive and young, much like "the fascinating Josephine," star pupil of Madame Tourniaire's equestrian display across the Ohio River at Covington, Kentucky.[4] She had the strange allure of being so traumatized by past events that she could not speak, a display of misery and longstanding suffering that rivalled Alexis St. Martin, currently exhibiting a gunshot wound that allowed you to look into his stomach.[5] The Wild Woman show claimed deep roots in the western wilderness, as did the forty members of "the Kansas tribe," who were in Newport performing "a regular war-dance in the full costume of their tribe" every afternoon and evening.[6] Patrons were told that their admission fee would be used to help restore the distraught woman to health, a charitable mission that might compete philanthropically against the concert for the House of Refuge or the Daughters of Temperance Pic-Nic.[7] A powerful mix of sex,

• 1 •

frontier danger, tragedy, and charity, the Wild Woman show survived for at least six weeks in this crowded market.

The exhibition shared another aspect with many of its entertainment rivals. There are good reasons to think that the Wild Woman show was a fake. Sold to the public as a display of a recently captured woman who had lived for years as a solitary feral in the wilds of what was not yet Oklahoma, it was almost certainly a hoax. In this fakery she had company on Cincinnati's other stages in the spring and summer of 1856. "Mons. Adrien" lured in customers by claiming to be "one of the greatest living magicians." Magic shows are, at their core, elaborate displays of deception.[8] Minstrel shows, of course, were also fakes, featuring whites posing as African Americans. The "Kansas tribe" members were not performing a "war-dance" in any real sense. The all-pervasive atmosphere of hoax and fakery was so strong that "humbug" was a watchword of the culture. As the advertisement for a patent medicine that cured twenty-two ailments, from cholera and dysentery to chapped hands and insect bites, boasted, it was "No Humbug—Try It."[9] A recent history of US currency in this era is called *A Nation of Counterfeiters*.[10] A discerning person looking for entertainment in Cincinnati might well agree.

The Wild Woman fit snugly into another entertainment context as well. There were many dozens of people put on display in the United States in the pre–Civil War decades. It was a common enough occurrence that one scholar has coined a term for the trend: the "human zoo."[11] The Wild Woman show was one such exhibit. It involved a cast of three people. Its modest scale makes it easier to understand, for it was a human-zoo show at its most basic. By analyzing this production in detail, we can understand the nuances in people's thoughts and actions when they were confronted with strangeness, sexuality, misery, and opportunity. To slow down and consider the choices attendees made about what to think and say about the Wild Woman, and the actions they took and did not take, is to put antebellum America's assumptions about gender and race under a particular kind of microscope. By stopping to think about one incident, we can get a firmer hold on very large questions. How different were the North and the South on the eve of the Civil War? What role did gender ideologies play in determining people's political loyalties? How much power did women have in the United States in 1856?

A detailed examination of the Wild Woman show reveals a disturbing truth about the writing of history: the limits of what we can know with certainty about the past, even if it is less than two hundred years ago. There is much that we do not know about the Wild Woman. For one, we do not even know her name, which, perhaps, is not too surprising since she never spoke. But it is perhaps more indicative of the historical confusion and silences surrounding this human-zoo show that we cannot even be sure of the name of its spokesperson. I have chosen to call him Northcott, but his name is also given with equal authority in other places as Northco, Northcoat, Norcott, and Northcote. Sticking with Northcott admittedly is an arbitrary decision and probably (given the odds) an inaccurate one. The omissions in the historical record mean that I have often resorted to educated guesswork; these guesses are always indicated by words such as "probably" or "likely." But for all of the gaps in the historical record, it is also true that what we know about the Wild Woman and the people who surrounded her is fascinating.

The brief outlines of the exhibit's history can be told quickly. Americans first learned about the Wild Woman of Cincinnati in late May 1856, when the story broke across the nation's newspapers. She had arrived in the city in the custody of a man known as Captain J. W. C. Northcott. Northcott claimed to have caught her, living as a feral, in the borderlands between Texas and the Comanche nation. He told his story first while traveling with the Wild Woman to Cincinnati, then again to the *Cincinnati Commercial* once they arrived in the Queen City. In this first stage of the show's history, reporters met Northcott, the Wild Woman, and a female attendant, and they described the Wild Woman in vivid, voyeuristic language.

As described by reporters, the Wild Woman was "a tall, young, white girl, graceful in her movements, and wearing the wild expression of a maniac."[12] She could not speak and never smiled. Nonetheless, she bore "in her visage a glow of intelligence." She had dark brown hair, "her complexion was fair, even delicate, and her features decidedly handsome. Her mouth is small and finely formed, her lips thin and red, but tightly compressed, and her teeth even and white."[13] Even in this abbreviated retelling of the "exhibit," inconsistencies and questions arise. How did the reporter know what her teeth looked like if her lips were held tightly together? Did he pry open her mouth as if she were an enslaved person on an auction block? Did he take Northcott's word for it? How did her face convey "intelligence" when she did not speak? The men who described this silent woman projected many of their own assumptions about women and femininity onto the Wild Woman, a blank screen ready to reflect whatever they wanted to see. In the process, they revealed far more about their own ideas and desires regarding women than they did about the actual woman standing before them.

Perhaps it is not surprising, given that dynamic, that almost every newspaperman brought an element of sexual suggestion to his descriptions of her. In doing so, each followed the lead of the people who staged the show. The initial *Cincinnati Commercial* story includes a sentence so salacious that some editors took it out when they reprinted the article: "We saw a tall, gracefully formed, young white girl, scantily but neatly clad standing with a stout rope about her waist and attached to a bed post."[14] Northcott's capture narrative reveled in fantasies of male mastery. He claimed to have lassoed her and then wrestled her to the ground, despite her screams and blows, all while she was wearing only skins tied together with "grasses" and "bits of leather."[15] Later, her attendant said that the Wild Woman only drank from a cup placed on the floor and she was "on all fours."[16]

The Wild Woman was placed on exhibit at twenty-five cents per visitor for almost two months. In early July, the police broke up the show, and Northcott fled, never to be seen again. The Wild Woman ended up before the probate court, which was empowered to determine people's sanity and whether they would be committed to an asylum. The court heard testimony from eleven doctors as to whether she was a true feral, an insane victim of Northcott's cruel greed, or a con artist feigning her symptoms. The doctors split in their diagnoses, and the judge ruled that, "although this whole matter might be a humbug, he would not at present dismiss this 'wild woman,' but would send her to the Lunatic Asylum."[17] About one month into her stay at the Southern Ohio Lunatic Asylum in Dayton, a Shreveport newspaper claimed to have learned that the show was a hoax perpetrated by local residents Joe Williams and Ann Eliza Paul, his mistress. This story was reprinted widely in August. Meanwhile, the Wild Woman, still in the asylum, appeared to regain her speech, her sanity, and her real identity—which was not Ann Eliza Paul of Shreveport—and was released on September 18. After pledging that she would go back to her family in Texas, she disappears from the historical record, like Northcott and her attendant before her, bringing the whole episode to a close.

This book is organized in a loosely chronological fashion. Chapter 1 examines the Wild Woman show as it burst on to the scene locally and nationally, paying particular attention to why it was successful. The first element of its success was the story told by Captain Northcott about how he had found, battled, and mastered the feral woman he now had with him. Almost certainly made up in its entirety, his story was tailored to appeal to antebellum Cincinnatians, especially the white men who would make up most of the show's potential market. The other key ingredient of the show's success was the appearance and behavior of the Wild Woman herself. The Wild Woman's looks and alert, emotionally laden actions kept many Cincinnatians guessing about the truthfulness of Northcott's tale. Given the unlikely nature of what he said about her past, her stage presence (either entirely faked by a con artist or the natural behavior of a traumatized young woman) must have been considerable.

Chapter 2 chronicles the downfall of the Wild Woman exhibit and analyzes how and why the show was terminated by the local government. After many weeks of public display, the Wild Woman had found erstwhile allies among the city's reformist women, who saw her exhibition at the end of a rope as exploitive and damaging. The local women mobilized the government to force an end to the coerced exhibition of a woman they believed to need care, not gawkers. This occurred in July 1856, when police broke up the production and took the Wild Woman and her female attendant into custody, pending an appearance in probate court the next day. The gendered diagnosis upon which the reformist women, Judge John Burgoyne of the probate court, and the Cincinnati medical establishment agreed contained its own implications. While the court's decision liberated the Wild Woman from her rope and exhibit hall, it also wrapped her up in a different identity and dispatched her to confinement in the asylum for care. Soon after, all three of the principal figures of the show would disappear into the vast sea of American fluidity.

An analysis of the Wild Woman episode in chapter 3 shows how people in different political parties and sections of the country reacted to the fact that a white woman was on public display while tied to her bed and unable to speak. Political parties disagreed about the meanings of the show and even about the nature of women. Democrats tended to see the Wild Woman as an unscrupulous and sexualized con artist, while Republicans consistently portrayed her as a virtuous victim of male cruelty. While political historians have found many factors explaining why Americans favored one political party over another, there is no scholarly consensus on the relative importance of policy debates, constitutional theories, ethnic and religious differences, or other cultural factors such as region of origin or family history. The fact that newspaper editors aligned with the Republican, Democratic, or Know Nothing Party had different reactions to the Wild Woman tells us that partisan identity was rooted in part on what people thought about the sexes and their proper places in society. The different gender ideologies of the northern Republican Party and the more southern focused Democrats suggest a growing cultural division between North and South. Even though the current historiographic tendency is to find few differences between the North and the South, the Wild Woman exhibit suggests that while some northerners agreed with southerners on how to understand and enjoy the show, there were many others who were upset by it. While inherently a cultural event, the Wild Woman episode has important lessons to teach us about American party politics and sectional cultures on the eve of the Civil War. Political parties and regions whose gender ideologies diverge strongly can find themselves at war with one another more easily than when they agree on such matters.

The final chapter also tackles a large question for historians: how much power did women exercise in the patriarchal society of antebellum America? The United States was deeply patriarchal in law and politics at this time; men barred women from access to the ballot, elected office, political conventions, and juries. Men also exercised near monopolies on the most lucrative professional careers. As oppressive as those restrictions were, however, historians have uncovered evidence that women gained personal and social power in these decades as educators, writers, social reformers, religious activists, and political partisans. But to what extent did these empowered women shape the events around the Wild Woman, a woman apparently very much in need of assistance?

The first three chapters show men staring at the Wild Woman and trying to figure out what she, a silent woman, meant. The final chapter changes perspective to try to see the world from her point of view. While we know far too little about her to know what she saw with her famously big eyes, we can empower her memory by imagining several different ways that she might have experienced her own exhibition. By doing so, we explore what it means to be on exhibit, to feel the full force of American patriarchy and its consequences for the women who had to live in it. Exhibitions of human beings were, and are, about power. By learning about the Wild Woman, we perhaps may feel the extent to which American women have experienced powerlessness in certain times and places, especially when it mattered most.

1

THE CAPTURE AND EXHIBITION OF A WOMAN

The Wild Woman show claimed to give people the opportunity to see what a woman would be like if she had lived alone in the wilderness, apart from all civilization. While looking at the young woman, visitors also met the two people who appeared to run the show. A female attendant, Ann Walters, sat with the Wild Woman and probably talked about her habits and tastes. Captain J. W. C. Northcott would retell the history of his pursuit and capture of the feral woman to paying customers. Analyzing the story Northcott told of his hunt and what he presented to the spectators of the exhibition is important to understanding what drew antebellum Americans to the show.

Working from the premise that the Wild Woman show was a humbug, the choices its creators made as they designed it reveal their expectations of the potential audience. Why did they invent the particular tale that Northcott gave to editors and visitors? They crafted a tale that blended sensationalism with charitable intent and intellectual curiosity in an attempt to bring in a wide audience while also protecting the show from charges of sexual impropriety. In doing so, they wrote a story that highlighted racial concerns and male mastery in ways that appealed to white men.

In considering the performance given by the Wild Woman herself, we do not know if she was an actor who created and played her role consciously or was a traumatized or disabled woman who was involuntarily used by Northcott and Walters. If she was a fully consenting performer, she could have been the driving force behind the entire exhibition. Although Northcott appeared to be in charge of the show, and certainly that was how every observer at the time understood the exhibition, we should be open to the idea that the Wild Woman, or even Walters, may have been its main creator and chief tactician. In that case, placing Northcott in the most important speaking role as hunter and exhibitor would be a decision that catered to the audience's preconceived ideas of who should be in charge. Regardless of who created or wrote the show, it was the Wild Woman whose performance would make or break the enterprise.

The show, after all, seems to have been a financial success. While we lack records regarding its ticket sales, the Wild Woman exhibition was profitable enough to stay open for at least six weeks before there was talk about moving to another city. It opened in late May and was shuttered on the verge of its departure from Cincinnati in mid-July.[1] We also know that it could afford a ticket collector, even if we only know of his presence because a janitor reportedly saw him talking and laughing with the supposedly speechless Wild Woman. Six weeks or more was a good run, the show staying longer in one city than earlier human-zoo attractions such as Barnum's Joice Heth, Captain Morrell's South Sea "cannibals," or Sam Patch, the waterfall jumper near Niagara Falls. Extremely popular shows might stay longer in bigger cities, especially New York, but Cincinnati had only 161,000 residents by 1860. Overhead on rented rooms for living and for the performances would have been substantial, but there was never any talk that Northcott left behind unpaid bills, even after he had fled and people had largely turned against him.

While the longevity of Northcott's stay in Cincinnati points toward his production's profitability, there are unexplained elements to its run. The Wild Woman show appeared in at least three different venues, all within a few blocks of one another. On June 24, one could see the Wild Woman at 55 West Fifth Street.[2] One week later, she was displayed at the southeast corner of Fourth and Vine Streets, "next door to Porter's Gallery."[3] She moved on from there very quickly. Next, a story covering her trial placed the exhibit at Bacon's Building on the northwest corner of Sixth and Walnut Streets.[4] Northcott, in other words, moved his show at least twice, not counting the United States Hotel, where he had first shown the Wild Woman to the editor of the *Cincinnati Commercial*.

Why would Northcott have moved from one venue to another? Since all of the exhibit spaces were within a few blocks of one another, it seems unlikely that the moves were calculated to open up new markets. One possibility is that he may have taken the Wild Woman on the road for brief stretches of time over the course of June and the first half of July. Northcott ran an ad in the *Cincinnati Daily Gazette* on July 8 announcing that he had "returned to the city with the Wild Woman, [and] will hold exhibits for a few days prior to her departure to the East."[5] We do not know where he had taken the Wild Woman in the intervening days or why. Did the performers, especially the Wild Woman, need a rest? Had she become unmanageable? Did they play small venues in the region? Regardless, if they did this more than once, it would explain the show moving from one venue to another in the city.

Nearing the end of its run in Cincinnati, the production gave no outward signs of commercial weakness. Even on July 8, the show stayed open eleven hours a day, from 9 A.M. to noon and from 2 P.M. to 10 P.M. Nor were ticket prices discounted; adults still paid a quarter to get in and children a dime.[6]

Northcott enjoyed a uniquely powerful position in the world of the Wild Woman show. He was the official storyteller. His words would shape how people thought about the Wild Woman both before they arrived at the exhibit and, since he probably attended her public hours, when they watched her. He may not have invented the story or written the final draft, but it was his role to sell it to editors and customers. While Walters also probably talked with spectators, Northcott was the public face of the show during these weeks. His version of events is our natural starting point.

CAPTAIN NORTHCOTT'S STORY AND THE HOAX TRADITION

Read today, it seems almost certain that nothing in Northcott's story could possibly have been true. Some may disagree with that conclusion, but inconsistencies in the story and its presentation eventually convinced almost all Cincinnatians that the show was a hoax. In addition to his tale's overall improbability, Northcott's exhibition bears too many similarities to classic pre–Civil War hoaxes to be seen as anything but a clever reworking of that tradition.

A hoax in antebellum America was a particular form of entertainment. P. T. Barnum was an early (but not the first) practitioner, and he has left the most insightful description of how it worked. In a hoax, he wrote, a person put on display something that the public would want to see but that they might reasonably think was a fake. It then became a battle of wits between the exhibiter and the paying customers to see if the showman could convince his audience that the display was genuine. The showman won if he could keep up the illusion of authenticity long enough for the public to feel that it had gotten its money's worth while trying to figure things out. Barnum claimed, probably rightly, that people felt no animosity toward the exhibiter of a fraud as long as they had been entertained long enough to have a pleasant afternoon or evening on the town.[7]

In Barnum's eyes, the best hoaxes were ones that stretched this battle of wits between showman and customer over three distinct visits. A person would be enticed to visit the first time because of the showman's advertising campaign, which trumpeted the show's authenticity. Doubts, however, would inevitably creep in either during the visitor's initial examination or as society and the media debated and discussed the exhibition. Ideally, Barnum wrote, this would prompt a second visit that might well fuel the customer's doubt. In a perfect world, this would cause a third trip to the show, during which the patron would try to figure out how the deception was perpetrated. As one historian has written, it was an "implicit competition between patron and promoter, each one seeking to outwit the other in a game of deception and exposure."[8] Unspoken by Barnum was the fact that he would also have received the price of admission three times from a single patron—a successful hoax, indeed.

A quick look at Barnum's first hoax reveals the ways this worked in practice as well as how it may have served as a prototype for Northcott's Wild Woman show. After experimenting with a variety of careers as a young man, Barnum hit upon the idea of displaying Joice Heth to the public in 1831. Heth was an aged woman who he claimed was 161 years old and the enslaved nurse who had taken care of the very young George Washington. After a fashion, Barnum had papers to prove this. He was not the first person to have come up with this idea; he had bought Heth from someone who had already been charging people to see Washington's nurse, a role she could only have had if she was fantastically old. Barnum, however, did a better job of promoting his version of the show, and it did well financially. For her part, Heth played the part convincingly, even though her participation was involuntary and coerced. Scholar Benjamin Reiss writes persuasively about the physical threats and violence that Barnum would have used to dictate her active participation, noting that the showman was her owner and an experienced slaveholder with few scruples about abusing his human property. This abuse could have happened even though the exhibition mostly toured in northern states. Only rarely, particularly in Rhode Island, did questions of slavery and Barnum's ownership of Heth jeopardize the tour's financial success.[9] Acknowledging the Heth exhibit as a possible template for understanding the Wild Woman show foregrounds the grave moral concerns about coercion and abuse-of-power imbalances that marked so many human-zoo events.

Did people believe that they were actually going to see a woman who was both 161 years old *and* the nurse of George Washington? It seems hard to believe that so many could be so gullible. But Barnum had some things going for him, even looking beyond Heth's talents as an actor. Perhaps most importantly, he had announcements and editorials in newspapers vouching for his show's possible truth. Check it out, these editors urged, and decide for yourself. That was all Barnum could hope for; as he noted, the best customer was one who visited several times to decide about a show's authenticity. In 1831, few people thought that editors were influenced by the advertising dollars given to their newspapers by exhibiters like Barnum. Even fewer considered the chance that something more like actual bribes might have been paid, though these do seem to have changed hands. Racism no doubt played a part in creating audience credulity as well; with many Americans convinced that Africans differed from Europeans in significant ways, why would it be impossible that Heth had celebrated her 161st birthday? Here, we might note that Susie King Taylor, a self-emancipated Union army nurse, began her autobiography with, "My great-great-grandmother was 120 years old when she died."[10] She made this statement in 1902, and there is no reason to think that Taylor fatally damaged her credibility by doing so. So, it is likely that people in 1831 went to the Heth exhibit thinking that they might see and even touch a woman who had held the infant Washington. The similarities between Barnum's hoax and Northcott's Wild Woman show will be readily apparent.

Perhaps the most obvious parallel between the showmen's behavior was their concerted work to guarantee press coverage. Northcott started cultivating media attention even before he and the Wild Woman arrived in Cincinnati. Prior to the show's opening, he had arranged for the *Cincinnati Commercial* to run a story about his feral woman. We cannot know if he paid for this coverage, but it was everything a showman might have wanted. Northcott's relationship with other papers in the city suggests that money bought media attention. Throughout the show's run in Cincinnati, there was a correlation between when newspapers ran editorials plugging the production and the appearance of advertising for it. For example, the *Cincinnati Daily Times,* which ignored the Wild Woman for a month, ran a favorable report about it on June 26. The editor admitted that he had "been inclined to consider the exhibition a humbug, but after investigation we are of a different opinion." Northcott then placed ads in the *Times* for June 26 and July 5, 7, and 8. Much the same thing happened at the *Cincinnati Daily Gazette*, which first ran an editorial about the show on June 30—again, many weeks after the show had opened. While it gave only a lukewarm report, the write-up was still publicity, and it gave Northcott some space in the story to refute his (by then) numerous critics. On July 3, the *Gazette* was listing the show in its City News space under the heading "Amusements, &c., To-Day." By July 8, Northcott's paid ad ran in the *Gazette* in a big, bold font.[11]

The newspaper coverage generated by Northcott, shaped by his money, provides historians with the most detailed accounts we have of the Wild Woman and the presentation staged around her. Thus, the limitations of the extant sources force us to look at the Wild Woman through Northcott's eyes. But before we overhear Northcott talking to his first newsman, we need to imagine the moment when someone first thought about turning a woman they knew as a nonferal person into an exhibit in the human-zoo phenomenon that captivated antebellum America. How did someone think of this? What triggered that moment of (possibly very cruel) inspiration? Was the show the brainchild of Northcott or of Ann Walters, soon to be known as the Wild Woman's attendant? Or was the originator actually the woman who became "wild"? Did she at some point tell her friends that she could act like a feral person, perhaps even offering a demonstration before mapping out how it could be made to pay?

Whoever thought of the scenario first, it was a bit of genius. The idea of feral people had a long history in Western Europe at the time, and people in the young United States inherited this fascination. Americans had heard reports of feral women and wild men throughout the decades before 1856, and the stories had commanded media attention. It is therefore likely that the show's inventors were familiar with such accounts. Still, it was a notable creative leap to go from knowing about the idea of wild humans to pretending to have caught one—to invent a capture narrative, rehearse it, test it for holes, and realize that you know a woman who could act (or be misunderstood) as a feral. The staging was of very questionable morality or even cruelty, though the degree of moral error depends on the extent of the woman's ability to grant informed consent to the enterprise. That is a question still very much without an answer.

We do not really know how old Northcott or the two women were in 1856. No reporter ever seems to have described him in detail, so obsessed were they with looking at the young Wild Woman. Since we do not know the age of either Walters or Northcott, we do not know how far back their cultural memories would have reached. But most of the men who looked at the Wild Woman would have been alive during at least four nationally known "wild woman" episodes. All four occurred in the 1840s—one in 1843, two in 1845, and one that began in 1848 and ended in 1854. Of these, two had their start in the Southwest, where the show's principals may have lived prior to their arrival in Cincinnati. It is intriguing to note that the episode that took six years to fully run its course, culminating less than two years before the Wild Woman took the stage, transpired where the show's participants lived—at least according to their own accounts.

It seems certain, then, that the originators had some familiarity with the traditional details of wild-woman stories. If they were from the Southwest, they would have lived where the stories filled the cultural air; even if they came from elsewhere, the news enjoyed a national appeal and circulation. Using three digitized newspaper databases to locate and chart wild woman accounts (the Library of Congress's Chronicling America; the Readex Corporation's Early American Newspapers; and the American Antiquarian Society's Historical Periodicals Collection, Series 4), we can find feral-woman stories copied from newspaper to newspaper, usually either with few alterations or as brief summaries of events. For example, the 1843 case (discussed in chapter 2) was reproduced in at least ten newspapers, ranging from Augusta, Maine, to Pensacola, Florida.[12] An 1845 story from the Southwest, which seems to have begun in a newspaper in Shreveport, Louisiana, called the *Caddo Gazette,* ran in at least ten other newspapers.[13] While a less bizarre story with fewer details from Maryland in 1845 appeared in only four papers from Baltimore to New York City, spotting a feral woman was clearly big news.[14] Northcott and his allies noticed this and moved to capitalize on the American fascination with women living alone in the wild. That earlier attention had been established with nothing more than reports of occasional fleeting glimpses, odd footprints, or a strange campsite. The inventors of the Wild Woman show must have believed that the reaction to the idea that one had been caught and could be seen would be even bigger—and more profitable.

NORTHCOTT: CAPTURING THE WILD WOMAN

As the show's public face, Northcott assumed the responsibility of telling the story of how the feral woman came to be under his control. While there are many things we do not know about the Wild Woman exhibition, we know the story that he told about her capture. This comes to us first from the show's emergence in public sight and then again from its end, with almost no alterations and only a few additions. It tells us how antebellum Americans thought about men and women, whites and Native Americans, and how the power structures of the society were enacted and reinforced.

Once we assume that the story of the Wild Woman's capture was an invention, we can realize that the show's scriptwriters could have created any number of different plots explaining how a feral woman had come into Northcott's possession. For example, they chose not to have her surrender herself to him at his farm or ranch. They did not have her welcome him as a fellow human the moment she saw him. Instead, they spun a tale about her fierce resistance to him when he arrived. Their goal in telling the story this way would have been to make the exhibit as intriguing and popular as possible. To do this, they invented plot elements with appeal to both sensation seekers and scholars, lustful men and philanthropists. Their choices about what to include tell us what they thought people would want to see. The resulting show leaned hard toward the prejudices, interests, and cultural needs of its main prospective market: white men. The origin story Northcott told them offered reassurances that the unequal race and sex hierarchies that they enjoyed were both justifiable and safe from any challenges from the people below them. The script offers firm evidence with which to analyze the ideological underpinnings of antebellum American society.

The Wild Woman first appeared in an Indianapolis newspaper, the *Weekly Indiana State Sentinel*. It introduced the story through the correspondence of the "clerk of the boat" on which she was traveling, the *Hickman*. The clerk had apparently taken it upon himself to alert the editor that his boat had a feral woman on board, perhaps as part of a regular arrangement he had with the editor. But it seems more likely that the clerk wrote because Northcott offered him a reward for helping spread the word about his attraction. Regardless of his motives for writing, the man offered a condensed one-paragraph version of Northcott's story. We could think of the clerk's tale as a promotional trailer for the Wild Woman show.

One of the most interesting aspects of the letter is the emphasis it puts on Northcott's capture of the Wild Woman. Six of the clerk's nine sentences describe the hunting and capture of the woman, while the rest hint at her appearance and demeanor.[15] This seems a bit strange since, ordinarily, one would think that the woman herself would be at the center of the public's attention. Knowing what she was like and how she was dealing with captivity would seem to be the most intriguing topics. But the clerk, or Northcott operating behind the scenes, must have thought that her capture would be more interesting than a description of what living as a feral for years would do to a person. This focus on her capture would continue to be a prominent feature in all of the Wild Woman media coverage, and it alerts us to how ideologically rewarding the male victory in a literal battle of the sexes was to men. The story was as much about male victory over women in hand-to-hand combat as it was about the woman on display. In an unexpected reversal, the Wild Woman show was about men and their social position as much as it was about her.

The Indiana paper's paragraph was only a teaser for the main promotional story, which appeared in the *Cincinnati Commercial* a few days later. This much longer version in the *Commercial* described the editor's visit with Northcott, the Wild Woman, and her attendant at the United States Hotel in Cincinnati. It continued the clerk's fascination with Northcott's capture of the Wild Woman but now included considerable detail about the captive herself. The editor began with a sentence that called Northcott "her captor" and talked of being allowed to go "into a room where she is a prisoner."[16] This foregrounding of her lack of freedom was followed by a lengthy description of the Wild Woman. About midway through the story, however, the editor breaks up his piece with a subheadline: "STORY OF HER CAPTURE." This section continues for about half of the article's total length. Clearly, both Northcott and the editor thought that his capture narrative needed to be told and would command people's attention. Historian James Cook writes that this era's frauds and hoaxes "always involved at least a modicum of narrative—an entertaining story that delivered the truth."[17] In the case of the Wild Woman, the story took on added significance in light of the exhibit's inability to tell any tale for herself. Thus, we need to read the story for ourselves and ask why it would have appealed to enough people to keep the show afloat for a long run.

The hunting of the Wild Woman began, Northcott said, in the spring of 1855. Almost immediately, he filled his tale with details, presumably in the spirit of W. S. Gilbert, who joked in the *Mikado* about adding in "merely corroborative detail, intended to give artistic verisimilitude to an otherwise bald and unconvincing narrative."[18] Northcott claimed to have set out from Texas with eight other men on an arduous journey of three hundred miles into what is now Oklahoma. Their goal, he said, was to find gold along the banks of the False Wachita River, which was the name of a real river (now called the Washita).

It is tempting to think that this opening scenario was Northcott amusing himself and his more astute patrons by immediately setting up the tale as the pursuit of gold by going somewhere with a name including "False." He was telling falsehoods, in other words, to get people's money. Such playfulness would not be out of keeping with hoaxes; Mark Twain would write long, untrue, and bloody stories for his Nevada newspaper that he called "hoaxes." Twain would always insert into these stories factual bits that he felt would—or at least should—alert quick-minded readers that everything that followed in the column was untrue. But that was in Nevada in 1863 and 1864, and it is hard to say if Northcott could afford to add any additional skepticism to what his presentation would already incur.[19]

In any event, Northcott's gold-mining party rode toward what he called "Comanche territory" until, one night in March, he saw the Wild Woman for the first time. After initially assuming she was an Indian, he soon "saw by moonlight that it was no Indian, but a young white woman dressed in a robe of skins." As the *Cincinnati Commercial*'s editor wrote, Northcott "was amazed beyond conception" by this realization.[20] What was this white woman doing in the wilderness three hundred miles from Texas?

In Northcott's story, even his fellow gold prospectors refused to believe him. Unable to convince them to stay and pursue the woman, Northcott was forced to return to Texas. Always, he used words like "pursue" and "catch"; at no point, apparently, did he say he wanted to "help" her.

Northcott told the editor that he had remained fixated on the Wild Woman even after returning to Texas. A year later, he said, the moonlit encounter still haunted him. Early in 1856, he organized an expedition of six "hardy fellows to accompany him . . . on a hunt after the wild woman." All but one of the other men fell by the wayside as they journeyed north toward her territory. By the time Northcott and his remaining colleague reached the spot where he had seen her, it was March 1856. (The show would open in Cincinnati at the end of May, giving him at most three months to catch, extricate, and transport the woman to Ohio; the March date was the last specific chronological note he would provide, though we know that his steamer, the *Hickman,* left Little Rock, Arkansas, on May 10, 1856.)[21] Apparently quite skilled as a backwoodsman, Northcott located her "nest" after having spent a year away from the spot. It was, he said, "a kind of den, a little cave, or a long and narrow aperture among the rocks."[22] Having found her lair, Northcott waited outside it for two days and nights. One of his story's themes was that nothing in this venture happened easily. He had gained possession of the Wild Woman by tenacity, endurance, and skill.

Northcott's account now gets harder to figure out, even though, on the surface, it seems straightforward enough. It turns out that the woman was inside her cave and that "she came forth" after Northcott's two-day wait. She then disappeared into the landscape. The *Cincinnati Commercial*'s editor narrated what happened next, starting with an unusual admission of fear from Northcott: "He says that he had been afraid to enter the den, and that now his first care was to stop up the mouth of [the cave] and wait for her to come back. After a few hours she returned, and took alarm on observing that her door in the rocks was closed against her. He had two dogs which he set upon her, and after running about one hundred and fifty yards, she turned about as if confused in her fright, and fled towards the cave." This seems clear so far, but questions do arise: How did he know she was in the cave when he arrived? Where was the other man who had accompanied him? How did Northcott keep the dogs quiet for two days and nights, especially when they saw the woman emerge from the cave? How did this story hold up when people heard it?

It is troubling to think of the Wild Woman being pursued by two dogs. The rest of the tale is no better. As she ran back to the cave "worried by the dogs," Northcott claimed that he threw a lasso "over her neck and called off the dogs." The woman, however, continued to fight. According to Northcott, she gave "a spring, jerked him to the ground, and at a second leap threw herself, the noose having by that time fastened about her throat and choked her. He then tied her, during which operation she uttered such horrid screams that the hair stood upon his head, and he had the most singular and awful feelings he ever experienced." With his human prey caught and eventually subdued, Northcott explored her cave and found her reserves of food, including "large quantities of nuts and berries and roots." Provocatively, he also explored her bed, which he described as "a kind of a nest to sleep in." From this point on, Northcott became the absolute master of the woman whom he now referred to as "his pet."[23]

What was the Wild Woman wearing during all this? Throughout the exhibition, Northcott would walk a fine line, always approaching male sexual fantasy while never saying anything that would suggest an improper sexual relationship between himself and the woman. In this way, the Wild Woman's clothing presented the storyteller with considerable difficulties. On the one hand, Northcott had to clad her in something that would protect her from his grasping hands—or from being mauled by his dogs. As such, he told the editor that her "garments were so strong, ... that they protected the female from the teeth of his dogs." On the other hand, he needed to allow a certain amount of voyeurism and sexual fantasy about manhandling an underdressed woman in the wild. As such, he added that "the garment which she wore was of skins, queerly tied together with bits of leather, and also with a kind of grass."[24] That seems much more flimsy, allowing him greater access to her body. So what clothes was she wearing, then? It was up to individual readers to imagine for themselves just how extensively her body had been covered.

The question of the Wild Woman's clothing would hound Northcott for the duration of the exhibition. Every version put forth sounded improbable. His initial hedging during this interview allowed him some maneuver room even as it provoked early doubts. For the time being, however, he tried to have it both ways; he was both sexually chaste and suggestive at the same time. Northcott told the editor that he did not know what kind of animal the skins came from, which seemed unlikely given his apparent mastery of the wilderness. Her clothes were not, he thought, made from a bear or bison skin. Instead, he offered as his best guess two contradictory situations: "it was his opinion that she had found an animal dead, or that she might have been attacked by and have mastered some beast."[25] This seems like a jumble of ideas, almost as if Northcott was throwing out anything that came to mind. It seems unlikely that he had not anticipated this question. Instead, Northcott probably was allowing his audience to choose which kind of Wild Woman they wanted to imagine. Did they want a peaceful, largely helpless version of femininity who could only clothe herself by chancing upon an already dead creature? Or did they prefer a more formidable woman, one who could defend herself and kill a "beast" large enough to provide her with a pelt that would protect her from hunting dogs? This account allowed his

THE CAPTURE AND EXHIBITION OF A WOMAN • 19

audience to pick either version of feral womanhood, though it did so at the cost of specificity and perhaps credibility.

Northcott's tale of their return to Texas continued the tone of hunt, capture, and imprisonment that had permeated his story to this point. The trip back, he said, was a difficult three-hundred-mile journey. The other, nameless man and the two dogs proceeded with Northcott and the Wild Woman, now "with a rope about her waist," through the wilderness. This was a hard adjustment for the captive, Northcott telling the editor that "for five days after her capture, his pet refused to taste food, but then partook of red haws."[26]

Northcott claimed that he had bought a "hack" after they returned to Texas and that he had converted it into "a kind of cage." In this cell on wheels, he "conveyed her safely" until they reached the steamer *Hickman* at Little Rock.[27] It must have been quite a sight, and one suspects that Northcott offered the fewest details about this part of the story because any proffered facts could have been checked. The interesting thing for us to realize is that no one in Cincinnati in 1856 seems to have questioned how an imprisoned white woman could be transported from north of Dallas to Little Rock without exciting any protest from passersby. Perhaps enslaved women were transported involuntarily so often there that no one would have raised questions. What a comment that is about the gendered and racialized limits of liberty and freedom in antebellum America.

All of this leaves us with two interrelated questions. First, why would Northcott and the editor spend so long on the capture narrative? Second, why would this improbable tale appeal to so many people in Cincinnati and across the country? The Wild Woman's capture offered readers deep satisfaction by addressing two concerns shared by many people in the mid-1850s. The first aspect was a racial component that reassured white Americans about the justice of the racial order that they had created and by which they profited. The story did this even as it used racial concerns to heighten interest in the exhibition. Second, it offered men a renewed sense of their own mastery over women, a social status called into question by woman's rights conventions and the entrance of women into the civil society of education, religious activism, reform campaigns, writing, and publishing. The racial and sexual undertones of the capture narrative made the Wild Woman a popular success and helped spread her story into dozens of newspapers across the United States. They also served the conservative causes of justifying white supremacy and patriarchy.

THE POPULAR APPEAL OF THE CAPTURE STORY

The history of the Wild Woman exhibit in Cincinnati is almost entirely made up of people of European descent. There was, however, a substantial African American community in the city, numbering 3,172 people in 1850. By 1856, African Americans had formed cultural institutions, including churches, newspapers, fraternal orders such as the Masons, and the Colored Orphan Asylum. The city's Black population was not especially segregated residentially, and it was beginning to make economic progress from its origins as newly emancipated slaves. But the state and the city had a history of anti-Black legislation and riots that was not erased by the repeal of Ohio's discriminatory "Black Laws" in 1849. While Black residents had gained certain legal rights in 1849, they were stilled banned from jury duty, militia service, and quite explicitly from citizenship. In short, the city's track record of white rioters targeting Black neighborhoods—there had been three such incidents between 1829 and 1841—had not gone away.[28] It would probably not have been prudent for Northcott to have allowed a man of color inside to look at the Wild Woman or for any Black man to have attempted that feat.[29]

Northcott may have had all of that in mind as he crafted his promotional interview with the *Cincinnati Commercial*'s editor. Certainly, his narrative seems to have been written primarily to draw in white men. Since such people were often acutely aware of their race and believed it to be of importance, Northcott tailored his story in ways that catered to race-conscious white men. Thus, even though the Wild Woman show seems to have been a thoroughly white affair, race was never absent from it. One requirement for a successful show, he seems to have thought, was to make it clear that his feral specimen was indeed white. His exhibit would lose the highbrow, sociological angle if the woman was an Indian; going to see a feral Native American would present no opportunity to study how a white person raised outside of civilization would act. The show's sensationalist dimension also relied on the Wild Woman's whiteness by presenting a rare opportunity to see a "scantily" clad but respectable white woman, who had a female attendant who silently vouched for her sexual morality on stage and off. In that sense, the show's novelty both as a sociological study and as a sexual attraction relied on her being understood to be white. While the male audience, in person and in print, often found women of color to be sexually desirable or intriguing, the Wild Woman offered the allure of novelty as well.

So, it was vital for Northcott to stress that he had very quickly realized that the Wild Woman was not an Indian. That he had been able to immediately determine her whiteness despite the utter improbability that a white woman, dressed in skins, would be in such a place was abundant testimony of her race. That he did so by moonlight reinforced the idea of just how very pale she must have looked. The speed of his determination vouched for her racial identity and reassured readers that they would be getting their money's worth by seeing an authentic white feral.

The swiftness of his realization had another effect as well. The immediate clarity of the Wild Woman's racial category validated the racial divisions in American society. Racial differences must be obvious and profound for Northcott to have been able to make such a quick, surefooted mental leap. For any white person hearing his story, his racial identification reinforced the idea that race-based laws such as slavery or Indian removal were justifiable.

Northcott's tale of the Wild Woman's capture had a second racial appeal. Since many exhibits from America's human zoo featured people of color from around the world, it initially seems odd to find a white woman on display. But cultural critic Kevin Young argues that race was always a component in hoaxes even if the visible players were all white. Most often, he writes, these hoaxes played on the dramatic tension that arose when whiteness is perceived as being in danger. To prove his point, he analyzes Barnum's exhibition of a "Circassian Beauty." Circassians were thought to be the origin of the white race, with their descendants still living in the Caucasus Mountains. During the middle of the nineteenth century, many Americans believed that these people were being killed or enslaved by brown-skinned Turks. As a result, Barnum's exhibit of an underdressed Circassian Beauty "represented the height of white beauty under threat of swarthy violence."[30] White audiences, especially white men, could pay to see the Circassian Beauty and think that they were participating in some way in the rescue of the woman from a horrible fate at the hands of inferior, barbaric men.

The Wild Woman exhibition bears out Young's point that seemingly all-white hoaxes profited from the appeal of whiteness-in-danger themes. Northcott placed considerable emphasis on his intrusion into Comanche territory in order to capture the Wild Woman. Her residence there would, to antebellum Americans, have placed her in immediate and continuous danger. Later, several doctors would testify in court that the Wild Woman had already, in fact, been the victim of Comanche violence (as will be discussed in the next chapter). White men seemed to have enjoyed fantasizing about violence against white women, perhaps because it justified a system of sexual subordination predicated on an all-important role for men as women's protectors. White Cincinnatians would be inclined to think well of any man who had saved a white woman from the Comanches. They could also enjoy the sensation of aiding Northcott in his rescue by handing over their quarters.

There is another possible dimension to the inclusion of the Comanche menace in this invented story. The tale proved that whites could equal or best the Comanches on their own turf. Seen in this light, the Wild Woman herself proved the adaptability, courage, and toughness of white people by surviving alone in a hostile environment. Not only did she survive, but she did so while eluding capture by the Comanches. In that sense, she was capable of anything the Native Americans could do, and even more. More spectacularly, Northcott beat Comanche men to the Wild Woman, arriving first to claim the prize of an attractive young white female. Women in Western culture often serve as a reward for men who accomplish heroic quests or defeat dragons; Northcott had won the competition against Native American men by finding and securing the Wild Woman.

The ideological appeals of Northcott's rescue of the Wild Woman from Comanche violence had an even broader dimension. Historian Laurel Clark Shire writes that white women in frontier communities played several crucial roles in the imperialist expansion of the United States. They not only provided vital labor, of course, but also served an ideological role in justifying the taking of land from Native Americans. This role was, not surprisingly, premised on feminized whiteness being placed in danger. Shire writes that white women "represented national growth as the spread of domesticity and civilization and rationalized the violence of territorial expansion as the protection of white women and their homes."[31] Frontier women were powerful actors in the permanent seizure of native lands, yet their gender and race presented them to other Americans as "innocent" victims of Indian cruelty. Northcott's story cast him as a hero for saving the Wild Woman from the supposed violence of Comanches, reminding white Cincinnatians of the necessity and justice of westward expansion. In this way, the Wild Woman show performed the ideological work of justifying American expansionism, a vitally important cultural and political idea in Ohio, a state only a bit more than fifty years old in 1856. Not that Americans needed a lot of reminding; when an English woman visited Cincinnati in 1856, she marveled that such a large city had grown "upon ground where sixty years ago an unarmed white man would have been tomahawked as he stood."[32] The traveler presumably heard that line from people in Cincinnati, evidence that the residents were primed to welcome Northcott in his role as a rescuer of white womanhood in distress.

The showman also pitched his tale directly at his most likely audience—men. It is hard to read Northcott's capture narrative as anything other than the story of a man hunting a woman, whom he then subdues by brute force, ties up, and imprisons. His use of force in wrestling her to the ground and carrying her away suggests rape, and her clothing reinforces the impression that he had sexual access to her body. Northcott certainly knew that there were overtones of rape in his story, and he left them there for their suggestive value even as he went out of his way to steer clear of accusations of having sexually assaulted the Wild Woman. Note that he crafted his tale to always indicate the presence of a chaperone; why else was there a second hunter with him, one who served no purpose in the hunt or the capture scene? Why else were the captor and captive accompanied by a female attendant to Cincinnati?

But even as he protected his show's reputation from charges of indecency, Northcott also highlighted the violence that he used to overcome her feral resistance. This was not a story in which the rescuers were met with joy by someone looking to be saved and returned to civilization. All of the talk of chaperones did not mean that his male audience could not indulge in sexual fantasies of what they might have done in the wilderness with similar opportunities. When Northcott and his complicit editor wrote about how the Wild Woman had been choked by a lasso until he "tied her, during which operation she uttered such horrid screams that the hair stood upon his head," they allowed readers to entertain ideas of male mastery at the most elemental level.

In addition to allowing men the chance to imagine wrestling and overpowering a white woman in a place where civilization's rules held no sway, Northcott allowed readers to revel in a certain kind of masculinity. Historians have identified two different masculine ideals that overlapped and battled for cultural hegemony in the North over the course of the nineteenth century. The first model held up men as masters of their households. They were cast as patriarchs who controlled their dependents, including their children, domestic servants, farm laborers or apprentices, and, most importantly, their wives. This featured, in law and custom, the male's unlimited right of sexual access to his wife's body, a critical component in creating the many children who served as unpaid workers on family farms or businesses. Those unpaid laborers were especially vital in a subsistence economy that had little access to markets or to cash with which to pay workers. The patriarch who headed such a household was hardnosed, masterful, and in charge, at least in theory.

The second, competing ideal of masculinity became increasingly common as the century progressed, in large part because of the growth of a capitalist, cash-based economy that flourished in the nation's cities and along its expanding transportation networks. This ideal man would exercise self-control, not his mastery over others. No longer free to do as he chose on his own farm, this man knew that he had to go to work at a certain time, resist the lures of the commercial world, and stay sober, especially when at work. He also realized that it was not part of his role to have sexual intercourse with his wife (or anyone else) whenever he felt like it.[33] Children in cities cost money; they did not make it. The transition to this more "modern" masculine ideal, however, was slow and by no means without conflicts, both in the larger society and within individual men.[34]

Northcott's narrative described and celebrated the first, earlier type of masculine hero. He painted himself as a rugged man who mastered nature, a hunter who was self-employed and in charge of his own life and expeditions. A hunter and frontiersman, he met outdoor challenges with dispatch. Need to catch a feral person? There is Northcott returning to the cave, devising a plan, and readying his lasso. Need to physically subdue a screaming adult woman and transport her hundreds of miles against her will? Again, Northcott has the brute strength and mechanical ability to get the job done. The addition of the military rank of captain to his (probably wholly fictional) name added a military dash to his persona. Northcott gave men a model of an earlier and still very much respected manhood. The appeal of this vision of masculinity was no less strong for its irrelevancy in a city now peopled with wage workers, shopkeepers, and manufacturers who lived lives of industrious self-discipline. As historian Steven J. Ross points out, Cincinnati workers in 1856 had already largely transitioned out of artisanal workshops into the larger and more impersonal world of what he calls "the age of manufacturing."[35] The fact that Cincinnati men no longer lived in the masculine role depicted by Northcott may have helped him sell his story, since modern men often were nostalgic for the kind of liberty, independence, and mastery over others that they no longer could claim. In appealing to the older model, the Wild Woman show had a distinctly conservative feel.

Even more importantly, perhaps, the capture narrative imagined Northcott putting women back in the place they had occupied when men ruled over a patriarchal society. In 1856, that world must have been seen as in jeopardy, if not rapidly slipping away. By that time, men saw signs that their hold over women was fading; indeed, their hold over women had never been as complete as they would have liked. Historians have been able to chart women's fuller entry into public life as the 1800s progressed. While excluded from voting or holding office, by 1856 they nonetheless had a public presence in "civil society." Women managed and staffed benevolent organizations across the United States. They wrote and edited magazines, textbooks, novels, and histories. They spoke in public, often on issues with direct political applications such as prostitution and slavery. They wrote, signed, and circulated petitions that they sent to Congress, requesting legislation against Indian removal and slavery.[36] Starting in 1848, they held woman's rights conventions that targeted male privileges. For conservative Cincinnatians, Northcott had a response to all of this. He had confronted the wildest of women, one able to survive on the frontier by herself, and he had beaten her to the ground and tied her up. The evidence of masculine power was now exhibited before the paying public of the city of Cincinnati.

Northcott's capture narrative hit the public before the Wild Woman show opened. What did people make of his story? Even the editor of the *Cincinnati Commercial* voiced doubts. He wrote about the Wild Woman's clothes, "there is an air of improbability about this that the strange and almost terrible reality of the woman herself does not quite dispel; and we have not room here and now to argue the point."[37] By stating some reservations, however, he was conforming with the usual journalistic practices regarding how to promote hoaxes perpetrated by paying advertisers. As we have seen, Barnum believed that hoaxes worked even if people had doubts about the veracity of the show. Perhaps an exhibit even worked better, and solicited more repeat business, when people questioned its truthfulness. The *Commercial* editor's doubts played into this dynamic, even as they offered him a shade of protection if the show blew up as a fraud.

The editor's conclusion to his story played on this element of skepticism wonderfully. He remarked that the Wild Woman and Northcott's adventure seemed "to be a veritable realization of romance." "Romance" took on a number of different meanings here, including the sense of a fiction that seems too improbable to be true as well as the more modern definition of a story that could end in Northcott's marriage to the Wild Woman, or at least her seduction. But the editor closed his article with a statement hedging his bets on the show's truthfulness while also promoting it: "If this is a hoax—and it was so wonderful that we are not able to give it full credit—the girl... looks the character she is made to personate so consummately, that the like was never before heard or dreamed of." To go see someone so "wonderful" and to see a "girl... the like was never before heard or dreamed of" was an appeal some men would find irresistible.[38] Even if it was a fraud, it seemed likely to be worth the price of admission.

THE WILD WOMAN'S PERFORMANCE

Knowing what the Wild Woman exhibition looked like can help us understand what Cincinnatians found fascinating about the display.[39] Determining what the audience saw at the show enables us to learn what people wanted and expected women to be, and how they should act around men. With the power dynamics between men and women shifting in the 1850s, the Wild Woman gave male commentators the chance to consider how women should behave and what they would be like if shorn of all the trappings of civilization by a lonely life in the wild.

Newspaper accounts provide the most detailed reports of what people saw when they entered the Wild Woman show. Most of the city's editors wrote about it, starting with the *Cincinnati Commercial*'s lengthy promotional piece. There is also an engraving of the Wild Woman that depicts her being examined by curious men and women. This artwork has strengths and weaknesses as a historical document, but it is a striking record of what the Wild Woman endured during her days before the public.

The show fell within the cultural norms of antebellum America, though it pushed the boundaries of good taste enough that it was eventually shut down. Americans had grown accustomed to seeing human beings, including Barnum's Joice Heth, placed on display. Almost all such presentations mixed sensational content with high-minded goals. Northcott kept within that cultural formula, mixing educational content and charitable intentions with a lurid story and an underdressed young woman. He erred only in that the Wild Woman was white, a fact that would eventually solicit unwanted (from Northcott's point of view) sympathy from Cincinnati's activist white women. But her race was a choice forced upon him by his star's appearance and by the reality that only a white woman would make for such a popular show. A Native American or African woman would have been assumed to be at home in the wilderness, hence devoid of the appeal of novelty.

The tendency for human-zoo shows to mix elements that were intellectual or charitable with the sensational was not reserved solely for that kind of exhibit. Americans tended to think of leisure as either highbrow, indicative of good taste and social status, or lowbrow, unworthy of the attention of discerning people.[40] Historian Steven J. Ross finds that wealthy antebellum Cincinnatians thought of recreations in two categories, "productive and nonproductive leisure." "Productive" recreations were those "benefiting the material, moral, social, and intellectual life of the individual." By contrast, "nonproductive" entertainments had no redeeming moral or intellectual purposes.[41] Both kinds of leisure had their audiences, though. The trick for shows like Northcott's was to appeal to both audiences, not only because that would maximize ticket sales but also because having a "productive" purpose ascribed to the show protected it from hostile judgments by ruling elites.

Northcott's Wild Woman had many predecessors in the human zoo, each with their own mix of sensationalism and anthropological or charitable content. One of the first exhibitions was staged by Captain Benjamin Morrell, who toured from Albany to Washington, DC, in 1831 with two men from the South Pacific islands of Uneapa and Ninigo. Morrell had kidnapped the two men, whom he called Dako and Monday, while on a trading expedition into the Pacific. Scholar James Fairhead writes of the physical and psychological pain inherent in Monday's experiences in the cold and very foreign world of New York City. He relates the man's prolonged attempt to escape his captivity and of his eventual death during his imprisonment by Morrell. That the captain sold tickets to see the men in part by playing up their cannibalism was in keeping with the emerging sensationalist element of the human zoo.[42] That was the cheap, degrading element of such exhibitions.

As befitted a human-zoo show, however, Morrell's South Sea "Cannibal" attraction had a highbrow element as well. The captain claimed, with some small grain of truth, that only by exhibiting the two men could he afford to take them back to their homes. It was quite common for exhibitors to claim that shows were staged for the benefit of the exhibited. In addition, Morrell's show appealed to intellectuals who wanted the opportunity to learn about the culture and language of the two men. As Fairhead writes, it drew in "eminent doctors puzzled by human diversity."[43] As a promotional pamphlet for the show claimed, the two men were "exquisite exemplars of humanity." Fairhead notes that while "the 'cannibal' hook certainly helped to draw the crowds," it was also true that "Americans' interest in global humanity went beyond the sensational."[44] The Wild Woman show sought to emulate that broad appeal.

The human zoo, in other words, attracted a wide range of Americans. Barnum's Joice Heth show affords us another example of how this worked. For everyone who wanted to see a 161-year-old woman because the idea was just so weird, another wanted to have the elevating experience of touching a hand that had held George Washington. In another example, the display of fifteen Native American leaders at Barnum's American Museum in New York City in 1843 is hard to excuse, but we must also point out that among the visitors to the show was Lydia Maria Child. One of the most egalitarian white thinkers of her day, Child was a radical abolitionist and advocate of interracial marriage who had sacrificed a popular literary career to promote abolition and racial justice. Immersed in the racial disputes swirling around her, she made time to see the Sac, Fox, and Iowa men when she had the chance. Nor did she do so secretly; Child wrote about it in the newspaper she edited, the *National Anti-Slavery Standard*.[45]

Looking at other examples of human-zoo shows can help us understand the limits of the dual attractions of scholarly or charitable sales pitches and crude sensationalism. Some productions now seem devoid of redeeming qualities. These include Barnum's What Is It? show, which positioned a person of color as a missing link on the evolutionary chain. But even something as deplorable as the show called The Aztec Children, which asked if the children of color on display were "'specimens of a historic race now extinct' or merely 'idiotic dwarfs,'" seemed scientific enough at the time for it be staged at the New York Society Library in 1852.[46] The Aztec Children was sold to some people as grotesque or horrible, while others believed they would see something of cultural or historic value.

One last example will help establish the cultural boundaries within which the Wild Woman exhibit hoped to operate. While not from the human

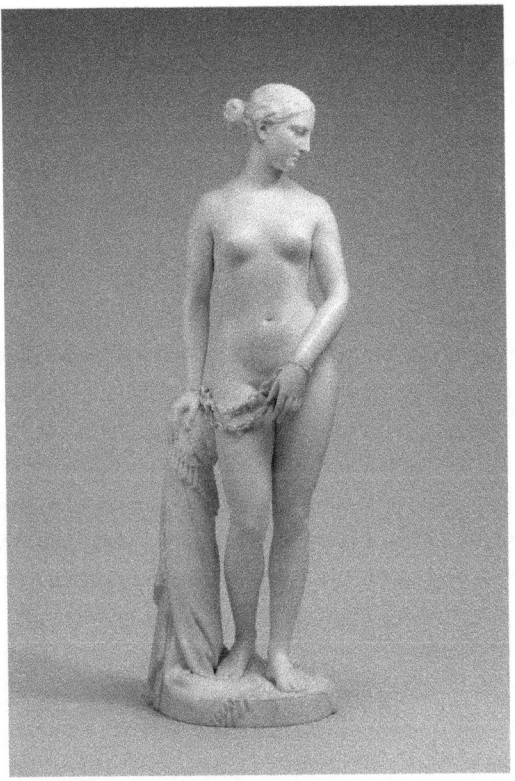

Hiram Powers, *The Greek Slave*. Courtesy Corcoran Collection, National Gallery of Art, Washington, DC (Gift of William Wilson Corcoran).

zoo, it suggests how a highbrow element could provide a protective cultural legitimacy for a potentially risqué exhibition. The carefully orchestrated unveiling of *The Greek Slave*, a tall marble statue by the Cincinnati-raised sculptor Hiram Powers, shows how this could work. The sculpture was certainly going to cause a sensation, being an idealized female nude. For Americans who took clothing seriously, a sculpture of a naked woman in chains could be seen as a threat to public morals. But the artist's supporters worked hard to teach the public how to view such a work of art. The main defense, presented in an accompanying brochure, was that the woman's modesty and virtuous character doubled as her clothes. In other words, she was dressed in her own innocence and virtue. Anyone could view this statue without scandal, they argued, because the woman depicted was as free of sin as the most dressed person in the room.

The Powers statue proved an artistic and commercial triumph, with the artist eventually carving—and selling—five such pieces. He had balanced fine art and cultural respectability with an attention-getting subject. There was refinement and sentiment to be gained by viewing *The Greek Slave,* just as touching Heth's hands might make people better by connecting them to President Washington. As Bostonian Caroline Healey Dall wrote in her diary after viewing the sculpture: "All else I have done today, sinks into insignificance beside the sight of, Powers' beautiful work of art.... How glad I am to have lived to see this work of Art—so spiritual."[47] When one of the Powers statues came up for auction while the Wild Woman was on display, the *Cincinnati Daily Enquirer* proclaimed that it "would be a rare ornament for any public or private institution, association, or for the mansion of any gentleman."[48]

The analogy between *The Greek Slave* and the Wild Woman helps us see that, while Northcott hinted at the sexual aspects of the Wild Woman's youth and good looks, he had to guard against going too far in that direction. While Powers's backers steered clear of sexual impropriety, the fact that they worked so hard to impress upon viewers the modesty inherent in the subject's innocence tells us that sensitivities about female sexuality remained a powerful force. Northcott walked right up to the line demarcating the extent of propriety and stood for almost two months with one foot on the side of charity and anthropology and the other on the side of steamy sensationalism.

All of this becomes apparent by analyzing what we know of how the Wild Woman looked and acted when on display. When the *Cincinnati Commercial*'s editor first encountered her, he was clearly startled by what he saw. "The first impression was similar to that of being in the presence of a fierce maniac," he wrote.[49] The editor of the *Cincinnati Daily Gazette,* who visited weeks later, had a similar reaction. "The only striking peculiarity about her is the wildness of her eye," he thought, "which gives her the appearance of a lunatic, and the spectator finds it difficult for some time to free himself from the impression that he is in the presence of a crazy woman."[50] But the Wild Woman's apparent psychological state—"maniac," "lunatic," "crazy"—was by no means the only thing that caught the men's attention.

The newspapermen also paid attention to the Wild Woman's appearance. The *Cincinnati Commercial*'s editor made it clear in his second sentence that his judgment of the show would include a provocative assessment of her looks, dress, and vulnerability. He was "introduced ... into a room where she is a prisoner," making it oddly clear that he was being "introduced" to a room and *not* to the Wild Woman herself, to whom no such civilities would be extended. He saw upon entrance "a tall, gracefully formed, young white woman." She was, he observed, "scantily but neatly clothed standing with a stout rope about her waist and attached to a bed post."[51] Not everyone who reprinted the *Commercial*'s story found it appropriate to include that sentence, finding the idea of a "scantily" clad woman tied to a bed too risqué for their paper, though many others included it. The disagreement about whether to include that line suggests that editors, even early on, had a difficult time deciding whether to prioritize a sensationalist story or to safeguard their community's moral standards.

Most journalistic descriptions of the Wild Woman continued to focus on her physical attractiveness in ways that had nothing to do with what a person would be like after years alone in the wilderness. The *Cincinnati Daily Enquirer*, an early but skeptical visitor to the Wild Woman when she was still on board the *Hickman*, rated her looks highly, if in need of a makeover. "She is a good sized person," the editor thought, "a handsome form if well dressed."[52] But the *Cincinnati Commercial*'s editor described her most thoroughly, and it was his article that spread across the country. Having already put her in scanty clothes and tied her to a bed, he then itemized what people would see if they came to look at her. Some of his description assessing her psychologically will be analyzed later, but much of what he wrote could have been written about a woman he had met at a dance or seen on the theater stage. This included a lengthy physical description: "her hair was long and thick, hanging in heavy matted masses and wiry tangles about her face, neck and shoulders, and in color dark brown. Her complexion was fair, even delicate, and her features decidedly handsome. Her mouth is small and finely formed, the lips thin and red, but tightly compressed, and her teeth even and white."[53] The editor, and his readers through his words, were engaging in what theorists call the male gaze, where men see and evaluate each part of a woman's body.[54] As if in a male fantasy, the newspaperman even enjoyed the power to request how much of her body he will see: "becoming more composed, she sat down, and her nurse at our request brushed back the tangles of her hair, showing her cheeks and forehead. These were fair. The cheek was thin but its outlines were quite womanly, and her brow and temples show intellectuality of no mean or common order."[55] Only the *Cincinnati Daily Gazette* refrained from assessing the Wild Woman's physical appearance in terms of sexual appeal.[56] For the other men who wrote about her, it was fair game to discuss her body's ability to please their eye.

There must be a begrudging recognition of the show's marketing ability; it was in the van of American culture's descent into modern advertising. The show pulled together two parts of the culture that had thus far remained separate. His exhibit combined the public display of attractive women's bodies in respectable urban spaces and the phenomenon of the human zoo. Women's bodies had been on display in cities before the 1840s, but increasingly, American men saw attractive and sometimes underdressed women in public spaces. First, they encountered them as advertising gimmicks. Consider the famous example of Mary Rogers, known as New York City's "Beautiful Cigar Girl," who was paid to stand in the window of Anderson's tobacco shop as an inducement for men to come in and browse. Nor was such advertising a uniquely northern phenomenon. In Charleston, South Carolina, in 1853, a daguerreotypist placed an advertisement in the newspaper urging men to visit his store to see photographs of "a pretty lady in the bloomers."[57] Female entertainers also took to the stage as performers in "breeches parts" that put them before audiences in pants and, as dancers, in roles that showed more of their legs than had previously been acceptable to respectable women and men. Writing about Annette Nelson, Celeste, and Fanny Elssler, historian Sara E. Lampert finds them drawing large houses but limited by "a repertoire that privileged beauty and sexual desirability" that "trapped female performers in narrowing expectations about the qualities of a compelling star."[58] Cincinnati men would have believed that the Wild Woman show gave them a fair chance to see an attractive woman in a state of undress, all under the cover of a respectable study of feral humanity.

Against this rather sordid backdrop, Northcott posed as the agent of charity. Like other showmen at the human zoo before him, Northcott told the public that he was only doing this for the good of the person on exhibit. Barnum had falsely claimed that receipts for the Joice Heth show would be used to purchase her freedom. Captain Morrell answered critics of his "Cannibal" show by claiming that the islanders were "performing 'for their own benefit,'" in other words, to pay for their return home.[59] In keeping with this tradition of claimed benevolence, reports stated that Northcott "disavows any intention to make a speculation of her and says that he will only take money from visitors that he may use it for her benefit."[60] With forces mustering to close his show in late June, Northcott repeated "that he is doing this to civilize her" and that doctors "have advised him to accustom her to the sight of crowds and to the aggregate appearance of civilized tamed humanity."[61] Like other human-zoo operators, he stood balanced on the twin pillars of sensationalism and benevolence. It was not always an easy pose to strike, but it promised a large audience drawn from a broad spectrum of society. As such, Northcott offered more to the public than an attractive woman. He promised a feral person, one who acted as nobody they had ever seen before.

THE WILD WOMAN'S FERAL BEHAVIOR

The Wild Woman show would only be allowed to happen if Northcott could convince the public that his exhibit had a scientific interest in addition to its sensationalist dimensions. By staging the Wild Woman as a feral person, Northcott hit upon a topic that had interested people for centuries.[62] What would a person be like if raised outside of civilization? The answer could reveal which human characteristics and behaviors came from nurture and which from nature. Cincinnatians could now see such a person and assess with their own eyes how crippling it was for a young woman to live without the benefit of family and society. What they saw confirmed for many people how much a young woman needed social instruction, even if she had proven herself capable of surviving on her own in the wilderness.

The show's success was dependent on the Wild Woman conveying answers to those complicated questions, all without uttering a word. If she failed to convince customers that, until recently, she had been living alone in the wilderness, word of the show's fakery would spread. Eventually, most Cincinnatians came to believe that the Wild Woman was a hoax, but her performance won over enough believers to keep the show viable for weeks.

One of the best descriptions we have of the Wild Woman's performance comes from the *Cincinnati Daily Times*. They waited almost a full month before sending someone to see the show, a reticence that originated from an early inclination "to consider this exhibition a humbug." But the Wild Woman's performance that day changed their minds (though Northcott buying an ad may have been a factor, too). The *Times's* description is one of the rare ones that measured her behavior and her actions against the story Northcott told: "Her appearance from the first moment that the eyes rest on her, is, to one at all acquainted with the actions of a wild animal, sufficient to convince anyone that the story of her capture is true. Her restlessness, the cat-like rapidity of her motions, the expression of wonder and surprise, the timidity at the slightest sound all are convincing proofs of the above assertion."[63] In this description, we can see how difficult a role it must have been, at least if the Wild Woman was sane and acting. Her jumpiness, restlessness, and speed of movement would have been exhausting physically and mentally when maintained for eleven hours a day. She could never let her guard down while customers were present.

Few other editors wrote such a detailed report of the Wild Woman's movements. Most, guided by Northcott, observed the Wild Woman's conduct and marked certain of her behaviors as signs of her feral background. They found her manner and actions not only fascinating but also strange and not entirely pleasant. Most of their remarks assessed her use (or absence) of language, her eating habits, and her emotional range, including her capacities for fear and happiness. The editors judged her behavior as not up to their standards of feminine conduct, an uncertain but potent proof of her feral background. Were not all young, white woman trained to be pleasing to men? Assessing what these men wrote of the Wild Woman reveals what they valued in women as well as what they thought were natural elements of femininity.

The Wild Woman's feral history was most obvious, the journalists thought, in her lack of any spoken or written language. Northcott and the editors noted her every primal scream and utterance, always commenting on her inability to speak. It was, perhaps, the single most pronounced behavioral marker of her status. An example of this is Northcott's mention of the loud, primitive scream she gave when he attacked her in the wilderness and wrestled her to the ground. It was the kind of scream, he said, that made his hair stand on end, a reaction usually said to occur when humans confront something terrifyingly strange. Her lack of speech continued to fascinate her visitors, as much a sign of her feralness as the rope about her waist.

Which is not to say that everyone described her utterances in the same way. The *Cincinnati Daily Gazette,* which visited toward the end of her stay in the city, heard Northcott say, "she speaks no language, and rarely makes a noise above a whisper."[64] The Wild Woman, if we are to believe Northcott and the editors, may have grown quieter and calmer during her time in Cincinnati. Earlier descriptions of her speech placed greater emphasis on her volume, hence her distance from conventions of female speech. The

Indianapolis editor, the first publisher to tell her story, made it clear that the Wild Woman was removed from all recognized speech. "She utters no words," but "she has a howl or scream when she requires anything or when slightly hurt by combing her hair. Mr. Northcott informs me that she has not the slightest idea of uttering a word."[65] The *Cincinnati Commercial* was less interested with the volume of her grunts than with the woman's reaction to hearing conversations. Whenever Northcott and her attendant talked, its observer wrote, the Wild Woman showed "the most animated curiosity."[66] But speech was clearly beyond her, and their attempts to engage her had all failed.

One sign of her recovery, Northcott told the *Commercial*, would be when she could speak. His emphasis on this is confirmation of the importance of language to Americans as they sought differences between the wild and the civilized, between themselves and animals. The editor wrote of Northcott that "his great object is to civilize her, to teach her to talk, and to hear her story, for he thinks he is sure that she has talked at some day, and that she has a dim notion of having long ago been with folks similar to those she now finds herself with."[67] While a cynic may read that sentence as the perfect setup for the Wild Woman's next act, something like "The Wild Woman Remembers Her Past," it clarified her absence of language in the present and offered a way for people to engage with scientific questions about the nature of humanity and its use of language.

Northcott and the editors were also intrigued by the Wild Woman's emotional range. While knowing a language and speaking was an obvious product of being raised among social people, one's behavior is also likely influenced by interacting with others. How a feral person would behave toward others could be a fascinating topic, and Cincinnati editors visited with an eye toward seeing how the Wild Woman acted. Perhaps because of expectations that women's lives were lived by emotion more than by reason, many of the male writers focused on her emotional life.

The editors wrote a great deal about whether the Wild Woman appeared to be scared. On the one hand, Cincinnatians seemed to expect a feral woman, newly dragged into an urban context from her seclusion on the frontier, to show a good deal of fear. On the other hand, maybe she would not be afraid; part of her allure had to be that she had fended for herself among the Comanches, bears, snakes, and coyotes. Returning to the idea that the show was staged to appeal to the widest possible range of customers, the issue of how afraid the Wild Woman should act raises tricky questions for the show's organizers. The most likely formula for commercial success was for the woman to appear scared enough to be credible as a feral without being so timid as to raise humanitarian concerns. If she looked terrified, people might insist that the show be closed for the woman's own benefit. Northcott and the editors hedged their bets on this question by presenting the Wild Woman as a mixture of bravery and reticence. That was a broad and sometimes mutually exclusive range of emotions for her to convey. She was either a talented actor who tailored her performance for the perceived predilections and reactions of an audience or a traumatized woman who reacted differently to unique people and circumstances.

Acting through the clerk of the *Hickman,* Northcott planted the first description of the Wild Woman's emotional life. She entered public life as someone who "appears frightened when looked at."[68] This probably played better on paper than it would have to paying customers; it was to be expected that a feral woman would be scared to be held prisoner on a ship heading up the Ohio River. This would conform to expectations for female timidity, but who would want to actually see that? Who would pay to see an attractive woman cower into herself? Northcott needed a better spectacle, one that conveyed a range of emotions that pleased customers. The editor of the *Cincinnati Commercial* obliged with a complex but contradictory depiction of the Wild Woman. On the one hand, he described her as distinctly frightened. "She stood at the foot of the bed," he wrote, "partially hiding behind it and rocking slowly, but with nervous uneasiness, from one foot to the other, and staring fixedly upon us with great, bright, unwinking eyes, so widely opened that a ring of white surrounded the pupil, which with a wild and intense glare of the orb, gave it a strange and frightful expression." This passage reflects the gendered characterization of women as timid and in need of protection. The Wild Woman was supposed to have survived in an environment that would have killed most of the young men who paid to see her, but having her appear frightened would reassure them of their own command.

Still, she could not be too scared. She must also be "wild" enough to satisfy customers who wanted to see the wilderness in the person before them. Northcott's show satisfied this desire, too, giving patrons a look at what a woman would become without society to shape her. The result, at least for the *Commercial*'s editor, was a fearsome and decidedly unfeminine person. In a culture that valued women who provided (and received) sympathy and sentiment, the Wild Woman's face was an emotional void. The newspaperman could not find "any trace of humor in her face to indicate any human passion, the only organ of expression being the eye, and that does not seem to seek, or ever to have known, human sympathy." She was so disconnected from people and the sentiments of human or familial interaction as to appear unnatural. Many things could alarm Cincinnatians in 1856, but a woman devoid of emotion and incapable of human sympathy was really scary. This people would have to see.

Perhaps even worse, the Wild Woman was physically attractive but so unschooled as to be a lousy flirt. The editor emphasized that her attendant had told him that the Wild Woman's "lips never curled in a smile, and nothing like a laugh ever found utterance." Her inability to laugh and smile, in other words to make herself agreeable, meant that she would not flirt. The *Commercial* editor's odd word choice when describing her eyes gave away his fixation on sexual appeal; part of the Wild Woman's act was that she rarely blinked, but he wrote of her "great, bright, *unwinking* eyes," a less usual word to use than "unblinking."[69] Did he often expect women to wink at him? The fact that no one had ever taught the Wild Woman how to be charming to men proved her feral upbringing. Her widely reported inability to please with her expression was one of the primary markers of her maturation outside of women's traditional acculturation, keeping company at the top of the list with her lack of language and the stout rope about her waist. Certainly, men wrote about her lack of smiles often enough.

A final note on the Wild Woman's observed emotional range shows Northcott (and the *Commercial*'s editor) casting a wide net to interest as many customers as possible. She was described as so afraid as to hide behind her bed and without any "line in her face to indicate any human passion." But, strangely, this passionless, timid woman also was portrayed as ferocious. The Wild Woman had, readers learned, "a kind of untamed audacity." In a direct contradiction of his earlier sentences showing her trying to hide, the editor wrote, "there is nothing like timidity in her looks, only the discomposure, mingled with defiance, which gleams in the eye of the panther."[70] So, was it frightened woman or defiant panther? Northcott promised both. We might see these two personas as embodiments of the two words of the show's popular name: "Woman" enough to be scared, she was "wild" enough to lack social graces and to be ready, panther-like, to bring down an unwary customer. Promoted in this way, she was a freak among her sex. Welcome to the freak show: come see the white woman who was not a lady.

It is possible that the Wild Woman changed toward the end of her exhibition. The only description we have from near the end of the show paints a different picture from the promotional piece in the *Cincinnati Commercial*. The *Cincinnati Daily Gazette*'s editor visited the Wild Woman show only a few days before it was closed, and his briefer description mixes incredulity, promotional hype, and disapproval. According to his piece, the Wild Woman lacked the "brutal" expression the writer expected to see in a feral woman; instead, he saw a face that was "rather one of sadness."[71] Who would want to pay to see that?

We do not know why the editor of the *Gazette* noticed more than his counterparts when he looked at the Wild Woman's face. Maybe he was more critical because he doubted the propriety of displaying a white woman to the public while she was under restraint. Perhaps the Wild Woman had changed over the course of her weeks of confinement and display. Or it may have been the Wild Woman was a talented actor who changed her performance depending on what she thought a particular editor or customer wanted to see. There is much that remains unknown about the Wild Woman show, and we know even less about the Wild Woman herself. But the show's promoters believed that a woman who lacked language and social graces would be taken as a feral, that she must be timid enough to fit female stereotypes even as she appeared fierce enough to have survived in the wild.

WHAT DID THE SHOW LOOK LIKE?

So far, we have seen the Wild Woman through the eyes of editors, men who were no doubt influenced by Captain Northcott. But newspapermen are not the only source for what the Wild Woman show looked like. In 1857, a Cincinnati publisher issued a novella loosely based on the exhibition, *The Wild Woman; or, the Wrecked Heart*.[72] While the text of the novella is examined in the next chapter, the book's cover illustration helps us understand the visual appeal of the Wild Woman show.

But first one must ask, was the cover art an accurate depiction of what the exhibit looked like? The engraving seems accurate. The novel inside is clearly a very fictionalized backstory for the Wild Woman, explaining how she came to be controlled by Northcott and placed before the people of the Queen City. But the engraver got many of the details of the Wild Woman show correct, at least as far as we can know them. Her eyes, so often described as unsettling and large, are clearly on display in this depiction. They dominate the image. The Wild Woman is dressed in a modest enough way but clearly in more revealing and less structured attire than the woman on the right side of the cover. There is a rope around her waist. She is staring at the gentleman who is examining her but is definitely not smiling or engaging with him. This is all accurate.

And why would it not be? A Cincinnati publisher would have seen his primary market consisting of people who had cared enough about the Wild Woman to have seen her the previous year. Placing an inaccurate engraving on the cover would ruin the book's credibility even before a prospective buyer picked it up. It is also likely that the publisher could have hired an artist to create the cover who had seen the show for himself. For these reasons, we will analyze the cover as if it were an accurate representation of what people saw at the exhibition.

It is a bit surprising to see two respectable-looking women in the audience. This suggests that Northcott had convinced people that there were legitimate reasons to see the Wild Woman. The respectability of the exhibition is further supported by the expensive clothes worn by the man in black at the engraving's center and the woman to his right. The engraver also places the attendant near the Wild Woman, looking the part of an elderly chaperone. The Wild Woman has a demarcated space of her own (with the attendant) behind a barrier, making it hard for anyone to get too close to her. Admittedly, the engraving gives the Wild Woman very little personal space, but we might regard that as a necessary (but inaccurate) concession to the artist's need to compress many details into a small visual plane. Like Northcott and his claims of benevolence and scientific interest, the *Wild Woman*'s cover image contains enough elements of respectability to gain a spot in decent shops or parlors.

And yet there are strong visual clues that something sordid is going on. This is in keeping with the disapproving tone of the novel, which depicts the Wild Woman as the victim of characters resembling Northcott and his cronies. The artist conveys his disapproval of the show through two of the central male figures. The man in the foreground, formally dressed in black and holding a top hat, is clearly staring at the Wild Woman in a way that would have been frowned on in polite society. He is close to her, and his head is leaning in to get even closer. We cannot see his expression, but we can see the face of the man standing behind the Wild Woman. This patron is

The cover of the novel *The Wild Woman; or, The Wrecked Heart,* by Alice Galon (Cincinnati: Barclay, 1857). From the Collection of the Cincinnati & Hamilton County Public Library.

staring as well; the engraver has emphasized his eyes as too-large dark spots on his face, highlighted and framed by his raised eyebrows. An unprepossessing fellow, his head is bent slightly forward, as if he is appraising her underdressed backside. If we compare the men staring at the Wild Woman in this depiction with the crowd in an engraving of *The Greek Slave* on display, the difference between gawking and a tasteful consumption of fine art is evident. In the respectable audience, the central male figures are looking at their female companions, not at the sculpture. Other men have their backs to *The Greek Slave,* looking at paintings on the walls. Thus, the men on *The Wild Woman* cover are depicted as behaving badly.

Engraving of *The Greek Slave* on exhibit. R. Thew, *The Greek Slave*, in *Cosmopolitan Art Journal* 2 (December 1857): 220. Courtesy Library of Congress, Prints and Photographs Division, Washington, DC.

Other aspects of *The Wild Woman* engraving raise doubts about the respectability of the event. The attendant, while present, appears to be oblivious to what is going on. She is no match for the powerfully depicted man in black formal wear. The woman whose face appears just above this man's right shoulder is smiling, perhaps even smirking, hardly what we would expect from someone concerned for the well-being of the Wild Woman or intrigued by the humanitarian or sociological issues she raised.

But mostly it is the Wild Woman herself who suggests a risqué element to the scene. Her clothing and hair were neither fashionable nor proper for 1856. The rope around her waist pulls in her clothes, accentuating her figure. Her shoulders are left bare, and all of her clothes have an unstructured look at odds with the formidable constructions worn by the woman on the right. The overall look of her attire suggests a shift or undergarment more than an actual dress; there is no pattern or color on the material. The undecorated garment recalls the editor's comment about her being "scantily but neatly clothed." Her hair is too long, hanging down almost to her knees. It hangs loosely all around her, far from how respectable women would have appeared in public in 1856. It is, in fact, too wild.

The Wild Woman's hair and clothes would have been strong evidence for people in 1856 that she had been feral until very recently. Their deviation from the norm put her beyond respectable society. Historian Holly M. Kent writes that "fashion is its own distinctive language, which members of any culture must learn to both 'read' and 'speak,' as fashion is vital in defining, upholding, and subverting cultural ideas."[73] In her case, the Wild Woman was apparently as unable to use her culture's language of fashion as she was its spoken one. That she would appear in front of people with her hair and clothes as they were represented here spoke to how far beyond American civilization she had traveled.

To gain a sense of how her loose hair and unstructured clothes would have been understood at the time, consider the humiliation and self-reproach a young Tennessee woman felt when she was seen by a male houseguest while wearing "only one garment under my wrapper, and such a head." In other words, she had not done up her hair and was wearing only two layers of clothing, seemingly what the Wild Woman wore every day in public, oblivious of her social disgrace. The Tennessean recorded her feelings at having been seen in such a state in her diary: "Such a sight as I know I looked. . . . I never hated any thing as badly in my life. . . . The idea of a son of his seeing me in such a plight distresses me beyond measure. It is the first time in my life I was ever caught so, and I certainly hope twill be the last. I felt ashamed to look at him the whole evening."[74] Proper clothing was vital, for women in particular, and mistakes called for self-recrimination.

The Wild Woman's unrestrained hair would have been an equally noticeable marker of her distance from civilization. Portraits of young women from 1856 show a popular craze for tightly controlled hair, often curling behind the head in a tight bun. This can be seen in the photograph of Nancy Day Beach and her husband from 1855 or Leopold Grozelier's portrait of the fashionable star of 1856, Jessie Benton Frémont. This socially accept-

Mr. and Mrs. Moses Yale Beach. In this 1855 photograph, Nancy Day Beach sports the hairstyle of fashionable women of the mid-1850s, very much the antithesis of the Wild Woman's long and loose tresses. Courtesy National Portrait Gallery, Smithsonian Institution, Washington, DC.

Jessie Benton Frémont, by Leopold Grozelier, 1856.
Courtesy National Portrait Gallery, Smithsonian Institution, Washington, DC.

The Wild Woman portrayed as a fashionable young lady. Note her restrained hair style. Reproduced from *The Wild Woman; or, The Wrecked Heart,* by Alice Galon (Cincinnati: Barclay, 1857). From the Collection of the Cincinnati & Hamilton County Public Library.

able hairstyle also appears in the 1857 Wild Woman novella. An engraving in the book depicts the character destined to become the Wild Woman as a fashionable young lady, complete with stylish dress and an appropriately done-up hairstyle worthy of Jessie Frémont herself. To appear with loose hair, described by the young Tennessee lady as "such a head," was to give credence to stories that one was more comfortable living in a cave in the Wichita Mountains than in a Cincinnati parlor. To appear in public that way voluntarily was just unthinkable.

Taking her hair and clothing into account, as well as the allowance given to men to stare at her from up close, the overall picture is one of profound inequality between the observed and the observers. It is an unsettling image that can only be made right in our minds today by hoping that the Wild Woman fully consented to her treatment and laughed all the way to the bank. But we cannot be at all sure that she did.

CONCLUSIONS

In his history of feral children, Michael Newton remarks that their silence makes it possible for their witnesses to imagine different ideas of what being a wild person meant or entailed. Feral children become a way, in other words, to learn about the society that looks at them and comments. He writes of these children, "by becoming objects of speculation, they opened up the fantasies of a nation and, in the stories told around them, we glimpse into our dreams."[75] That is also true of what happened in Cincinnati when the Wild Woman, silent and unable to escape, appeared before the city's men, women, and children. What they saw—and how they interpreted her—tells us much about these observers.

What, then, were the "fantasies of a nation" when it considered the Wild Woman? What were America's dreams of women on the frontier? The show's planners went to considerable pains to allow customers to see in her a range of women when they came to the show. Visitors could fantasize about a silent woman tied to her bed, or perhaps to theirs. They could look into her eyes and imagine a person so lost to society as to be without language. They could imagine her either as afraid of people or as a courageously defiant panther. Like Powers's *The Greek Slave*, whose grace, beauty, and innocence taught viewers lessons in morality even as her nudity threatened to unloose scandalous thoughts, the Wild Woman could teach people the importance of society, language, and civilization, all while stirring up improper passions. Women could imagine her as a sister victimized by violence or heartbreak who deserved their sympathy, or they could see a woman whose all too apparent misfortunes or perhaps mistakes had brought her to an unenviable or perhaps amusing end.

As different as all of these possible versions of the Wild Woman might have been, they all shared one thing in common. If the Wild Woman show gives us an idea of what its originators thought Cincinnatians wanted to see, then we know that they sized up their potential market and decided that the city wanted to look at a powerless woman. She should be utterly powerless when people paid to see her: no speaking, no freedom of movement, no sartorial authority, not even the limited power of a flirt. It is disturbing to think that this production worked as well as it did. Powerless in appearance and behavior, the Wild Woman was no more empowered by the script's version of how she had gotten there. According to Northcott, he had been able to beat this woman alone, the mysterious second man who accompanied him there and back having somehow disappeared during the several days of the capture and battle. Her inability to defend herself against him reinforced the need for men to defend women on the frontier, serving as an ideological reinforcement both for aggressive action against Native Americans and for men having earned their dominion over women. Powerless and weak women served many ideological needs for American men in 1856.

We cannot even take comfort in the idea that some men and women probably showed up thinking or hoping that they could help the Wild Woman. Some might have fallen for Northcott's line that he was only accepting money from "visitors" to help finance her recovery. But it must have soon become apparent that no funds went to help her. The show just went on and on, with no underlying changes in script, with no new chapters added to the young woman's life. No customer ever seems to have intervened to free her from the rope that remained firmly about her waist.[76] Northcott's "pet" would remain in captivity on public display for over six weeks, a monument to antebellum America's passion for enchained women.

But this exhibition was not to last forever. Tying up a white woman in Cincinnati may have been acceptable for a month and a half, but resistance grew. People and their government were about to put an end to Northcott's enterprise. How and why they did so, and the stories that they invented about the Wild Woman to justify their actions, offer a different window into the minds of antebellum Americans. A powerless woman was not everyone's fantasy.

2

CLOSING THE SHOW AND TRYING A WOMAN IN COURT

The Wild Woman show ended abruptly in a Cincinnati probate court. The presiding judge, John Burgoyne, had heard complaints from women in the city about the forced detention and exhibition of a "white woman." He probably agreed with them, finding the display both unseemly and contrary to his antislavery politics. Soon, a host of men began debating the Wild Woman's background and sanity in Burgoyne's courtroom and in the media. Everyone had an opinion about her, including newspaper editors, the prosecuting attorney, the judge, and the eleven doctors who testified. Men on the street gossiped as the Wild Woman drove momentous national events from people's minds.

People in Cincinnati raised the traditional question asked of all hoaxes: Was the Wild Woman a real feral or was she faking her symptoms? But other men went beyond this dichotomy, imposing a new third option onto the hoax dynamic. They insisted that the Wild Woman was insane. As such, she was neither a knowing actor in a hoax nor a real feral. Instead, she was a victim of Captain Northcott, who presumably had found an emotionally or psychologically devastated person who already displayed the symptoms shown by his imagined Wild Woman: fear, speechlessness, a lack of comprehension of what was going on around her, and no knowledge of her own history. The invention of a third answer to the hoax/authentic question was the result of the introduction of gender and its ideologies into the discussion about the show. Faced with a blank and silent woman on whom they could project their ideas about femininity, men made of the Wild Woman what they wanted to see. Some wanted to see a duplicitous woman who charged them a quarter to look at her act and her body. Others could not stomach the idea that a woman would do such a thing but found themselves unable (as a result of medical testimony, if nothing else) to believe that she was a feral. Facing that unappealing choice, they made her something else: an innocent but insane victim in need of medical care. The Wild Woman's day in court shows us a range of antebellum gender ideologies in action; the exhibition would not survive such turmoil.

THE WILD WOMAN ENTERS PROBATE COURT

The end of the Wild Woman exhibit came so suddenly that it caught people by surprise. Even the Wild Woman herself seems to have been taken aback by the speed of the show's closure. As with most of her history, there is much that we do not know about the production's end. Some things, however, are certain. The basic timetable of the shutdown is one of them. It happened quickly.

All seemed to be going well for Northcott on July 8, when he placed an ad in the *Cincinnati Daily Gazette* announcing his show's new venue and his plans to take his exhibit to an eastern city. We might wonder, though, if he was as confident as his advertising copy. As early as June 30, the *Gazette* had run a lukewarm story about the production and went so far as to mention that "many people object to visiting her because they regard it as a great inhumanity that a white woman should be led about by a rope to be exhibited as a wild animal to a curious multitude."[1] Nevertheless, Northcott risked reopening the Wild Woman show at its new home at the southeast corner of Fourth and Vine Streets, solidly in the downtown business district, "next door to Porter's Gallery, opposite the *Gazette* office."[2] Perhaps he needed income. There would be considerable expenses involved in traveling to a new city, procuring quarters there, and buying favorable publicity from the area newspapermen.

Behind the scenes, opposition to the Wild Woman's public display was building. Even before Northcott took out his advertisement for July 8, women from the Walnut Hills district of Cincinnati had decided to take action. According to the *Cincinnati Daily Enquirer*, "some individual waited on Judge Burgoyne, at the request of a number of ladies residing on Walnut Hills, stating that suspicions were entertained that the female on exhibition in this city as 'a wild woman,' . . . was insane, and suggesting that some measures should be taken to investigate the matter."[3] As this was going on, Northcott was away, having decided to go with the Wild Woman "a short distance" out of town.[4] Perhaps he had heard that there might be trouble, or perhaps he was merely giving himself and his attraction a bit of a rest before they left to conquer a new market. Either way, Judge Burgoyne could not touch them outside of the city limits. When Northcott announced the show's return, however, Burgoyne was waiting for it.

Northcott's gamble that he could hold his show over for a few more days did not pay off. The police closed the exhibition on July 9, arriving so unexpectedly that the Wild Woman was said to have blurted out her first audible words: "What are they going to do with me?"[5] She was supposed to have said these words to her attendant, Ann Walters, but whether her sudden command of English was due to surprise and fear causing her to tap deeply into her memory or she lost her hold on her role is unclear. Indeed, we do not know with certainty if she even said the words since the fact of her speaking is not directly attributable to a reliable source. Northcott was not arrested or even questioned, and he apparently would later visit the two women in the jail. It was not against the law to stage a hoax, though if the court ruled the Wild Woman insane, might he then be guilty of kidnapping? Northcott's future looked uncertain.

The two women were taken to the Cincinnati jail, so their futures were very much in doubt. In some ways, the situation looked very bad. Judge Burgoyne had "issued a warrant for the arrest of the woman," and he "directed the Sheriff to retain the Custody of her, to give time for the service of subpoenas, on a number of physicians."[6] Thus, the Wild Woman was locked up overnight. If found to be both sane and faking her feral status, could she receive jail time? Would Northcott—and where was he?

Yet the Wild Woman's cloudy status also had a brighter—if not actually bright—side. She had been arrested and jailed, but Burgoyne's status as probate judge meant that his court could only determine her sanity, not her criminality. She may not have understood that but perhaps recognized that, while "taken to jail," she was not placed in an ordinary cell. In newspaper accounts, the Wild Woman and Walters seem more like guests than inmates. As one reporter wrote, the Wild Woman was "taken to jail, where a room in the front part of the building was appropriated to her and a female attendant."[7] Her detention was only "in pursuance of a new law passed on the subject of lunatics," and physicians had been called only "to testify in an examination as to her sanity."[8]

How much of this did the Wild Woman know or understand? We cannot know the answer to that question, although she may have gained confidence during the day after her initial response to having the police arrive at her door. The only thing we know of her conduct while under arrest is inconclusive as to her state of mind. When a man on a staircase at the jail got too close to her, she took action to ward him off. As a newsman reported, she "seized one individual by the beard, and nearly pulled it from the roots, as a chastisement for his tenacity in approaching too near."[9] Her action does not allow us to understand her thinking. She might have grabbed the man's beard because she was incapable of expressing herself, or she may have been acting her part as a feral woman. She might have panicked, or she felt confident that such an aggressive response would enhance her act. Regardless, the next day would prove to be an especially difficult one for the Wild Woman, almost certainly her worst since arriving in Ohio.

With the Wild Woman detained in the jail pending her hearing, Cincinnatians could think about little else. The *Cincinnati Daily Enquirer* reported on their obsession, providing an unusual opening into the obscure world of sidewalk and barstool chatter. "The arrest of this strange creature was the principal subject of gossip about the city yesterday," it reported. The Wild Woman even drove the twin political crises of the time from conversation, the article declared, noting that "Kansas and Sumner were apparently forgotten for the nonce."[10] To momentarily forget the politically motivated killings in Kansas Territory and the bludgeoning of US senator Charles Sumner, all amid a presidential election cycle, meant that the Wild Woman had achieved a very high level of local notoriety.

What the gossiping Cincinnatians were saying was even more enlightening than their level of fascination. The people speculated, as many had all along, about who the Wild Woman was and how she had gotten that way. In many ways, this was P. T. Barnum's ideal humbug, with people willing to pay for repeat visits to test their own theories about the authenticity of the exhibit. But now the stakes were much higher for the Wild Woman, and the gossips of the city laid out and debated all of the options for her possible identity as well as her most likely fate.

This gossip serves as an introduction to what the court and its doctors were likely to think. The physicians' testimony and the speculations on the street align snugly, which in turn signals that the doctors determining the Wild Woman's future carried with them almost no expertise or specialized knowledge. The state of medical training in the United States was low in the 1850s, and the men summoned by the court brought with them no ideas that had not already been bantered about in the city's parlors and bars the previous night.

Public opinion, the *Cincinnati Daily Enquirer* thought, was divided about the Wild Woman. But there was a growing consensus on one point: "nearly everybody is of the opinion that she and the 'captain' are unmitigated humbugs." Of course, seeing her led off by the police would have tended to sway opinion in that direction. But that point of view did not have the forum all to itself; indeed, if it had there would have been far less to talk about. The *Enquirer* observed that "a few still cling to the original hypothesis respecting her wildness," but an alternative explanation for her behavior had appeared as well. Neither feral nor a fraud, the Wild Woman might instead have been "driven insane by some severe nervous shock, possibly by the killing of her husband and children by the Indians, and while in this condition took to the woods, and was then discovered by the 'Captain.'" Judge Burgoyne would hear several of the subpoenaed doctors advance similar theories in his court.[11]

Strangely, the *Enquirer* writer ended his article about gossip with a question, written in poor Spanish: "Quien save?" Having presented the rival theories about the Wild Woman, he ended by asking, "Who knows?" though he should have written "Quien sabe?" His question pointed toward everyone's continued bafflement about the Wild Woman, but it is intriguing to note that he thought to introduce Spanish into the *Enquirer*'s pages, an almost unheard-of act in an American English-language newspaper in 1856. Certainly, he did so without any great fluency. Still, he must have done so to continue to implicate outsiders in the Wild Woman's story of hardships. Why was she the way she was? Indians were one possibility, but darker-skinned Spaniards or mixed-race Mexicans were yet another. Either way, critic Kevin Young's thesis that American human-zoo shows often rested on some foundation of "whiteness in danger" at the hands of darker races seems oddly reinforced by this story of the gossip running through the streets of Cincinnati.

Arrested on Wednesday, July 9, the Wild Woman received her sanity hearing the next day. She was escorted by a Deputy Sheriff Shattuck and Walters, her attendant, from the jail to the courtroom. Throughout the walk and during her initial appearance in the crowded court, the Wild Woman looked and acted as she had while on display. She was "dressed in a loose cotton wrapper, pinned in front," and her hair was "disheveled," both strong indicators that she was not conforming to middle-class standards for a woman's appearance.[12] Even more telling was that "a long leather strap was fastened around her waist, an end of which was held by the attendant, as she led her from place to place."[13] For Cincinnatians, the short procession to the probate court was an opportunity to see the Wild Woman free of charge. Had things gone better for the exhibitioners during the rest of the day, this parade through the city's streets would have been good publicity.

The spectators who filled Burgoyne's court also saw the Wild Woman for free that day, and they were treated to a full display of her behaviors, as well as glimpses of her clothing, hair, and rope. At least three Cincinnati papers sent reporters, and they agreed that the Wild Woman looked terrified in the courtroom.[14] The *Daily Gazette* writer observed "the wild stare of her eyes, and the unvarying expression of subdued terror, [which] were the most peculiar features of notice in her appearance." He then described what this looked like: "Though invited to sit down, she seemed disposed to remain on her feet, as near to the wall as she could get, where she rolled the dilated pupils of her dark eyes from object to object, with an apparent apprehension of her own security."[15] The *Daily Times* offered a similar description, reporting that in the face of a courtroom "very full at the time of witnesses and spectators, she seemed disposed always to get her back to the wall, and to prefer a standing posture.... She appeared wary of the approach of any other person."[16] She had reason to be concerned.

She was now one of only two women (Walters stayed as a witness) in the courtroom, a point we can sure of since one of Judge Burgoyne's first acts was to clear all spectators from the room. After this was done, those remaining included the judge; the county prosecuting attorney, Joseph Cox; eleven male doctors; a witness called Mr. Canon; and at least three newspapermen. There was probably also a stenographer. No defense attorney was present to counterbalance Prosecutor Cox. While the Wild Woman would certainly have been familiar with being stared at by strangers, the almost entirely male crowd may have been less familiar, and Northcott was nowhere to be seen. Other elements were new, including the setting and the degree to which these men had power over her. The courtroom was a new and menacing place.

They, like so many other men, assessed her appearance, including her sexual appeal. The *Cincinnati Columbian* described her as "young and good looking" before going into greater detail: she "has unparalleled eyes.

The dark portion is as large as a dime—They are kept staring open so as to show a ring of white around the large circle; the flesh beneath is of a dark color, and the face pale; . . . the hands lie listlessly by the figure, the fingers as listlessly turned towards the palm of the hand."[17] The *Cincinnati Daily Gazette* agreed, calling attention to the fact that she "is decidedly pretty, if not a handsome woman."[18] No matter what her state of mind, the Wild Woman could not have been comfortable in this crowd.

The only other woman in the courtroom was Ann Walters, who may or may not have been much of a comfort to her. While Walters would have been familiar and had been employed to care for her, she would soon offer testimony against her in order to clear her own name. Relations between the two afterward proved frosty. With at least seventeen men in the room and only the dubious protection of Walters to rely on, the Wild Woman had every reason to want to keep her back up against a wall.

Regardless of who she was or her state of mind that morning, the Wild Woman panicked at the judge's next words. After clearing the court, Burgoyne announced that he "desired that the physicians should make such examinations as they might deem proper, in order to form an opinion as to the condition of her mind."[19] Newspaper coverage of what happened next varies, not so much in what they thought occurred but in terms of how much detail each was willing to offer its readers. Clearly, the Wild Woman offered a strong physical resistance to undergoing an examination by the eleven men. For their part, the doctors seem to have been willing to use physical force to remove the Wild Woman's clothes. Her resistance, only partially successful during the ensuing struggle, proved tenacious enough to convince the men to try a different approach. One of the doctors jammed a chloroform-soaked rag over her mouth and nose. The Wild Woman then supposedly exclaimed, "Oh, my!" causing one doctor to observe, "That is English as any rate."[20]

This episode, with its violence and resemblance to a gang rape, left the newspapermen to determine how much detail they should give to their readers. Editors would have considered several factors before they decided what to include. They certainly had the power to embarrass the medical men and the judge if they chose to do so.

Most, however, chose to protect the men in the courtroom. The *Cincinnati Daily Gazette* largely skipped over the incident, saying only that "it was then determined by the physicians that chloroform should be administered to her, and, while under the influence, she was examined by the medical men present."[21] No mention was made of what had occurred between the judge's order and the decision to sedate her, an omission that protected Burgoyne from any criticism that she had been mistreated in his court. This could have been a politically motivated choice by the editor of the pro-Republican *Gazette*, since the judge had a strong antislavery record. Still, it had the undeniable consequence of glossing over the Wild Woman's intense vulnerability.

Other newspapers allowed slightly fuller coverage than the *Gazette*, perhaps because they lacked any political reason to protect Burgoyne. The *Columbian* noted only that a "complete medical examination was made" after "the woman exhibited much modest reluctance toward the inspection."[22] Its readers, however, did not learn what form her "modest reluctance" took or what had brought her to the point of expressing it.

The *Cincinnati Daily Times* offered a much fuller description of the events. While most of the press glossed over the details of how the doctors conducted their examination of the Wild Woman, the *Times* offered a detailed and disturbing account that reflected poorly on the men involved. The doctors began, it reported, by trying to calm the Wild Woman with a glass of water, which prompted a display of feralness not recorded elsewhere. Subsequent attempts to disrobe her brought forth resistance. The *Times*'s account is worth quoting in full:

> She appeared very timid at first, but finally gained courage, and permitted the approach of physicians. Her agitation increased. A glass of water being placed before her on the floor, she stooped down on all fours with the rapidity of lightning, and drank with her mouth inserted in the tumbler. The attendant was then requested to divest the woman of part of her clothing. The Wild Woman resisted the process, betraying a singular modesty for a woman so very long banished from the haunts of civilized society, and unable to speak any language. Her breasts were exposed, however, when the physicians with one voice exclaimed, "She has been a mother, and has nursed."[23]

The reporter's derision is hardly warranted, given how any person would react to having almost a dozen men—even if understood to be doctors—stand and stare at them as someone else undressed them. But for the journalists at the *Times*, her modesty was only proof of her being a fraud.

The reporter for the *Times* then criticized the Wild Woman in the next paragraph for being immodest. His sensationalist account continued: "After some time it was proposed to administer chloroform. She was led to a table in the centre of the room, and stepped upon it from the floor without indicating that modesty developed when her bosom was exposed. Drs. Dandridge and Murphy then forced her down upon the table, when Dr. Wright administered the opiate.—she meantime screaming violently."[24] The image of a nearly naked woman "screaming violently" while being forced down onto a table in the middle of a courtroom is one of the indelible images in the history of the Wild Woman. It is an indictment of both the court and the medical establishment that it actually happened. The men in the courtroom had now succeeded in doing to her for real what Northcott had claimed to have done: subdue her by brute force so that men could look at her. As they had been while hearing the captain's story, most men again seem to have been fine with such violent action. Just as Northcott's tale had met with a certain leering fascination, the journalists of Cincinnati (and presumably their readers) decided that the doctors' subduing of her either did not warrant attention or presented it only as a sensational event. Notably, the *Times,* while covering the assault on the Wild Woman, expressed no sympathy for her. Instead, they gloried in the events of her undressing and mocked her for her modesty and her immodesty in rapid succession. She could win no praise however she behaved, receiving only bruising and scorn from these men.

That someone then proceeded to do a phrenological reading of her head while she was under the influence of chloroform seems like a comic afterthought compared with the doctors' use of force, and yet there is something appropriately unprofessional about the court allowing a phrenologist access to the Wild Woman's unconscious head. Phrenology was not based on medical science—but then, the doctors' assault on her was not medically sound either. Consider this: how would examining an unconscious woman help the doctors determine her sanity? Sanity could be known only by talking with her or by evaluating her actions, not by looking at her body. What would be gained by taking her clothes off? Who had decided on this manner of examination—the judge, one of the doctors? The sources do not say. For the record, the Wild Woman was deemed by the phrenologist to lack "hope and resolution" while "her organ of cautiousness is largely developed." (Who could blame her for lacking hope or being cautious, given her situation?) She was, this man thought, by "temperament melancholy."[25] By the end of the day, the doctors' ability to determine the Wild Woman's degree of sanity would prove to be no more credible than the phrenologist's diagnosis.

THE RESULTS OF THE EXAMINATION

Different men had always seen different things when looking at the Wild Woman. She was a blank slate in a feminine shape upon which, time and again, men wrote what they thought women were and what they valued in them. Lying exposed and unconscious on a table in the middle of a courtroom, the Wild Woman once again became the receptacle for men's ideas about women. The examination and their individual conclusions would not get them closer to a consensus, a diagnosis, or the truth.

In the end, the doctors' ideas proved to be wildly at odds with one another and yet limited to the same interpretations flowing through the city's gossip mill. The Wild Woman's silent body inspired diagnoses so at odds with the rational possibilities for her background that we might do well to call them fantasies. Although called doctors and given power over her fate, these men produced uninformed fantasies of sex and sexuality that betrayed their own limited visions of who women could be. For this they received from the government seventy-five cents per man, a rate that at least one Cincinnati doctor had the cupidity to grumble was too low.[26]

The physicians could come to no consensus regarding the issue before the court: was the Wild Woman sane or insane? Perhaps we should not be too surprised about their lack of agreement. Knocking her out and removing her clothes would seem to be an unpromising path for making such a diagnosis of her mentality. Yet the doctors would have answered that a woman's sanity was dependent on the proper use of her reproductive organs. Women's whole essence, they seemed to think, was so wrapped up in reproduction that only by inspecting her vagina and breasts could they understand her psychological well-being. One after another, the doctors fantasized about sex, violence, childbirth, and child-rearing, all of which was another way of saying that they, as men, held the key to women's mental health. Women existed to have sex with men, to bear their children, and to raise those children. When the doctors looked at the Wild Woman, they fantasized about her sexual history, often without evidence to support the stories they told each other about the unconscious woman lying exposed before them.

To add one more complaint against these eleven doctors, they often simply lost track of the purpose of their testimony—determining the Wild Woman's sanity. Instead, they veered off into the question of whether or not she had been feral. Perhaps this was because the Wild Woman's unconscious body offered more concrete answers to that question. Yet even these answers revealed only if she had always been feral, which of course was desperately unlikely, or had become that way only after reaching maturity. That question was not really germane to the reason that they had been subpoenaed.

The doctors' testimony split on the question of her sanity. A quick count suggests that two believed she was feigning insanity, presumably to continue her humbug. Eight of the doctors believed that she was insane and had been the victim of the nefarious and now absent Captain Northcott. A final doctor, William Hamilton, suffered from indecision, saying "he was of the opinion that, with some degree of insanity, there was more or less of feigning."[27] Some other doctors admitted that they were not entirely sure, but Hamilton's testimony was a small masterpiece of fence-sitting.

The physicians who deemed her a fraud got in the first word. Dr. Marmaduke B. Wright deposed first, as befitted his established reputation as a medical professional and civic leader. He was not always a pleasant person, apparently; an 1894 biography described him as "a born controversialist" who was "as well known politically as professionally."[28] A recent arrival from Columbus, Wright had plunged into the leadership of Ohio College and Know Nothing politics, having left behind his Whig Party background.[29] Given that the doctors who spoke after him had so little actual evidence to go on, we can only wonder if their testimony was swayed by their dislike (usually) or alliance (only rarely) with the argumentative new man in town. In any event, Wright's words failed to sway most of the others. But he did establish a pattern of offering "evidence" for his point of view that drew from many sources, including having seen the Wild Woman when she was on exhibit.

Wright began the medical testimony with, "my opinion is that it is a case of feigned insanity." He was the only doctor to testify twice; when word swept through the courtroom that Walters was ready to testify to the fraudulent nature of the exhibition, Judge Burgoyne asked Dr. Wright to come back to the stand to explain more fully his reasoning. His answer then revealed his long familiarity with the Wild Woman show: "I was from an early period of [the] opinion that there was feigning; I had suspected the nurse, who, I observed, dressed and undressed the woman in the dark; I think the woman was but faintly under the influence of the chloroform; she resisted its action;

the manner in which she has remained on the present occasion fixed in her position, gaze and studied aspect, gives me the impression that she is feigning."[30] Wright, in other words, had been to see the Wild Woman before and had already established his opinion of the show's authenticity. What he had seen in the courtroom had not changed his mind; indeed, if he spoke literally when he said he had "observed" the nurse undressing the Wild Woman "in the dark," he already knew that the exhibitors were hiding something about her body that would indicate that she had not been feral her whole life.

Wright did not find any unqualified support for his diagnosis until the tenth doctor stepped forward. That man, Dr. Williams, said that he "was of opinion that the staring of this woman was not of that involuntary character which was observable in insane persons; and the change in the expression of her eyes led him to suppose a great deal of her actions were assumed."[31] While other doctors would allow the possibility that the Wild Woman might be a fraud, only these two men would stake their professional reputations on this conclusion.

The men who assumed her to be insane offered depositions of a more fanciful sort. Their physical exam had proven that the Wild Woman had lived part of her life "in civilization" by finding evidence of pierced ears, vaccination marks, and scars consistent with medical bleedings from both arms. They also believed that she had given birth to at least one child. They then proceeded to invent a life story that would explain those realities and yet drive a healthy, "civilized" woman insane. Some invented biographies that had her fleeing into the woods of the Wachita Mountains, apparently reluctant to discard Northcott's feral-capture narrative entirely.

The second physician to testify, Dr. Alexander S. Dandridge, began a long string of depositions in favor of finding the Wild Woman insane. Like those who followed him, Dandridge presumed that she had been driven to insanity by a traumatic event related to reproduction. His explanation of her mental state began with the fact that he, like Dr. Wright, had had previous contact with the Wild Woman. In his case, Dandridge had seen "her the day she arrived" and had, he said, believed her to be insane even then. (Either Dandridge was lying or he had had no influence with Northcott, who claimed to have consulted with doctors who had advised him to put the Wild Woman on display to familiarize her with other people, apparently having said nothing about insanity or committing her to an asylum.) In court, Dandridge said that her illness "may have originated in child-birth." Further, "she may have held the relation of a mother and experienced the loss of her child; I think her reason is upset, yet there are indications that she feigns."[32] In imagining a traumatic backstory for the Wild Woman, Dandridge's testimony would prove popular, though some of his colleagues imagined and testified about more violent stories.

Dr. John A. Murphy stepped up next. He concurred with Dandridge, though he went further by offering a specific diagnosis. The Wild Woman, he said, "had probably puerperal mania—that she has been a mother is clear." Puerperal mania has fallen out of use as a medical term, but one scholar writes that it "was believed, by alienists as well as obstetricians, to be a common cause of a form of insanity which was usually manic, often severe and occasionally fatal."[33] Murphy stated that Northcott had presented "the sheerest humbug" by putting an insane woman on exhibit, and he advised that she be sent to an insane asylum.[34]

With one of their number willing to put an actual diagnosis before the court, and finding it go unchallenged despite its lack of evidence, other doctors grew more assertive and invented additional causes for her madness. With Dr. Murphy having opened the door to puerperal mania, the next medical witness, Dr. Hiram Cox, found the temptation to elaborate on this diagnosis impossible to resist. Cox was the sole practitioner of eclectic medicine among the eleven testifying doctors. Eclectic medicine sought to use botanical cures in place of the traditional medical practices of the day. Doctors like Cox (as well as hydropathic practitioners who sought health in water treatments) did not routinely deploy the "heroic" practices of regularly trained doctors whose "cures" included bleeding and the taking of extremely strong emetics, including regular doses of mercury-based products.

On this day, however, Cox and his alternative approaches to healing produced a diagnosis similar to that of the standard allopathic practitioners testifying before him. Cox began his testimony with a qualification that he, unlike Dandridge and Wright, had only seen the Wild Woman "for the first time last Sabbath." He added another qualification, admitting his diagnosis "is but speculation." In that he was right. But it did not stop him from testifying "that her condition is a result of puerperal derangement; there may also have been the loss of a child; if she was found in the woods, it is possible she had been taken by the Indians, have had a child and lost it, and the condition in which we see her ensued."[35] Cox's introduction of Native Americans into the medical narrative was without any basis in evidence. His phrasing at least admitted his uncertain footing; he filled his testimony with words such as "if," "speculation," and "it is possible." Also, he talked of her having been "taken by the Indians," a turn of phrase that could mean either her capture, her rape, or both. Such a severe turn of events, he said, "may have caused her insanity and deprived her of speech."[36] He concluded by saying that she had been a mother and at some point had been bled, a common treatment for puerperal disease.

While Dr. Cox hinted at the possibility that the Wild Woman may have had children by an Indian man, Dr. Samuel G. Menzies followed that testimony by introducing sexual assault by Native Americans as a clearly stated possibility. "The woman had perhaps been a mother more than once," elaborating, "she may have been violated by the Indians; I consider her insane at the present time."[37] That Menzies had no evidence for this statement did not discourage him from imagining what he must have found an intriguing idea; perhaps his own actions and those of his colleagues earlier in the proceedings planted the idea of rape in his mind.

Dr. Menzies had one more invention to pass on to the judge before he sat down. While he imagined her rape by Indians as a negative extreme, he also created a positive fantasy for the Wild Woman. Sadly, he had no evidence to support his happier fantasy either. Menzies informed the court that "she had been a cultivated woman, and the mother of children."[38] There was no reason for him to find her "cultivated," unless having pierced ears or a desire not to be undressed in court qualified her for that status. There was no evidence, certainly, that she possessed learning, artistic abilities, or social refinements. Menzies perhaps found it more tantalizing for a cultivated lady to be raped by Indians than for a lower-class woman to be sexually assaulted. His flights of imagination may have begun to strike observers as embarrassingly tenuous. Menzies's remarks were the high-water mark for creative imaginings of the Wild Woman's past by the Cincinnati medical establishment. The tone of testimony for the rest of the day became more sedate.

It is interesting to note, however, that in 1857, a local doctor complained in an article mentioning the Wild Woman trial that the practice of allowing doctors to appear at lunacy trials "subjects the entire profession to public derision." He continued, offering only a backhanded defense of doctors who bestowed on the courts poorly thought-out opinions: "It is no disparagement to the general character of a physician to say that he is not competent to give testimony on the spur of the moment in a doubtful case of insanity, and especially after the current of popular sentiment has been flowing in a particular direction."[39] It seems as though either the author, Dr. George Blackman, had a very thin skin or that the medical field had received sustained criticism for its testimony in probate courts. The doctors' showing in the Wild Woman's case indicates that they had earned that "public derision."

For whatever reason, the remaining physicians offered less lurid and fictive testimony. Dr. Fred Seymour, whose testimony was offered late in the proceedings, concurred with most general medical understandings of the day regarding what he took to be the Wild Woman's insanity. "I think it is not feigned," he said, "but she has at some time experienced a severe shock, the effects of which still continue; I thought there was much feigning at first; I do not think so now; it is a species of mania."[40] Dr. O. M. Langdon also found her insane, and he laid out a reasonable causation that did not invent new stories about her medical history. He argued "that the probable cause of her insanity was her confinement, or something attending upon it." Sensibly, he urged Judge Burgoyne to get her into "seclusion."[41]

THE TESTIMONY OF ANN WALTERS

In many ways, the most fascinating witness of the day was the Wild Woman's attendant, Ann Walters. Her legal position as the day began was uncertain, and we might feel sympathy for her. Could she be detained on criminal charges—perhaps kidnapping—after the hearing? Since we cannot know with certainty who the Wild Woman was, the true relationship between her and Walters is also unknowable. Did Walters physically care for a woman who was in genuine need of help? Did she care about the Wild Woman even if they were partners in a hoax? We do not know the answers. But we do have two newspaper accounts that include Walters's lengthy testimony, complete with its rich details about the Wild Woman's life during her exhibition and Walters's interactions with her.

A maddeningly poor witness, Walters's testimony was internally contradictory, offering support for any theory offered about the Wild Woman and her state of mind. It cannot all be true. But if we read the *Cincinnati Daily Gazette*'s coverage, which has her testifying at two distinct points in the proceedings, then her self-contradictions make a certain sense.[42]

Walters started her statement with a colorful and detailed account that backed up Northcott's story. She offered information about the Wild

Woman, her capture (as told by Northcott), and her own role in presenting a true feral to the community. According to the *Gazette,* she spoke as the medical examination of the Wild Woman was being conducted, only to be interrupted so the first nine physicians could testify as to the results of their inspection. None of the doctors gave very much credence to Northcott's story, though some were willing to entertain the idea that she might have found her way to "the woods." After hearing their testimony, Walters realized that Northcott's story, like the man himself, would not be around much longer. As a result, she changed course and proceeded to tell a different story when resuming her testimony. No longer likely to be the attendant at a feral woman show, she must have been newly uncertain of her place, her future, and perhaps her criminal liability. Walters reacted to her new vulnerability by telling a range of different stories that cast her as a victim who had been hoodwinked by Northcott or even by the Wild Woman herself. It was not a pretty performance by the end, with hints of desperation, lies, and a good bit of turning against the Wild Woman, who had until then been either her ward or her colleague in deception.

Walters began the day by offering a vivid performance as the attendant who helped Northcott bring a feral woman before the public in order to get her the help she needed. This part of her testimony offers details about the Wild Woman unavailable elsewhere, a window into how Northcott's story had evolved over the past six weeks. Walters comes across as a glib and inventive storyteller. Either Judge Burgoyne or Prosecutor Cox asked her questions during this portion of her appearance in the courtroom. Their interrogation probed at weak points in the show's script, perhaps either to trip up Walters or to convince her to break from the established narrative. She would have none of it, however, and stuck to Northcott's story despite any temptations she may have felt to abandon the leaking ship of the Wild Woman exhibition and save herself. In the process, she managed to insert new stories and details into the capture narrative and the picture of the Wild Woman's life in captivity.

The court, for example, raised the issue of how the Wild Woman had created her clothing. Doubters had wondered how skins had been procured and turned into clothing, but Walters now said that the Wild Woman had carried "an old piece of a knife." Other dubious parts of the story received attention. Did the Wild Woman bear any tooth marks from having been caught by Northcott's dogs? Walters denied having seen them, stating, "I mostly washed her in the dark; I could manage her better in the dark." Doubts about why a feral woman would even be modest came out as a question: "Was she modest from the beginning?" Walters readily replied, "No; I learned her to be so." The court even asked Walters if she had "ever struck her?" That was an easy one to answer: "Never." But then we might follow up that question by asking about the ever-present rope around her waist.[43]

Walters's answers to direct questions played it safe by maintaining the Wild Woman show's credibility and potential profitability even at this late date. While we know that the production was over for good, that may not have been obvious to Walters. In fact, if she and the Wild Woman had convinced the court of her feral nature, then the hearing would have been a publicity bonanza for the show. With Cincinnati's reporters writing down her words, Walters seized the chance to introduce new sensational elements into the public record. Such exciting testimony could also have the benefit of distracting the court from the implausible parts of the exhibit, an important tactic given Prosecutor Cox's tendency to look into the weakest parts of the narrative.

From Walters, people now learned that the Wild Woman enjoyed soft music, had used her knife against one of the Northcott's dogs, and had been a mother (though she claimed to have noticed that only over the past "day or two"). In a bid for gothic thrills and publicity, Walters testified that Northcott, while inspecting the cave where the Wild Woman had slept, had "found bones, which he supposed to be those of a female," located outside of the entrance.[44] Amazingly, this detail had not found its way into earlier accounts, suggesting that Walters had either made it up on the spot or that Northcott had introduced it in the last few weeks. Perhaps even more surprisingly, Walters's examiner was not sidetracked by the extraordinary statement that a human skeleton had been found just outside the cave.

Nor was the court diverted by the tantalizing prospect raised by Walters of the undressing and washing of the Wild Woman. Instead, the questioner merely followed up this topic with a query about whether Walters had ever hit her. Faced with such a determined line of questioning that next approached the Wild Woman's diet, she tried humor to divert people's attention. She replied that the Wild Woman "will eat a cabbage as quick as a cow will."[45] She also added that she "eats like a monkey, and drinks on all fours."[46] All of Walters's evidence so far backed up Northcott's story, and her appearance in court proved that she was an effective spokeswoman who probably had a speaking role while the exhibit was open. Certainly, the idea that visitors could see a woman tear into a head of cabbage or get down on all fours to drink water would have boosted public interest if the show survived its day in court.

When Walters spoke again, however, she had decided to change the direction of her testimony. By this point, she had heard nine doctors testify to their doubts about allowing the show's continuation. After six of them had testified, a reporter noted that "all the witnesses hitherto examined, who believed her insane, in reply to a question, concurred in expressing their opinion that the public exhibition of the woman was calculated to injure her."[47] In saying this, they concurred with the mental-health reformer Dorothea Dix, who believed that "delicacy and modesty" were inherent parts of a woman's mental and physical nature.[48] No longer willing to defend Northcott's shredded story, Walters now said that she had become convinced over the past "several days," or even just "yesterday," that the Wild Woman was sane and in league with the captain to enact a humbug.[49]

When the court asked why Walters had changed her mind about the show's authenticity, she described events that probably had occurred only the night before. According to Walters, she first became suspicious about the Wild Woman's authenticity when Northcott had entered the women's bedroom, and "I saw him lying down by the side of her bed."[50] The Wild Woman and Northcott then shared a close and quiet discussion, according to Walters, who added that she had not been able to hear their conversation. Even though she had not heard the Wild Woman speaking, she became convinced that "it is all a hoax."[51] Walters also came to question the veracity of Northcott's story when she heard the Wild Woman exclaim, as the police arrived to take her into custody, "Lord of mercy, what are they going to do?"[52]

It is not clear when this discussion between the Wild Woman and Northcott had occurred, but the *Cincinnati Daily Gazette* account records Walters as having said that he "was with her in the jail, but not alone." While this report stretches credulity in the sense that this would place Northcott in the prison even as the deputy sheriff was supposedly searching for him, the *Cincinnati Daily Times* records Walters as saying in court "that she had not seen or heard of him since last night," which would have been at the jail. Further, in a different story, the *Times* stated in its own voice that "Captain Norcott was also at the jail, though not as a prisoner."[53] Thus, two newspapers place Northcott in the Wild Woman's room (with Walters, presum-

CLOSING THE SHOW AND TRYING A WOMAN IN COURT • 65

ably) on the night between her arrest and her trial. Apparently, the police were not looking for him very diligently.

That Walters told the court about these two episodes of the Wild Woman using language is not unquestionable evidence that such discussions happened. During this second burst of courtroom testimony, Walters was clearly looking after her own interests. Making up evidence that cast her as the victim of a duplicitous pair of con artists would have seemed like a good way to safeguard her own position. Nor would she stick to this second version of events. Once she returned to the jail, Walters reverted to the Northcottian script. There was no consistency to her accounts, and it is unreasonable to trust anything she said. Even when she did not contradict herself, there was often no independent corroborating evidence to support what she said. For example, Walters claimed that prior to arriving in Cincinnati, the Wild Woman was "in Little Rock [where] she was exhibited at fifty cents a head."[54] While the show may have found a venue in Little Rock in order to rehearse and fund its opening on a bigger stage, neither the *Arkansas State Gazette and Democrat* nor the *Little Rock True Democrat* made any mention of it.[55] And then there was the attendant's most dubious testimony.

Walters proved willing to say just about anything once the evidence of the Wild Woman's body shredded Northcott's version of her past. With the doctors saying that the woman was insane and that public exhibition was hurting her, Walters looked to protect herself. One route forward was to side with the men who had just testified. During her second testimony, she told the court that she "thought the woman had been taken off by the Camanches [sic], and had children by some of them, that she escaped and got lost on the mountains."[56] Another way to try to save herself was to incriminate the Wild Woman and Northcott as a humbug. Presenting herself as a victim of their lies, Walters claimed that the captain had not paid her a cent of her promised wages. Having begun the day repeating the script from the exhibit, she now closed her appearance in court with claims of the Wild Woman's sanity and ability to converse as well as Northcott's financial indebtedness to her. It was quite a shift. Amazingly, Judge Burgoyne would prove to be receptive to parts of her final version of events. By the end of the day, Walters had earned the *Cincinnati Columbian* reporter's description of her as having a "motherly appearance" but one laced with "much shrewdness."[57]

In a stunning reversal, Walters changed her story back again by the next morning. Interviewed by a *Cincinnati Daily Times* reporter at the jail on Friday, July 11, she reverted to Northcott's narrative. Stuck in an upper-story jail room with only one window, and that "strongly protected with iron bars," Walters had only the Wild Woman for company. She continued to behave as the Wild Woman, acting timidly in front of the reporter. Having been seated on the floor, she "jumped up the moment we entered, and ran to the farthest corner of the room, where, fixing her large black eyes upon us she remained almost motionless." Walters played along with the Wild Woman act for the duration of the interview, coaxing her to relax and encouraging her to interact with the reporter and "Turnkey Bloom." Never did she again express her belief that the Wild Woman was feigning her feralness. By the conclusion of the interview, Walters had definitively reversed her position to its original stance: "There ain't no sham there," she told the reporter. And she should know, Walters added defiantly: "Didn't I see her when for five weeks she was kept in a cage like a tiger?" She expressed no doubts now. "'I tell you thar's no sham thar,'" she repeated. The reporter was unconvinced, declaring himself "very much disposed to differ with the attendant." He predicted that the Wild Woman would recover from her faked insanity "in a short time" if she was sent to the Southern Ohio Asylum at Dayton.[58] Knowing what we know now, we might guess that the Wild Woman had, when left alone with Walters, been able to convince or coerce her into changing her story back again. A different reporter, who saw the two women part company the next morning, remarked that "no tears were shed" by either of them.[59] Whatever the cause of her changing testimony, Walters now comes across as one of the least reliable sources in a sea of untrustworthy evidence.

Judge Burgoyne heard from two more doctors after Walters left the stand for the second time, but they added little. A final witness, a Mr. Canon, who ran a store underneath the Wild Woman's lodgings, said that she had a "fondness for his little boy," whom she caressed by playing with his "ears hands, legs and other parts."[60] With that, Burgoyne adjourned the court until the next day, Saturday, in the hopes that Northcott could be brought in. Rumors swirling around the city, however, said that "he had left for New Orleans."[61] He would not be found.

JUDGE BURGOYNE'S VERDICT

So, how would Burgoyne rule? Would he rule the Wild Woman an insane victim of the cruelty of Northcott, an Indian, or someone else? Would he instead find her sane, a humbug who might then find herself in legal peril? The doctors had not given him a clear path. There had been more votes for insanity than feigning, but several had hedged their bets and admitted that either was a possibility. Walters, who knew the Wild Woman better than anyone else, had clarified nothing. There was also the city's gossip to keep in mind, and it was running toward feigning and a hoax. Also, the *Cincinnati Daily Gazette*'s trial coverage had concluded with a note that a janitor in a building where the Wild Woman had been exhibited claimed that "one day after the company was gone he saw the 'wild woman' and the ticket-seller laughing together. When he approached to hear their conversation, the woman resumed her stare and the ticket seller looked sheepish."[62] The judge would have read that issue of the *Gazette* before his court reconvened. (Burgoyne was generally antislavery and likely to take the Republican-leaning *Gazette*.) There was enough doubt in the air to allow him to rule either way.

The *Cincinnati Daily Times*, for example, was extremely skeptical about claims of insanity. By the end of the court hearing, it found that Walters's testimony about the Wild Woman's hoaxing was "conclusive." Its reporter even made a joke about the extent to which public opinion had swung toward seeing the show as a humbug. "The imposture is absurd," the paper declared, "and we doubt whether any person can be found in the community who have been to see the Wild Woman."[63] It was so clearly a hoax, in other words, that no one would want to admit to having been hoodwinked out of a quarter by so blatant a fraud. Subsequent events only confirmed the paper's conviction that it had been a humbug, starring a sane actor. It sensed that among those attending the sentencing, "the general impression is that the woman is feigning insanity, and that the story of her capture in the Wachita mountains is all a humbug."[64]

Either way, Burgoyne's verdict was now due. The next day his court was, in the *Cincinnati Daily Enquirer*'s words, "densely thronged with spectators anxious to get a peep gratis at the strange individual, who now became the 'observed of all observers.'"[65] The Wild Woman's reappearance was accompanied by Walters and, pointedly, two deputy sheriffs. Gone was the rope, though, proof of the demise of the Wild Woman story in court the day before. Also gone was "the fierce stare of a falcon eye," replaced or at least "moderated into an expression of comparative softness." She was "dressed more carefully than on the former day," and her hair, though still hanging loosely, "had evidently lost much of the wild appearance which heretofore attracted so much attention."[66] She was a wild woman no longer.

Her changed appearance prompted the *Enquirer*'s reporter to try for rhetorical eloquence. His words were the funeral oration for the Wild Woman show, and they captured both the allure of the feral woman and the start of the Wild Woman's retreat into the confines of respectable femininity: "The mystic wreath that hung over her brow, and suggested tales of dense solitude, 'twilight groves and dusky caves,' seemed to have departed with the discovery of the many facts irreconcilable with much of the romance of her history; and as she became more assimilated to truth, softness and feminine grace, she became less an object of interest and curiosity." To be feminine was to be boring, no less for the observed than for the observer. The Wild Woman and her power to command public attention was dead, leaving behind a domesticated woman who would attract only very limited attention in the months to come.

Ultimately, Judge Burgoyne issued the only verdict that was open to a man of his sensibilities. He ruled that it was the court's "duty not to discharge her, but would have her taken care of, and see that such medical treatment as her case required should be furnished to her, and such accommodation as would have for its object the amelioration of her condition." Burgoyne admitted that there had been "a strong disposition on the part of some" to find that it "was all a humbug," but he chose the path that guaranteed that he would not be releasing an ill woman out on the street.[67] If he had read Dix's tracts on mental health, he also knew that prompt therapy was crucial to recovery.[68] Rendering the Wild Woman insane instead of a hoaxer also preserved the gender ideology by which Burgoyne and other reformers lived. Many reform movements, from temperance to abolition to anti-prostitution campaigns, were predicated on presenting women as morally pure people all too likely to be victimized by unscrupulous men. The idea that the Wild Woman could be a willing actor in a con would violate that stereotype of womanhood. As scholar Kathleen De Grave writes of female con artists, such women "elicit a much more nervous laughter, because they make it clear that the false ideal [of femininity] will have to change."[69] The only way to keep the Wild Woman true to an imaginary ideal of femininity was to paint her as insane, an abnormality among her sex. Burgoyne ruled that she would stay in the jail until Monday, when she would be transported to the Southern Ohio Asylum in Dayton. The woman who had been a star until her arrest on Thursday would be institutionalized by the end of the day on Monday.

Burgoyne took one more action after he issued his verdict. It is a credit to his generosity, though perhaps to his gullibility as well. He noted that

Walters "had been deserted by the gentleman at whose solicitation she traveled from her home in Texas, and was now anxious to return, without the means to do so. He suggested, therefore, the raising of a fund to defray her expenses." The courtroom was packed. Would people donate money to Walters, or were they skeptical about her honesty and worthiness? A reporter noted that the fund reached a total of "about $8," including the $5 given by the judge himself.[70] That lack of generosity is one measure of how much credibility people extended toward Walters and her stories.

THE WILD WOMAN'S INSANITY

The Wild Woman spent the next several months at the Southern Ohio Asylum, labelled insane by Judge Burgoyne and most of the doctors who had examined her. This verdict stands out in the history of the human zoo. At every other such exhibit, there had been only two possible realities to imagine: it was either authentic or a fake. Some of the doctors stuck with those two choices, especially Wright and Williams, who dismissed her as a humbug. But most of the men had proven to be open to a third answer. This group started with the judge, who had brought her into his probate court to determine, not the legitimacy of the show, but the sanity of the exhibited woman. Even before him, a group of women in Walnut Hills (and their spokesperson who had carried their concerns to Burgoyne) had come up with the idea that the Wild Woman might be insane. This was new territory for a human-zoo culture, and it is worth noting that it started with two newly empowered elements in society: publicly active women and an antislavery judge. (Those groups will figure prominently in chapters 3 and 4.)

Also intriguing was the creativity shown by the doctors who favored an insanity verdict when they invented a personal history for the Wild Woman that would have deprived her of her reason. Where did they get their ideas for how insane women looked and acted? Where did they get their idea that a woman's insanity must have its roots in the death of her children or in sexual assault? Reproductive issues were not listed as primary causes for insanity in the medical literature of the day. Historian David J. Rothman records the leading causes of mental illness from asylum reports from 1845 and 1861 as ill health, religious anxiety, financial losses, too much studying by students, frustrated ambitions, overexertion, and many other causes that have little to do with courtship, sex, or children. Perhaps tellingly, these other causes seem to have afflicted mostly men. For them, "disappointed love" appears far down on the list of causes.[71]

The Cincinnati doctors followed the medical tradition of finding different causes for insanity in men and women. As early as the beginning of the 1800s, male doctors "increasingly attempted to root diseases of the mind in the bodies of women," writes historian Brenna Holland. There were, she notes, "deeply gendered ideas about madness that circulated at this time."[72] According to Dr. Benjamin Rush, the female body and its reproductive organs made it prone to mental illness. In short, when doctors looked at the Wild Woman, all they saw was her body's reproductive function. From there, telling tales of rape was perhaps a predictable outcome. Given her sexual vulnerability—a woman tied up by Northcott in the wilderness, placed on display by her bed in Cincinnati, and then forcibly undressed in the courtroom—thoughts of rape were probably already in the physicians' minds when they invented their diagnoses that morning.

The doctors also drew on a rich culture of stories about insane women when they created their fictive narratives about the Wild Woman. Readers of Jacksonian-era newspapers and literature would have encountered many crazy women over the years, and there were enough parallels between these figures and the Wild Woman to enable the doctors to draw on their earlier cultural lessons when considering her case. There were, notably, several examples of women driven to insanity by the loss of loved ones or children. In some cases, they ended up living in the woods apart from civilization. Tellingly, their condition displayed itself through their eyes and disordered hair, both trademarks of the Wild Woman show. To understand how Judge Burgoyne and the doctors, as well as the Walnut Hills women who set them on this diagnostic path, came to find the Wild Woman insane, we need to look at some of these antecedents of the woman they thought they saw when examining the woman in the courtroom.

Some of the stories the men might have drawn on were nonfiction, or at least items that presented themselves as such. One of the first "true" newspaper stories about a feral woman made its appearance in 1843. The report started in the *Baltimore Sun* on January 30, and it was picked up the next day by the *Philadelphia Public Ledger*. From there, it spread to at least thirteen other newspapers. Although a small minority of all of the newspapers then in business, they covered much of the country, with the feral-woman story appearing frequently not only in New England and New York state but also in Pennsylvania, Ohio, and even Florida. The story ran in traditional newspapers as well as in two Christian publications and the *American Masonic Register*. Reports of a feral woman were big news in 1843, just as they proved to be in 1856.[73]

The 1843 feral woman's story began, curiously, in Cincinnati. No names are given in the story. There, the future feral woman was courted by a man, only to have her father oppose the blossoming romance. She then chose to elope, the news story continued, and the couple made it as far as Louisville. There, the man promised marriage, seduced the woman, and then abandoned her. The woman learned of his flight, and immediately "fainted and fell in the street." This began her descent into insanity. Deserted by her lover, she returned home only to find that her disobedience and elopement had killed her father. Her mother then cursed her and shut the door on the young woman. Bereft of all family, her suitor, and her virtue, she retreated to the woods, where she caught birds and "devoured them raw."[74]

This woman's life in the wilderness, which somehow involved her walking from Cincinnati to the outskirts of St. Louis, bears some resemblance to the tales told by Northcott and the courtroom doctors. This feral woman survived on "berries, nuts, fruit, and such game as she was enabled to catch," all while she lived through two winters "in an old deserted cabin on the banks of the Missouri. She filled it nearly full of dried leaves in the fall and would creep into them in cold weather." The woman later said she "had made up my mind to die in the wild woods, and never again to suffer a human being to speak to me," but her resolve failed after a fire destroyed her cabin and her food stores. Facing a severe winter and already "badly frostbitten," she abandoned the woods, appearing outside a home "almost naked, and apparently quite wild." She survived, the newspaper reported, only long enough to become "quite rational" and to tell her story.[75]

The popularity of her story, whether true or not, reflects the culture's belief that young women's sexuality held destructive and disruptive powers. Tales of seduction and its fatal consequences for young women had been a mainstay for American readers starting with Susanna Rowson's *Charlotte Temple* in 1791 and Hannah Foster's *The Coquette* in 1797. Such works meant to inspire sexual caution. As a prototype of the story Northcott told, the 1843 news had an early version of her diet, her long stay in the wilderness, and her description as "almost naked" and alone. As an early version of the doctors' stories about the Wild Woman, it placed a young woman in the woods because of sexual wrongs and the sudden death of her father.

The 1843 account claimed to be true. But there was also a strong tradition of wild women in American fiction that laid the groundwork for the 1856 exhibit. Catharine Sedgwick's important 1822 novel, *A New-England Tale,* introduced readers to Crazy Bet, a character who lives in the woods independently, though she does interact with town residents. Sedgwick's description of Bet included features that the Wild Woman would later exhibit, most especially her loose hair and prominent eyes. With her head wrapped in "a full leaved vine, by which she had confined bunches of wild flowers," Bet has long hair "streaming over her shoulders; her little black mantle thrown back, leaving her throat and neck bare."[76] Almost always outside and frequently encountered at night, Bet's "eyes were in a fine 'frenzy, rolling from earth to heaven, and heaven to earth'; she looked like the wild genius of the savage scene, and she seemed to breathe its spirit."[77] At a crucial point in the novel, Bet acts as a guide to the young heroine, Jane, through "a wild trackless region" of New England.[78] She takes Jane along a path "none knows but the wild bird and the wild woman. Have you never heard of the 'caves of the mountains'?"[79]

Bet, the self-proclaimed "wild woman," knows of caves in the mountains, unkept hair, unusual eye movements, and open-neck clothing. In addition, Sedgwick's explanation for how Bet came to be this way could have served as the model for the Cincinnati doctors, albeit thirty-four years after the book's publication. Bet had been full of sensibility as a youth, only to have her mind become "unsettled" when her fiancée drowned on the eve of their marriage.[80] After his death, she "would range the woods, and climb to the very mountain's-top, to get sweet flowers, to scatter over the mound of earth that marked his grave."[81] For Sedgwick, Bet's emotional freedom and expressiveness served as a positive counterpoint to strict Puritan theology, and her eventual death on her lover's grave marked a reunion and a final coming to rest. For our purposes, it is important that her insanity begins with the loss of a lover and the traditional female path to fulfillment that he had promised. As with the Cincinnati doctors decades after her, Sedgwick could imagine female insanity as the product of familial loss.

As important as Sedgwick was to American culture, Harriet Beecher Stowe would certainly have had the most influence on the Wild Woman's fate in court. Her best-selling novel, *Uncle Tom's Cabin,* had been popular since its publication as a standalone book in 1852. Its influence in Cincinnati would have been especially strong, given that Stowe had lived in the city for eighteen years, leaving only in 1850.[82] Her former neighbors would also have had several opportunities to see theatrical versions of *Uncle Tom's Cabin;* as historian John L. Brooke has shown, several touring companies brought the play to Cincinnati in 1853 and 1854.[83] The Queen City, he writes, "attracted the greatest number of dispersing productions of *Uncle Tom's Cabin.*"[84] The educated doctors, and certainly Judge Burgoyne, would have been familiar with Stowe's character Cassy, who lives on the Simon Legree plantation, the location for the novel's most dramatic scenes. Like Sedgwick's Crazy Bet, Stowe's Cassy closely resembles how Northcott, Walters, and the doctors would come to represent the Wild Woman.

Born into slavery, Cassy is raised in a convent, where she is protected by her benevolent owner, who is also her father. This man dies when she is fourteen, however, and by age fifteen, she enters a romantic union with a man she loves, who is also her new owner. By the time poverty forces him to sell her seven years later, they have had two children. Her next owner then abuses her and sells away her offspring. As Cassy retells the story of her children literally being torn away from her, she says that "something in my head snapped, at that moment."[85] This derangement leads her to kill her two-week-old son, an act that she tells Tom is "one of the few things that I'm glad of, now. I'm not sorry, to this day; he, at least, is out of pain."[86] In the eyes of Stowe, Cassy must be morally excused from having murdered her son because her madness was the natural outgrowth of her family history and of slavery. The deaths of her father and the man whom she first loved, the sale of her children, and her succession of coercive sexual relationships, culminating with her purchase and abuse by Simon Legree, drive her to madness and murder. It was entirely to Cassy's credit as a woman that she had been "stung to madness and despair by the crushing agonies" of her life.[87]

Stowe's descriptions of Cassy while she lives on the Legree plantation bear interesting correlations to how men wrote and talked about the Wild Woman. As with Sedgwick's depictions of Crazy Bet, Stowe's representations of Cassy in her madness focus on her eyes and her manner. Stowe makes it clear that the Cassy whom readers meet on the Legree plantation has lost her reason. She writes that Cassy has "a wild, long laugh" that ends "in a hysteric sob."[88] Only Tom, a saintly Christian slave, can calm her, at which time she shows none of her "former wildness."[89] A few pages later, however, Cassy is once again seen having broken "out into raving insanity."[90] This lunacy is caused by "the hideous yoke of her servitude," but it is insanity nonetheless.[91]

Cassy's eyes, like the Wild Woman's, are the true sign of her mental anguish and illness. Readers are immediately introduced to the wildness of Cassy's eyes. "Her eye was the most remarkable feature," Stowe writes, "so large, so heavily black, overshadowed by long lashes of equal darkness, and so wildly, mournfully despairing. There was a fierce pride and defiance in every line of her face, ... but in her eye was a deep, settled night of anguish."[92] As bad as that seems, her eyes become more excited and wilder as the novel moves to its showdown between good and evil on the plantation.

Though enslaved and abused by Simon Legree, Cassy slowly gains ascendency over her oppressor, in part because of his alcoholism and superstitious mindset. Cassy's eyes, signs of her mental instability, are important factors in her empowerment. She can terrify Simon "with a sharp flash of her eye, a glance so wild and insane in its light as to be almost appalling."[93] On the verge of her escape, she stares at him with "that strange light in her eyes that always impressed Simon with uneasiness."[94] Like the Wild Woman, she possesses a "strange, unearthly expression" that is conveyed largely through her eyes when she "sat fixing them on him."[95]

Two things are going on here. First, we can see how unusual it must have been for women to look at men in anything other than a supportive or flirtatious manner. One who looked directly and steadily at a man must have been quite unusual. That Cassy and the Wild Woman did look directly at men, even angrily, may have been enough to convince Stowe's readers or the Cincinnati doctors that something was amiss with a woman's psyche. Second, anyone who had recently read *Uncle Tom's Cabin* was likely to have remembered Cassy's manner and visual appearance, including the descriptions of her eyes. Perhaps those behind the Wild Woman hoax recognized how much it would help their show's credibility if her eyes were the main feature of her wildness. But it need not have been the exhibitors' idea; the doctors, Judge Burgoyne, and the women of Walnut Hills were the ones who read insanity into the Wild Woman show. The Walnut Hills women, Stowe's neighbors until six years ago, would have read *Uncle Tom's Cabin* closely. As middle-class women on the verge of antislavery politics but not there yet, they were Stowe's target audience. As readers of Cassy's scenes, they knew the manner and eyes of insanity, and that was what they came to see in the Wild Woman. They also knew its causes.

There is one more detail in Cassy's backstory that may have sealed the diagnosis of insanity for the Wild Woman. It comes right after the character is sold by her first lover, the man whom she considered to be her husband for seven years. She later tells Tom that she was, at that moment, so upset, "I couldn't speak."[96] The destruction of families could render a woman insane and speechless—any reader of *Uncle Tom's Cabin* would know that much. It seems almost inevitable that people who thought the Wild Woman to be insane would devise a backstory for her that involved the destruction of her family.[97]

And that is exactly what happened in 1857 when an author sat down to write a sensationalist novella that claimed to be the Wild Woman's autobiography. It gives the Wild Woman the name Alice Galon and, with it, a backstory full of misfortunes. The author jams the story with seductions, counterfeiting, forgery, gambling, an evil school principal, and no small number of murders into less than eighty pages of text. The result is, in many ways, completely divorced from anything to do with the actual Wild Woman exhibition. Alice Galon's time on display happens only in the final two pages and offstage in a way that sheds no insight into the show. The entire plot serves only to explain how Alice came to lose her sanity and her ability to speak. Its author follows in the footsteps of Sedgwick and Stowe by locating her insanity in extreme familial loss.

Alice, the novella explains, was rendered speechless and helpless through the death of her closest family members. Her seduction by Clarence Withrow brings her momentary happiness but lingering moral doubts. Clarence's murder of Alice's brother, James, who had sought to bring her home, is only the first blow. Additional losses follow as the months go by. News of her seduction soon kills her father in a scene reminiscent of the 1843 news story. When Clarence then plots to abandon their baby girl, Alice's transformation into a helpless victim begins; as Clarence explains, "now she looks wild, her eyes seem to have expanded to twice their original size." Alice loses the ability to speak. While she is incapacitated, he and his new lover murder Alice's child, sending her spiraling into a "singular species of insanity" that lasts for months. Clarence's counterfeiting schemes go awry, and in desperation, he takes "her to Cincinnati for exhibition!"[98]

The novella ends with an unspoken but clear endorsement of Judge Burgoyne's verdict and Alice's understanding of the case. The Wild Woman was both insane and the victim of "a mystery of wickedness too deep to comprehend." Like the other female characters who suffer extreme mental illness, Alice does so because of the death of her brother, father, and especially her own infant daughter. Cincinnatians are credited with saving her from an abusive man. The author concludes by praising the "kind citizens" who "wrested the innocent victim from the hands of her persecutors, and placed her under the kind protection of those who could sympathize with and heal her woes!" While wholly fictional and useless as a source for understanding the actual exhibit, the novella shows us the culture's ways of seeing the roots of women's mental health.[99]

Judge Burgoyne's verdict brought the Wild Woman show to its end. Captain Northcott and Ann Walters would not be seen again. He fled before the verdict was given; Walters waited only one day more. The *Cincinnati Daily Enquirer* reported, "it is said, [Walters] immediately took passage on a steamboat for her home, being apprehensive, as some think, that the place round here was getting too hot for her."[100] The Wild Woman, her name forever obscured, would continue to be the subject of rumors and reports for several months until her release from the Dayton asylum. The hearing had brought forth more media attention and gossip than any other aspect of the show, and public commentary revealed important ideas about women and insanity, about the medical profession, and about Walters's integral part in the dissemination of the Wild Woman narrative. For the first time, the traditional dichotomy of the human zoo—fake or authentic?—broke down in the face of a third option. In this case, the Wild Woman might not be real or a hoax, rather a victim in need of publicly ordered medical care. As they had for the past six weeks, the men in the courtroom looked at her and projected their own ideas of femininity, sex, family, and civilization onto the silent woman before them. But unlike the men in the exhibit hall, the steamboat, and the room at the United States Hotel, the Walnut Hills women, the doctors, and the judge saw an insane victim rather than a feral woman and acted accordingly.

So far, we have learned the details of the Wild Woman capture narrative, seen what the show might have looked like, and followed how it ended. The next chapter will explore what the public's reactions to the exhibit tell us about the political divisions in the United States as it stood on the brink of the Civil War.

3

SEX-TIONALISM AND THE GENDER IDEOLOGIES OF THE POLITICAL PARTIES

On the surface, the Wild Woman episode does not appear to have very much to do with politics. No politicians held forth on its merits or its fakery. It inspired no new laws or policy changes. And it cannot be tied to any election or campaign platform.

Yet the ways men and women reacted to the Wild Woman can help us answer two of the biggest questions scholars have about the Civil War era and its politics. First, historians have asked why people identified so strongly with the political parties they joined. Antebellum Americans displayed keen partisan loyalties that often lasted a lifetime. Political historians find the roots of this loyalty most often in rational policy debates about economic issues, the extension of slavery, federalism, and foreign policy as well as the strengths of candidates and their biographies.[1] Others see voters influenced by their racial beliefs or by their ethnic and religious identities. All of these factors played especially strong roles during the mid-1850s, when slavery became increasingly controversial and the Know Nothing Party called for curtailing the access of immigrants and Roman Catholics to US citizenship.[2] For still other historians, including myself, political allegiances were also determined in part by a person's beliefs about family, marriage, and gender roles. Parties expressed distinct stands on issues such as prostitution, divorce, and women's empowerment in marriage and public affairs. They sought to enlist (male) voters by emphasizing either unchecked patriarchal authority or the promise of women as willing and powerful allies in private and public life.[3] Not surprisingly, Republicans, Democrats, and Know Nothings also expressed different opinions about the Wild Woman show, diverse reactions consistent with the gender ideologies they promulgated throughout the country.

Second, scholars have recently been debating the extent to which the North and the South differed during the antebellum years. While most historians in the late twentieth century believed that substantial cultural, economic, and political differences existed between the two sections, many recently have stressed the similarities shared by the South and the North. The ways in which southerners and northerners discussed the Wild Woman enable us to see how the sections differed in their reactions to the event's central image: a woman publicly kept captive and tied to her bed. Nor was the Wild Woman of Cincinnati the first or the last feral woman to blaze her way across popular culture in the 1850s. Looking beyond the Cincinnati episode, other wild-woman stories elicited different responses from northern and southern observers, especially as the 1850s progressed. In opposition to recent claims of regional similarities, sectionally distinct reactions to feral women suggest that northerners and southerners lived in two different cultures.

The importance of the political and sectional disagreements about gender that emerged from the Wild Woman show are hard to overstate. Historians know that gender is a fundamental marker for how people understand their society and their place in it. Open conflicts are more likely to break out when people see an outside group as holding different gender beliefs or practices. This is especially true if these beliefs appear to pose a threat to their own gender systems. The different ways that political parties and regional cultures interpreted feral women provide a key to understanding why the South and the North readied themselves for open hostilities in the late 1850s.

THE WILD WOMAN AND THE POLITICAL PRESS

Cincinnati newspapers have reliably shown us what the Wild Woman exhibit entailed and why it appealed to enough customers to keep it viable for over six weeks. But to analyze the production's larger place in national politics, our scope must broaden to include newspapers from around the country. Much of the national coverage was little more than the wholesale copying of stories from Cincinnati papers, sometimes in full but often in severely abbreviated versions. Nevertheless, editors around the nation often glossed these reprints with their own comments and occasionally deleted certain lines from the Cincinnati reports. Analyzing what stories were repeated or altered and correlating those editorial decisions with the presidential endorsements the newspapers made later during the 1856 campaign reveals the position of each major party on the proper roles of men and women in American society and culture.

During the initial burst of coverage following the show's opening, editors printed similar content regardless of their political affiliations. Increasingly, however, they diverged in their opinions as the Wild Woman show entered July. Politically aligned editors occupied different positions on the production by the time it unraveled, then diverged completely after the Wild Woman was taken to the Dayton asylum, treated, and released. By analyzing disagreements between each party's newspaper editors, we can understand what they thought about women and men.

In 1856, three major political parties competed for votes. The oldest and most established was the Democratic Party, which traced its ancestry back at least as far as Andrew Jackson's election to the presidency in 1828. It would win in 1856 behind its presidential candidate, James Buchanan. The Democrats won votes in both the North and the South with a platform favoring white supremacy over Native Americans and African Americans, national expansion, religious freedom, European immigrants' rights, and a limited role for the federal government in economic policymaking. It also supported patriarchy, asserting male rights to exclusive control over government and family while opposing the woman's rights campaign in the aftermath of the Seneca Falls convention of 1848. While more successful in southern states, Buchanan would also carry five northern states to secure his victory.

The opposition to the Democratic Party in 1856 was splintered and in flux. The party's traditional opponent in the 1830s and 1840s, the Whig Party, had all but disappeared by the time the Wild Woman show opened. In its place were two new parties, the Know Nothings (formally called the American Party) and the Republicans. These groups vied for the loyalty of the same pool of potential supporters, which included former Whigs, new voters, and any Democrats who might be lured away from the old party of Jackson. Because they mostly shared the same constituency of anti-Democratic voters, the two new parties' positions overlapped to a degree. Both appealed to evangelical Protestants, approved of the federal government's intervention into economic issues, and desired economic development. They disagreed, however, about the primary danger confronting the country in 1856.

The Know Nothings regarded Roman Catholics and immigrants as the main threat to American traditions and democracy, while the Republicans warned voters about the dangers posed by slavery's expansion to the West and North. For men who disliked the Democratic Party, choosing which opposing party to back often came down to what scared them more, Catholics and immigration or slavery. Complicating matters further, many Republicans were uneasy about immigration and Catholicism, and many northern Know Nothings worried about slavery's territorial growth. Both parties included men and women open to significantly enhancing women's legal rights and levels of political activity. Both alike and different, the Republicans and the Know Nothings would occasionally agree about the Wild Woman even as they eventually came to different stands on the show.

One other crucial political factor in 1856 was that most southern states did not allow the Republican Party to campaign within their borders. There were exceptions in some counties of the Upper South, but as a whole, southern politicians and violent mobs managed to make sure that the antislavery Republicans could only field candidates in northern states. For their part, the Know Nothings would spend 1856 slowly splitting into northern and southern wings, with antislavery Know Nothings running in the North and proslavery Know Nothing candidates fielded in the South. By the time voters went to the polls in October and November, the Republicans would be the dominant anti-Democratic party in the North. Thus, when the Republicans, an exclusively northern party in 1856, articulated a unique position on the Wild Woman by the end of the production, theirs was a sectionally distinct voice that highlighted the gendered differences between the North and the South on the eve of the Civil War. While not all northerners questioned patriarchy's tolerance of men's abusive behaviors, only northern voters could back a party that raised that concern as an issue.

Despite the differences in the political parties outlined above, partisan editors of all stripes reacted similarly during the first part of the Wild Woman episode. When the story first broke in Indiana and Ohio, newspapers across the country copied these reports with no differences based on the editors' political allegiances. This uniformity of coverage indicates that editors had not yet thought through how the silent woman played into their larger partisan ideologies.[4] Most Americans first learned about the Wild Woman when the *Cincinnati Commercial* published its long interview with Northcott in late May. Reprints of the story appeared across the country. Democratic, Know Nothing, and Republican editors were equally interested in the story and showed a reluctance to editorialize, choosing instead to reprint the full *Commercial* story or to summarize it.[5] Editors from across the political spectrum ran the whole report, including Democratic papers in Dallas, Nashville, and Chicago; a Know Nothing paper in Louisiana; and three midwestern Republican papers.[6] The same roughly equal distribution across partisan newspapers is apparent if we include abbreviated versions of the *Commercial* story. Two Republican papers from Vermont and one from New Jersey followed this practice, but so did Know Nothing ones in Tennessee and Virginia as well as Democratic publications in Pennsylvania, Massachusetts, and Indiana.[7] Individual editors decided whether or not to include the salacious sentence about the Wild Woman's scanty clothes and the rope attaching her to the bed, but there was not a partisan pattern to this choice.

The closing of the Wild Woman show brought greater partisan differences in coverage. There was a dramatic increase in the number of stories in Republican papers and a sharp drop-off in attention from Democratic editors. In addition to rising or falling levels of interest in the story, the content of party editorials began to vary. Partisan editors reacted differently to the idea that the episode may have been a humbug, with a woman consciously playing the lead role in a deception. They also displayed far different levels of interest in the Wild Woman after she went to the Dayton asylum, with only the Republican press concerned about her ongoing treatment and recovery.

THE DEMOCRATS

Nationally, Democratic newspapers lost almost all interest in the Wild Woman exhibition when the court closed it down. This is especially striking because the Democratic paper in Cincinnati, the *Daily Enquirer,* provided the best and most extensive coverage of the Wild Woman after the trial closed. (The Republican *Daily Gazette* came in a close second.) The *Enquirer* ran four stories in July as the Wild Woman was taken to Dayton and began undergoing treatment. It followed this in August and September (when she was released) with four more stories. Most of the *Enquirer*'s later reports were from someone who had been to the asylum and found that she was recovering. Always, though, the details of what had been learned about her past were withheld; Dayton officials never disclosed her case history.[8] It is noteworthy that the extensive coverage by the Democratic *Enquirer* did not stem from its party's gender ideologies. Quite simply, the *Enquirer* was the largest and best paper in the city, with an extensive staff and a constant demand for news to fill its densely packed pages. Its full coverage, however, means that it is analytically meaningful that other Democratic newspapers nationwide failed to reprint its stories. Through their exchanges with the *Enquirer,* Democratic editors across the country had access to free updates on the Wild Woman's recovery and yet failed to use them. The almost complete silence in the national Democratic press was the product of an ideologically driven lack of concern about the Wild Woman, not the result of a lack of news about her.

Despite the local Democratic paper's fine coverage of her recovery, the party's editors around the country showed no interest in the fate of the Wild Woman herself. With the show closed, there was little left to concern the Democrats. The only storyline that interested them ran about a month after the trial, when a Shreveport newspaper claimed it had proof that the show had been a humbug perpetrated by three of their town's residents. It stated that the cast consisted of Joe Williams (as Northcott), Ann Eliza Paul (as the Wild Woman), and "the wife of a man named Bond, who keeps a cake shop" (as Ann Walters). This item usually ran as a brief story in other papers. Editors loyal to all three parties ran the short version, though it is notable that Democrats chose to do so less often.[9] Perhaps by this time, almost a month after its end, the Wild Woman show had already faded into obscurity for them.

But there was also a longer version of the Shreveport story circulating in the nation's press. Notably, only Democratic newspapers in the databases reprinted this longer story, and the only ones to do so were published in the North in Columbus and Indianapolis. The longer version gave readers more details about Paul's transformation into a hoax, but only in a way that gave all of the power, intellect, and agency to Joe Williams, the lone man in the story. According to this longer account, "some gentleman in the vicinity [of Williams] last winter killed a bear of a tawny color. The skin was tried on Ann Eliza, whom Williams [then] carried before a male friend, to obtain his opinion as to the possible success of the disguise. The friend told him it wouldn't do, and it was abandoned." Not to be defeated, the would-be hoaxer then heard "a description of the capture of a wild man in that vicinity, which was intended as a hoax, [and] applied it to his mistress, and was reaping the benefits of the fraud till the courts of Cincinnati rudely interfered and put a stop to the speculation." The Democrats, it seems, were bemused by the makeshift ingenuity of the "tall, big-whiskered carpenter" named Williams and his success in staging a profitable show out of a cake-shop-owner's wife, his own mistress, and lots of gumption. In this Democratic telling of the show's backstory, the man thinks up every idea and takes all of the actions. "The skin was tried on Ann Eliza," the report said, not even giving Ann Eliza the agency to put on her own outfit. Dressed in the bear skin, she was carried, not even given the power to walk. She did not, in this account, enact the role of the Wild Woman; the part was simply "applied" to her.[10] This is a very masculinist version of events.

The fact that the Democratic editors who reprinted this longer version were based in the North suggests that they found it a useful way to counter Republican attempts to portray the Wild Woman as an innocent victim, an argument Democrats in the South did not have to refute. Its presence also suggests that these men supported a patriarchal vision of society with considerable vigor. While Republicans and some Know Nothing editors wrote about the Wild Woman as a wronged victim of male power, these Democrats imagined and then presented to the public a Wild Woman who was both complicit in the hoax and utterly passive at the hands of the masterful, bewhiskered carpenter, Williams. Their support of patriarchy was no less than that shown by white men in the South, who embraced male rule with the same passion they showed for white supremacy in this period. While some historians have seen northern Democrats nudging closer to a Republican position on slavery's expansion into the western territories, even to the point where Abraham Lincoln feared that his party might nominate Stephen Douglas for the Senate seat he coveted in 1858, the question remains: what kept the two parties and their voters separate?[11] There are several answers, but one of them must be that Democratic men were far less willing to entertain the idea of sharing private or public power with women than their Republican foes. The northern Democratic vision of the woman on display in Cincinnati as having her role "applied" to her and being carried to her private audition is evidence of the passivity that they expected from women. Republicans did not reprint that story, as many of them agreed with the court that the Wild Woman was not even a hoax.

The handful of Democratic editors who reprinted either version of the Williams and Paul story enjoyed its confirmation of what they had already concluded: the show was a humbug. News that the Wild Woman was a deception warranted only a bemused smirk and a collective yawn. The *Dallas*

Herald introduced its short version of the story by telling readers that the exhibition had been a hoax, "as we supposed." The *Columbus Daily Ohio Statesman* issued the longer report by announcing that its readers "will be amused" by the confirmation of the deception.[12] Democratic editors simply did not believe that the Wild Woman was a victim worthy of their readers' concern. To declare the show a humbug was enough for them. To take the Wild Woman off the stage, to no longer be able to stare at her, was to lose all interest.

It would be easy to say that Democratic men cared about the Wild Woman only as long as she was scantily clad. That would make sense in terms of what we know about the gender ideologies of the party nationally. In both the North and the South, Democrats seemed comfortable reporting on men paying to see the Wild Woman tied to her bed. Given the party's endorsement of slavery (with its legalized sexual abuse of enslaved women), northern urban brothel culture, and its angry dismissal of the woman's rights campaign, this is not surprising.[13] Democratic disinterest in the Wild Woman's day in court, the possibility that she had been wronged by a man, and her subsequent recovery highlights the extent to which Democrats cared about her mostly as an underdressed, tied-up young woman they could watch through a thin gauze of respectability. Even on the rare occasions when editors did carry reports about her treatment, they laced their news with sexist humor. One brief item in the Democratic *Cincinnati Daily Enquirer* ran only two sentences, and the first one was nothing more than a joke at the expense of women: "We learn from a gentleman who recently visited Dayton, and saw the Wild Woman at the Lunatic Asylum, that she has entirely lost her wild appearance, but has not recovered that without which no woman is herself—namely, the full use of her tongue." The second sentence then added only the most general note about her insanity and the doctor's optimism that she would be cured.[14] Patriarchy in politics extended to patriarchal pleasures and ridicule in the exhibit hall.[15]

As harsh as that sounds, Democrats can be credited with a better understanding of who the Wild Woman was, at least if she was a willing actor in a humbug. The party's gender ideology envisioned women as capable of a full range of behaviors, including dishonest ones, while the Republicans and the court saw them only as innocent victims. Democrats were not indignant about the hoax, nor were they surprised that a woman could have been an agent in deception. In that sense, they imagined women as capable of a broader range of personalities—a fuller scope of human qualities—than Republicans did with their narrow perception of women as virtuous angels.

THE KNOW NOTHINGS

As the Democrats lost interest, the Know Nothing partisan press ran more stories, with six Millard Fillmore–supporting papers reporting on the Wild Woman story as it came apart. One joined Democratic editors in reprinting the Shreveport story that the show was a fraud.[16] Two others, however, reported on the trial that sent the Wild Woman to the Dayton asylum, something that no Democratic paper outside of Cincinnati bothered to do.[17] Another praised the woman who had played the feral in the exposed hoax, saying that "if her wildness has been acted, then she is an actress of no ordinary capacity."[18] These Know Nothing editors differed from their Democratic peers in their greater willingness to cover the trial and to credit the woman at its center. Their agreement with the Democrats in some things is in keeping with Know Nothing strength in the South, but the party clearly was staking out its own positions on the gendered issues raised in Cincinnati.

The most notable Know Nothing divergence from Democratic coverage came in two newspapers that wrote about her sympathetically. Refusing to believe that she was a willing participant in a humbug, they wrote of her instead as a victim. An Iowa paper wrote of her as a "poor, wronged woman" and thought her derangement stemmed from "griefs . . . connected with her child or children. What anguish she may have suffered, what terror, what depth of misery may have torn her heart we cannot tell." In noting her "anguish," "terror," and "misery," this editor echoed the doctors who had invented tales of the Wild Woman's personal history. He hoped that "kind usage, human sympathies, the sweet influences of her own sex, and especially the melting, touching, subduing tons [sic] and caresses of children will at length bring the sorrowing creature to herself again."[19] This was an especially gendered diagnosis and prescription: Female insanity was caused by family problems, so women and children could cure them if applied properly. Another Know Nothing editor assumed that the woman being taken into court was scared and reprinted a story that claimed she had written "in a round, handsome hand" the words "I, I afraid" when asked by officers for her name.[20] Unlike the Democrats who assumed the Wild Woman had knowingly humbugged the public into paying a quarter to look at her, these two Know Nothing editors from Iowa and Tennessee portrayed her as a wronged victim, a woman grieving over lost children and afraid of what lay in front of her.

Given the same blank screen of a woman's body on which to project their party's ideas of womanhood, Know Nothing men could not come to a consensus. Their lack of agreement on what to say about the Wild Woman mirrored the party's confusion about what positions to take on woman's rights legislation or women's political activism. In Massachusetts, the Know Nothing–dominated government passed a married women's property law in 1855 that allowed a wife to work without her husband's consent and to keep her wages; she could also gain an easier divorce if deserted by her husband and find a smoother path to securing alimony and child custody.[21] Historian Mark Voss-Hubbard has found some women publicly organizing to help elect Know Nothings. He concludes, however, that the movement overall "was infertile soil for women's political activism." His finding that the nativist party "marginalized women's direct participation in the movement" seems to be borne out, especially in the southern states.[22] Two studies of the Know Nothing Party in Maryland find almost no involvement by women in politics or any legal reforms concerning woman's rights.[23] As historian Jean Gould Hales writes of the nativist position on women's activism, it was "a complex blend of conservatism and liberal reformism."[24] Clearly, there was no consensus about gender roles in the Know Nothing Party.

Unable to agree on a national position on woman's rights, it is not surprising that the Know Nothings found little common ground when they thought about the Wild Woman. Some agreed with Democrats that she was a hoaxer, while others wrote that she was a victim who deserved sympathy. Democrats agreed nationally to uphold patriarchal rights, and Republicans generally believed that women deserved more say in public and private. Unlike their rivals, however, the Know Nothings had no coherent gender ideology or perspective to unite it. They would pay a price for this, coming apart as a political party within the year.

THE REPUBLICANS

Republican editors also came to life as the Wild Woman show unraveled. The Republican Party was a diverse coalition, ranging from socially conservative former Whigs to radical antislavery men and women from a variety of political backgrounds. It also included some opportunists, such as James Gordon Bennett of the *New York Herald,* who stayed only for the 1856 campaign. The Republican reaction to the Wild Woman reflects its various constituencies. The more conservative elements of the coalition printed stories that also appeared in Know Nothing (or even Democratic) newspapers. They also wrote about her recovery in ways that reflected a traditional understanding of what roles women should enact. The party's more radical newspapers wrote about her exhibition and recovery in ways that were critical of patriarchy.

The newspapers of the more conservative wing printed stories that can also be found in Know Nothing organs. At least seven Republican papers ran brief reports that the show was a humbug, often using the same Shreveport story that opposing editors reprinted.[25] Some also ran the same "I, I afraid" account that Know Nothing editors reprinted, while the pro-Frémont *New York Herald* copied the story about the Wild Woman's anguish, terror, and misery that could be healed only by the company of other women and the "caresses of children."[26] The Republicans and the Know Nothings vied for the loyalty of the same anti-Democratic voters. That they would share some similar ideas about the Wild Woman is not surprising.

But Republican editors also broke new ground. This can be seen in the pages of the radical *Cincinnati Daily Gazette* even while the exhibition was still open. The *Gazette* was never comfortable with the idea of displaying an enchained woman. It showed its displeasure initially by not giving the exhibition any publicity in its pages. The paper did not list it in its local-events section until June 24, at least a month after the production had started.[27] The *Gazette* then waited another week before sending someone across the street to interview Northcott and run a story about the Wild Woman.

The *Gazette*'s belated story was not like the puff piece that the *Cincinnati Commercial* had run when the show opened. It raised questions about the production that other local papers had left unasked. Its reporter was skeptical when he looked at the Wild Woman, perhaps also discomforted. Noting her "fair complexion," he snidely commented that it was "as though she had never been exposed to the weather." He had other doubts as well. "The expression of her face is not brutal, as might be expected of a woman who had lived all her life as a mere wild beast," he observed, "but is rather one of sadness." Instead of accepting Northcott's story, the journalist imagined his own version of her: "the only striking peculiarity about her is the wildness of her eye, which gives her the appearance of a lunatic, and the spectator finds it hard for some time to free himself from the impression that he is in the presence of a crazy woman." This might have been the birth of the lunacy interpretation. It is more likely, however, that the reporter had heard this idea in reformist circles and carried it with him when he attended the show. Unlike other witnesses, he thought she might be as old as thirty-five, a notable change from the early twenties that other men chose to see. Most importantly, he wrote that "many persons object to visiting her because they regard it as a great inhumanity that a white woman should be led about by a rope to be exhibited as a wild animal to a curious multitude." To answer this charge, Northcott was allowed only the unconvincing reply that doctors "have advised him to accustom her to the sight of crowds."[28] In a bit more than a week, the production was closed by Cincinnati police. After that happened, the pro-Republican *New York Tribune, New York Herald,* and *Cincinnati Daily Gazette* stayed on the story, running long transcriptions of her day in court.

Republican newspapers dominated the coverage of the Wild Woman after she was admitted to the Southern Ohio Asylum.[29] To run stories in these months required editors and readers to care about the person when she was no longer wild or on display. Five Republican papers ran such stories; their only company among newspapers outside of the city was a lone Democratic item of only three sentences.[30] The Republican journalists reported on her recovery with satisfaction. An antislavery judge had said she was insane and had recommended treatment, and now she was responding. The Wild Woman's reported recovery was a victory for the new party and its actions in closing the show.

Republican editors celebrated the Wild Woman's recovery in ways that validated and reinforced their party's emerging gender ideologies. The antislavery party embraced a spectrum of beliefs about gender, ranging from conservative endorsements of patriarchy to reformist calls for broadening the rights of women. This breadth of opinion about women's proper roles is reflected in how its newspapers thought about the Wild Woman's recovery. On the one hand, her happy ending was sometimes rendered as proof of a conservative model of womanhood. On the other hand, even that circumscribed ideal was turned into a radical critique of society's gender system by faulting the ways men had behaved around the Wild Woman. Republican gender ideology proved more reformist than that of their electoral rivals.

After the Wild Woman had been in the asylum for a month, a Republican paper in New Jersey updated readers on her treatment. This story shows both a limited idea of how women should behave in public and a realization that men were to blame for hurting her very badly. There was no doubt in this item about whether she was really sick; Republicans (unlike Democrats) believed her to be mentally ill. According to this story, her condition had been diagnosed as "the peculiar but not uncommon phase of monomania, which manifests itself in refusal to converse—patients of this description being found in every Asylum." While in this state, the report continued, she had been subjected to a "very great alarm" that had put her "under the influence of fear, [and] was taught to deport herself according to the wishes of her inhuman exhibitors." The journalist, however, issued an optimistic outlook on her recovery, although one that was producing an extremely passive woman. The Wild Woman had "improved remarkably in docility and personal appearance." Her eyes no longer had that "peculiarly wild glare that characterized them a few weeks ago," and her hair was "neatly dressed." Her conduct had also improved, at least in this man's opinion. "She is sometimes taken into the reception room to see visitors," he noted, "and behaves in a very womanly manner. She answers the questions of strangers only by motions of her head. She will talk at times, however, with a good deal of connection and coherence to those with whom she is familiar." Her complete recovery was expected.[31] The Newark report's satisfaction with her "very womanly manner" confirms that Republicans expected different conduct from men and women, including greater silence and docility from women in social situations.

About three weeks later, a Republican paper in Indiana printed another visitor's report on the Wild Woman at the asylum. Her return to feminine behaviors seemed to be continuing. The "monomania" was "steadily disappearing," and she was "rapidly progressing in confidence and development." On several days, she had left the asylum grounds with the institution's matron. The two women had gone on "shopping excursions through the city, and her air and appearance had become so subdued that she attracted no special attention." The Wild Woman had, he reported, "an excellent intellect, considerable cultivation and association with refined and intelligent society."[32] One can complain that a satisfactory Republican recovery produced nothing better than a subdued woman who went shopping. On the other hand, at least Republicans cared that she was alive, which was more than could be said for the men in the other two parties.

Republican updates on the Wild Woman continued over the next few months, emphasizing her return to traditional female social roles. A *Cincinnati Daily Gazette* story (that was reprinted in Vermont and Hawaii) stressed that her family had been discovered. The Wild Woman had family in Texas, it said, and she was the mother of two children who, in her absence, had been "raised in good life, and [she] is respectably connected."[33] A final update from a Republican paper in Ohio continued to embed the Wild Woman within a family network, observing that she had gone to Texas after receiving "a letter from her sister." Once there, the article said, she wrote to a friend in Cincinnati "stating that she found her children in good health, and that she is now with them at her sister's."[34] This final report put a familial stamp on a happy ending that buried the Wild Woman in the anonymity of a woman's place in the private household. The Republicans, it seems, were satisfied with this role for her.

But Republican editors then added an important idea that separated their party from the other two. As noted earlier, a New Jersey paper blamed the Wild Woman's illness on the actions of her "inhuman exhibiters."[35] As reformers, Republicans were willing to fault how some men treated women. A *Cincinnati Daily Gazette* story, like the New Jersey item, insisted that she had been "early deceived and duped by some miscreant." The Wild Woman's mental state "did not amount to mania" but, rather, was depression that was "the result of abuse and neglect." Treatment had saved her from a "deep, melancholy gloom," but all of her troubles had their roots in abuse by a "miscreant," almost certainly a man since Northcott was the likeliest perpetrator; men also victimized women in the Republican fiction of Harriet Beecher Stowe and others (as well as in reality).[36] It is important to note that the lone Democratic paper to report on the Wild Woman's life in the asylum copied from this exact story, only doing so, however, after removing the two sentences about her having been abused and deceived.[37] In the world of partisan Democrats, men were not to be faulted.

The final word about the Wild Woman confirmed the impression circulating in Republican circles that she had been the innocent victim of male misbehavior. Intriguingly, it started in two issues of the Democratic *Cin-*

cinnati Daily Enquirer, whose reporter spoke with sources who were Republicans. On August 23, the *Enquirer* reported that Judge Burgoyne and one of the doctors from the courtroom, Dr. Langdon (who had testified that the Wild Woman was insane and should be kept from public gaze), met with the head of the asylum, Dr. John Joseph McIlhenny. Both McIlhenny and Burgoyne were Republicans, even if the judge clearly maintained a working relationship with the men at the *Enquirer.* As such, the tale they told bears the imprint of Republican sensibilities. The Wild Woman appears to have spun her story to suit their desires. This seems especially likely since we know that she had recognized Burgoyne and Langdon.[38]

What we know of the story she told Burgoyne and Langdon is limited by the asylum superintendent's unwillingness to share information. But an account told about two weeks later claimed to reveal a fuller version of events, and some of its details align with the earlier trip by Burgoyne and Langdon. Both reports, for example, state that the patient had gained about twenty or twenty-five pounds and that her recovery was nearly complete. The later account also blamed a man for her recent insanity, in the process telling quite a tale. Whether true or just a story told by the Wild Woman in an effort to win McIlhenny's sympathy, it recounts a harrowing tale of seduction and deceit that reads like a Republican piece of fiction. The patient, it reported, had unknowingly "married a man who had another wife, and by whom she had two children. Finding herself deceived, her health broke and she was removed to the Warm Springs, Arkansas. How Northcote came into possession of her person and mastery over her will have not been explained." The woman should not be faulted, the writer explained, since "whatever may have been the offense or collusion of the woman, she certainly has sorrowfully and sadly atoned for them all in her misfortunes and her sufferings." More at fault was the man who exhibited her. Of Northcote (Northcott), the writer would only say, "if ever a fellow deserved hanging it was the monster who sought to gain a living by such infamous and unprecedented means."[39] This version of events was essentially Republican in nature, probably fed into the media by either McIlhenny or people affiliated with his institution. That it appeared first in the pages of a Democratic journal is a credit to the size and scope of the *Cincinnati Daily Enquirer,* the largest newspaper in the city. It is telling that none of its editorial colleagues in the nation's Democratic press thought the story worth reprinting.

Republicans presented an assortment of thoughts on gender throughout the Wild Woman episode and the 1856 campaign more generally. One part of the coalition inclined toward traditional ideas of feminine behavior. Many Republicans envisioned her recovery as nothing more than a path to becoming a subdued shopper with two children and good manners. This trend may have been reinforced by the Wild Woman herself, who no doubt just wanted her own release from the asylum. Had she claimed a reformist or woman's rights identity, she would only have jeopardized her chances for an early discharge. So why not tell the male doctors what they probably most wanted to hear? Why not say that all she wanted to do was to go back to her family? There was a wide swath of the party's male supporters who would have relished confining her activities to this restricted sphere. Even their depictions of Jessie Benton Frémont, the wife of the first Republican presidential candidate, John C. Frémont, and the politically savvy daughter of a powerful US senator, sometimes presented her as little more than a beautiful woman who was eager to work in the kitchen.[40]

In addition to this sharply limited role for women, there was a more radical element in the Republican writings on the Wild Woman as exhibit and patient. This was in keeping with the national party's more liberal wing, which sought a greater public role for women, including as active agents for disseminating the party's ideas. Novelists Harriet Beecher Stowe and Lydia Maria Child published books in 1856 that backed the party's platform, and ordinary rank-and-file women organized and attended party rallies. Female Republicans carried signs, rode on floats during partisan parades, and raised money for antislavery settlers in Kansas. Jessie Frémont, who some Republicans reduced to a passive trophy, more often was portrayed as an advocate (though usually in private) of her antislavery beliefs.[41] These more reformist Republicans found a way to use the Wild Woman incident to benefit their cause of empowering women in public and private life.

In Cincinnati, these gender reformers engaged with the Wild Woman case in several ways. First, Republicans seem to have cared about the Wild Woman, her illness, and her recovery. More importantly, they were capable of blaming men for behaving badly. Abolitionist radicals and the nascent woman's rights movement (whose memberships often overlapped) had critiqued male behavior as early as the 1830s.[42] Both movements' ideologies were based on the premise that men would abuse the almost unlimited power society granted them over their slaves and wives. Antislavery women novelists, historian Holly M. Kent writes, began to criticize men in their fiction in the 1850s. These authors, including Stowe, represented "white slave-owning men as hopelessly sexually corrupt and violent."[43] Cincinnatians saw, read, and heard this critique of men and slavery just before the Wild Woman arrived, when the city was convulsed by the trials that resulted from the attempts of the Garner family to escape from slavery. Their attempt to gain freedom had ended in Cincinnati, where armed slavecatchers surrounded the house in which they had taken refuge. As slavecatchers stormed the building, Margaret Garner killed her very young daughter, Mary, intending to keep the child from repeating her own life experience in bondage.[44] The abolitionist and woman's rights advocate Lucy Stone, speaking later in a Cincinnati courtroom after one session of the subsequent hearing, clarified why she thought Garner had murdered her own daughter: "the faded faces of the negro children tell too plainly to what degradation female slaves submit."[45] Stone's point was made delicately, but she made it clearly: Garner had been sexually assaulted due to her bondage, and she expected her daughter to be similarly abused if she lived long enough as a slave. Of all the Cincinnati newspapers, only the Republican *Daily Gazette* was willing to print that part of Stone's speech.

The Garner case was big news in the city during February, March, and April. It took weeks for the courts to sort through its legal ramifications, which hinged on whether Garner should be removed to Kentucky under the federal Fugitive Slave Law or tried in Ohio state courts for murder. Judge Burgoyne played a part in these jurisdictional battles, trying to save Garner from reenslavement by upholding Ohio's right to keep her for trial. It is hard to see how the judge and other Cincinnatians could later look at the Wild Woman, white in skin tone and tied up with a rope, and not think about the famously light-skinned woman who had appeared before him just months before. In both cases, as Stone had made clear about Garner, men were at fault for their abuse of unchecked power.[46]

Ultimately, the *Cincinnati Daily Gazette* was willing to question the display of a chained white woman, just as they had been willing to print Stone's criticism of slavery as allowing the rape of Garner. That was a statement about sex and power that no opposing editor would make. The gender ideology of the more radical part of the Republican coalition emerged in their willingness to criticize some men's behavior toward women. It is difficult to underestimate the importance of people taking this stance. If no one ever stated that there were problems with patriarchy, nothing would be done to change it. The public criticism of men's treatment of women underlay the urgently needed feminist reform of patriarchal American culture, law, and politics.

The Wild Woman incident shows how partisan editors reacted to an enchained woman being put on display in a northern city. Democratic men thought about women as sexual beings to be enjoyed or even deceived by. They saw no need to look beyond the hoax; the Wild Woman was not a victim nor did she deserve medical care. In contrast, Republicans saw women occupying a circumscribed role in society, limited by their virtuous natures from acting duplicitously. But they also thought that women of all races were often the victims of men, whose patriarchal powers and immoral natures needed to be controlled by municipal police and courts as well as abolitionist legislation. The fact that Republicans and Democrats could look at the same silent woman and project such different ideas of womanhood onto her is a sign that voters could choose their political identities in part on the basis of their ideas about gender. As men imagined and interacted with the women around them, those who became Republicans and those who became Democrats lived in their own cultural worlds. One of the chief divides between the parties was drawn along the lines of how men thought about women; in short, they had different sexual politics. Republican and Democratic men and women's political affiliations were not based exclusively on issues such as Bleeding Kansas or the annexation of Cuba. They were also rooted in heartfelt personal beliefs about the ways women and men should interact.

The existence of partisan divisions based in part on the gendered beliefs of Republicans and Democrats (with Know Nothings occupying a confused space between them) clarifies the important sectional divide running across the nation. Southern editors reprinted news of the show while it was being staged but rapidly lost interest in it after its closure. The few exceptions to this rule came from Know Nothing editors in the Upper South. Northern editors proved far more active than their southern peers in following the story after the police detained the Wild Woman; this is true regardless of the northern men's political affiliation. Northern Democrats published a long account about the origins of the hoax in Joe Williams's head, while some Know Nothings but mostly Republicans contested for the Wild Woman's innocence. They also asserted her need for medical care. By extension, this meant that they called for government intervention in the form of police, a judge, and a state-funded asylum. These government agencies were necessary to protect a woman from the man who had called her his "pet." To insert the government between a man and the woman he controlled was a radical infringement on patriarchal rights as Democrats understood them.

With Republicans as an exclusively northern political party competing against two others that were national in scope, the divisions between Republicans and their electoral foes represented a sectional fault line as much as a partisan one. Political differences were also sectional disagreements. The North and the South in 1856 had different sex and gender ideologies; we can call this important regional difference "sex-tional politics." This sex-tional politics would divide men and make political amiability hard to achieve during the Civil War era. We can also see the two sections' different gender ideologies applied to other feral women discovered across the United States during the 1850s.

CINCINNATI AND SECTIONAL DIFFERENCES

A quick glance at Cincinnati in 1856 seems to reveal that the United States was unified in important ways. Located on the Ohio River, the city was poised on the very southern edge of the North. Economically, Cincinnati traded with both the North and the South. Goods came into the city from all directions, often to be exported again to the North and East on canals and railroads or shipped South and West on steamships and flatboats plying the Ohio and then the Mississippi River. The city could not exist economically without both sections. Politically, it hosted a national Know Nothing convention in 1855 and the Democrats gathered from the four corners of the Union to nominate James Buchanan for president even as the exhibition was running a few blocks away. Sectional tensions did not interrupt these conventions.

Social ties also came together in the Queen City. Black Cincinnatians, for example, came predominantly from the Upper South; one study finds that 70 percent of adult African Americans in the city "were southern born."[47] Many of the white residents also came from southern states, and they found themselves sharing neighborhoods with northerners and numerous European immigrants by the 1850s.[48] Historian Bridget Ford finds deep social and cultural connections between antebellum Cincinnatians and the people of Louisville, including shared assumptions about race, education, and "a strikingly similar spiritual economy on both sides of the Ohio River."[49] Historians Anne E. Marshall and Christopher Phillips have argued in separate books that people on both sides of the Ohio saw themselves as part of a shared culture, with a rigid sectional understanding originating only because of the events and policy debates of the Civil War years, especially emancipation.[50]

Recent histories that analyze other places along the border between the North and the South have also downplayed the extent of sectional differences. Some of the first studies in this historiographic trend compare the social and economic structures in border communities. Foremost among these is the comparison between Franklin County, Pennsylvania, and Augusta County, Virginia, by Edward L. Ayers and Anne S. Rubin. Likewise, L. Diane Barnes argues that Petersburg, Virginia, displayed the economic and social characteristics of a northern industrial city and that such "economic diversification into the manufacturing sector was not a complete anomaly in the antebellum South."[51]

Some historians have also questioned whether the controversies circling around slavery, or even the institution's existence, created meaningful differences between the two sections. This argument for the unity of the nation, slavery not excepted, has been advanced on two fronts. First, there is the indisputable fact that slavery played a part in the founding of the northern states, ranging from New England in the colonial period straight across to the upper Midwest in the early national period, despite the 1787 Northwest Ordinance's ban on slavery in the five states (including Ohio) that would be carved out of that land. Historians have recently noted that some white northerners participated in the kidnapping of people of color from the free states both before and after the passage of the Fugitive Slave Law of 1850.[52] But some scholars have gone further, arguing that there were important similarities between slavery and the ways wage labor was enacted in the racist North through the 1850s. Historian Matthew Salafia has written that "one of the stunning anomalies of the Ohio River Valley was the similarity between the work regime of racial slavery and that of wage labor on the borderland. . . . Enslaved and free African Americans experienced characteristics representative of both slavery and freedom, as along the Ohio River wage labor and chattel slavery became points on a capitalist continuum rather than mutually exclusive categories for African Americans."[53] Racist laws and cultures united white Americans on both sides of the Ohio River, he argues, creating one culture, not two. The border between free and slave states seems to have been muddied.

The second way that some have attempted to collapse the distinctions between the North and the South has been to argue that the southern economy, while based on slavery, was as capitalist and modern as anything that was happening in the North. This new interpretation goes against an earlier idea that the slave South was a premodern economy and society at odds with modernity's wage labor. The antebellum North, in the older interpretation, was an industrializing economy based on wage labor and capitalism. Some current historians now interpret the South as vibrantly capitalist, even without the widespread existence of wage labor, because it was deeply immersed in global trade and financial markets. While this new vision of the South has been challenged by scholars who rightly argue that capitalism by definition always rests on a class of wage workers, not on unpaid, unfree labor, there is no denying that southern planters and merchants exhibited capitalist behaviors and operated within global capital markets.

As a result of these two ideas—that the North profited from its own decades of slavery and then carried a commitment to white supremacy into the antebellum period and that southern slaveholders were profit oriented and immersed in global and sophisticated financial practices and institutions—some historians have argued that the North and the South shared many more features than earlier scholars had recognized. As Edward Ayers observes: "The North and South, so divided by slavery, also shared a great deal. The South was more economically advanced and the North more racially oppressive than they often seem in retrospect."[54] An analysis of the Wild Woman exhibit clarifies the nature of the similarities and differences between American regional cultures in the mid-1850s.

Superficially, the Wild Woman exhibition bears all the hallmarks of a national rather than sectional event. Northcott and Walters presented themselves as southerners, and the Wild Woman would eventually claim to be from Missouri and Texas. Despite their apparent southern origins, their show prospered in Ohio, and reports of it found their way into newspapers in every corner of the Union. Northcott hoped to take his production to the East after he closed in Cincinnati. Like the city that hosted the exhibition, the Wild Woman show did not give any overt indication that civil war was a mere five years away.

But there was, in fact, a larger gulf between the two sections than these recent studies admit. Even as some historians have argued for sectional similarities, others wisely point to differences in regional cultures and even armed conflict across the border between slavery and freedom.[55] Gender ideologies constituted another major fault line between the North and the South by the mid-1850s. A sharp rise in gender conservatism in the South in the 1850s shattered a national consensus that had supported an expanded (but still constrained) "sphere" for women. Historians of the 1830s and 1840s have documented nationwide support for allowing women greater liberties in education, political participation, and benevolent work. For example, Mary Kelley and Jonathan Daniel Wells have shown that women's academies nationwide provided excellent educations for some white women, and that the schools enjoyed widespread support during the Jacksonian era. Elizabeth R. Varon and Ronald Zboray and Mary Saracino Zboray have proven that the Whig Party in the 1840s encouraged women to show their partisan loyalty at rallies, speeches, and conventions. North and South, women cheered on Whigs publicly. Democratic women also endorsed Andrew Jackson's politics across the country in the years before the party became uniformly conservative on gender after 1848. The pre-1848 gender consensus also endorsed women's benevolent organizations that publicly aided orphans, widows, and the poor as well as Christian causes such as missionary societies and Bible and tract societies. As historian John W. Quist has demonstrated, women led these groups whether they were in Alabama or Michigan. All of these forays into public life came with acknowledged limits, however. The ideologies underlying women's educational, political, and benevolent activism dictated that they did not act for themselves in these ventures into public life.[56] We should note also that even with their self-proclaimed adherence to a distinct sphere and its limitations, women still heard conservative grumbling about their public involvement in compulsory education, politics, and benevolence. Like the women's activism, the complaints were national in scope.

The Jacksonian era's national consensus arguing for an enlarged sphere of public activities for women did not survive into the 1850s. It evaporated as both northern and southern cultures changed in response to the tumultuous events of 1848, with its European revolutions, French emancipation, the end of the Mexican-American War, and especially the Seneca Falls woman's rights convention. Faced with growing support for abolition at home and abroad, as well as a vocal woman's rights movement, the white South retreated into increasingly conservative positions on women's place in society. Southern politicians like Virginia congressman Thomas Bocock sarcastically mocked Republicans about their "great doctrine of woman's rights" during congressional debates. Southern culture also became much less tolerant of female involvement in any political event. The fear of being smeared as unsexed made it extremely hard for women to attend campaign events in the slave states after 1848. Jane Crumpler DeFiore has analyzed Tennessee women who were politically active in 1840 and 1844 but finds none in 1848 or after. Elizabeth Varon's study of Virginia women finds a handful of female activists in the 1850s, though far fewer than greeted Henry Clay when he arrived in Richmond in 1844. Most female Virginians shed their partisan identity as they assumed the role of "sectional mediators." Even Petersburg editor Rebecca Brodnax Hicks, whose fierce editorials against male privilege earned her a reputation for being outspoken, drew the line at endorsing women's suffrage. Despite her self-imposed limits on her gender ideology, there was still a price to be paid. As Varon notes, Hicks's "ultimate reward was alienation" from southern society, and her paper was forced to fold. By 1864, she was living in Washington, DC, and married to a Union officer.[57] Jonathan Daniel Wells, who argues convincingly that a large number of women edited and wrote for southern periodicals, admits that "there appears to have been fewer published in the South in the years preceding the Civil War than there were in the 1830s and 1840s."[58] None of the ten major antebellum woman's rights conventions was held in a slave state. Likewise, no convention of radical women seeking to end slavery or prostitution met in the South.

As many southern women saw their "sphere" contract in the 1850s, their northern counterparts grew more assertive. Historian Anne Boylan notes the changes in northern women's political styles that happened during the 1830s and beyond. Women's benevolent organizations in Boston and New York City continued the same political practices they had followed between 1800 and 1840, namely a reliance on female "influence" over municipal officials (often relatives or husbands). Their deferential engagement with potential sources of public funding "did not translate into a gender analysis of women's position in the political economy," Boylan writes. Their political style fit into the national consensus on gender since it did not push women too far into the political arena. During the 1830s, however, they were joined, and challenged, by new groups of female activists. The newer women had more radical goals, increasingly confrontational tactics, and a wider spectrum of social support, including women from different classes and races.

Abolitionist and anti-prostitution women, Boylan writes, "began to forge a new style of female politics," one that "invited controversy as a means of publicizing their work."[59] Using political pressure instead of influence, these abolitionists became integral to what Richard S. Newman calls the "shoe-leather" politics of mass-action democracy.[60] Women taking to the lecture circuit to address the politics of slavery or circulating petitions to Congress for the abolition of slavery in the District of Columbia was never part of the national consensus on gender.

By 1856, parts of the Republican Party gave their blessings to women who took partisan stands during public campaign events. Again, the party was a distinctly northern organization, and its encouragement of women's partisanship contrasted starkly with their southern electoral rivals, who banished women even from the sidelines of electioneering. Elizabeth Cady Stanton's speech at an 1860 Republican rally in Seneca Falls represents the epitome of the northern party's willingness to be associated with woman's rights reforms. But its inclination toward women's participation in democracy on partisan terms was much more broadly based than a single event. At Republican campaign rallies across the North in 1856, groups of thirty-two women rode on floats under banners that supported Free Soil Kansas settlers. Large segments of the party turned their presidential candidate's wife, Jessie Frémont, into an informed and committed antislavery thinker. That Republican state legislators in Wisconsin came within a whisker of passing a women's suffrage bill in the late 1850s is proof that the North, while having many conservatives who agreed with the South's retreat from women's participation in aspects of civil society, was considering a new course.[61] The new gender ideologies of the reformist North also included fresh ideas about masculinity. Historian James W. Cook has found that regional differences in ideologies of masculinity caused Barnum's Feejee Mermaid show to succeed in the North but fail in the South.[62] Similarly, the South and the North received feral-women stories differently by the 1850s because of sectional divisions over gender and racial ideologies.

FERAL WOMEN, SOUTH AND NORTH

The South and the North experienced a minor flood of wild-women stories during the 1850s. None of the individuals was caught and exhibited in the same way as Cincinnati's, but newspapers found the stories alluring anyway. The regional patterns in media reactions to the sightings demonstrate that two distinct sectional cultures existed by the end of the 1850s. Some men in the North agreed with an almost entirely unanimous southern consensus about feral women, but many northerners developed a very different way to think about them. In these cases, the racial identities imposed on the feral women played important roles in driving northern and southern thinking.

There were two wild-women episodes in the South during the 1850s.[63] The first one played out over several years, between 1848 and 1854. It may have inspired the Wild Woman of Cincinnati hoax, if we assume that show was a humbug originating in the greater Shreveport area. This one starts as a classic wild-woman tale. According to the story, the woman lived in the woods and had only secretive interactions with the settlements along the bottomlands of the Navidad River in Texas. The first published reports ran in November 1848 and focused on the discovery of her "camp or den." The editor tied this lair to decades-old reports of a wild woman who had never been seen. The sex of this unseen individual was determined by "its track," which was supposedly that of "a small and delicate female." Her den contained "a most astonishing variety of little trinkets, such as pins, needles, knives, brushes, and several articles whose uses were entirely unknown, and all of the most ingenuous and exquisite workmanship."[64] The camp also included a Bible and two guns. While she stole clothing and medicine, this feral woman was also known to return some of the things she took.

Any historian reading this story would immediately suspect that the camp belonged to one or more escaped African Americans who had chosen a life in the woods over a life under the lash. But that was not a possibility, according to the editor. Again, the evidence lay in the footprints. "It cannot be a negro, male or female," he concluded, "because the track forbids that conclusion. We incline to think it a Mexican woman."[65] This is an absurd statement. Race cannot be determined by footprints. Yet one can see the need the editor must have felt to clarify the racial identity of the wild person. First, a "wild" person of African descent was unlikely to be considered news by his largely white market. Second, southern white culture could not admit that an enslaved person had escaped their clutches and lived on his or her own for the full ten years this one was said to have eluded discovery. Whether it made sense or not, the person's tracks needed to prove his or her non-African origins.

For more than a year, the Wild Woman of the Navidad lay quiet as a news item. But she did not disappear from the pages of the nation's newspapers forever. When her story reappeared in January 1850, she brought with her all of the racial complications and gendered concerns that had filled the initial reports.

Footprints again betrayed her gender, a statement of doubtful accuracy that still went unquestioned by an editor who was convinced the "foot marks... resembled those of a woman." Oddly, while her gender seemed certain, the identity of her species fell into question. With many white Americans increasingly unsure about where the dividing line between people of different races and animals lay, the Wild Woman of the Navidad landed awkwardly astride the boundaries. On the one hand, every person who had seen her "concur[ed] in representing it as a human being." On the other hand, it was "so covered with shaggy hair as to resemble an ourang outang [orangutan]." Her "reddish brown hair" was "very long upon the head and neck," which may have helped her escape from the lasso a pursuer named Glascock claims to have thrown over her head. (Could the author of Northcott's capture narrative years later have remembered Glascock's lasso?) She escaped "with the speed of a deer," further clouding this wild woman's species.[66] In this story, the Wild Woman of the Navidad played upon American interest in the uncertain boundaries between people and animals.

Perhaps the most interesting aspect of the 1850 Navidad story is its reception in the national media. The reported sighting proved almost irresistible to editors. Not surprisingly, the story found a home in the southern press, where some editors had recently defended slavery by questioning the humanity of Africans. Starting in the Victoria, Texas, *Texian Advocate* and the *Houston Democratic Telegraph and State Register,* the item reappeared in Alexandria, Virginia, and Natchez, Mississippi.[67] More surprising, perhaps, was the even warmer reception the Navidad wild-woman story found in the northern press. Versions of the report were printed in seven New England papers, two papers each from New York City and Philadelphia, and two in Ohio; among them was even a religious paper, the *Philadelphia Presbyterian.*[68] The Navidad wild woman, identified as human but bordering on animal, had a national appeal to a readership eager to find out where to draw that boundary.

The national curiosity about the Wild Woman of the Navidad revived over a year later when she was finally captured in March 1851. Newspapers nationwide again published the story, but the regional balance of interest was shifting. Eight northern papers still ran the report, but an additional six did so in abbreviated versions that omitted a racially offensive reference to "ourang outangs [orangutans]."[69] More to the point, thirteen southern papers reprinted the full version, and two others ran the short one. This shift in the sectional balance of coverage resulted, it seems, from the fact that the story out of Texas was now one about race and slavery instead of about a non-African woman running free in the woods. With that shift came an alteration in which part of the country found the Navidad incident appealing.

The capture report from 1851 notified readers that the wild woman was "an African negress who had fled to these wilds when the settlements were deserted just after [James] Fannin's defeat, and she had been wandering like an ourang outang for a period of about fifteen years." This statement directly contradicts the supposed evidence of her footprints, though that is hardly surprising. More notably, it turns her remarkable accomplishment of having retained her freedom for fifteen years into a racial insult; rather than a brave and resourceful woman intent on her own freedom, she instead was only "wandering," walking around without a purpose, "like an ourang outang." That slight rendered her subhuman. In addition, the story indicates that she gained her freedom not by consciously taking it, but by getting it passively out of the chaos of a military defeat.

In reality, however, the Wild Woman of the Navidad was a determined and resourceful person who did not give up. Her captors in 1851 mentioned some of her talents, though they did not recognize them as such. They noted that "she cannot speak any English, but converses freely with the Africans on the neighboring plantations." That points to her linguistic skills and to the willingness of enslaved people to support those who had escaped and were living away from white control. It also suggests that she was African, not African American, and that the other people enslaved around her in Texas may have shared similar backgrounds. The American southwestern frontier was inhabited by a diverse group of enslaved people, including some from the Caribbean and others imported directly from Africa before the federal government banned slave importation in 1808 (or brought in illegally afterward). The 1851 story also noted that she supported herself with what they called stolen food as well as "acorns, nuts and other wild fruits." She was a resilient woman and far more likely to have been a true wilderness survivor than the Wild Woman of Cincinnati.

Nor did the Navidad wild woman stay reenslaved for long. The details are lost, but at some point in the next three years, she regained her uncertain freedom. Depending on when she escaped, she may have been free for nearly all of that time. Given her accomplishments and her obvious desire for freedom, it is with sadness that one notes her reappearance in the historical record. In June 1854, an advertisement was bought by John McHenry, the sheriff of Lavaca County, Texas. He declared that he was currently holding "an AFRICAN well known as the Wild Woman of the Navidad" and wanted "the owner" to come and claim his property. There must not have been any immediate response, for the sheriff ran the ad again about six weeks later.

The notice itself is a very strange document. Read in its entirety, it changes the escaped person's sex several times. Note the inclusion of each of these terms in sequence: "man," "woman," "her," "him." This is the ad: "Committed to the jail of Lavaca county, on the 17th inst., a small black negro man, about 35 or 40 years old, an AFRICAN well known as the Wild Woman of the Navidad, supposed to belong to Beckford, late of Virginia. The owner is requested to come forward prove property pay charges and take her away. Otherwise he will be dealt with as the law directs.—John McHenry sheriff L.C."[70] Was McHenry having a bit of fun with the speculation that had earlier surrounded the detained person? Or was there enough uncertainty that he did not want the so-called owner to be confused about whether or not to try to claim the person he considered his property? In light of all of the speculation about the Navidad individual's species, McHenry's gender-flipping prose stands as a tribute to the ability of this escaped slave to throw into doubt the supposedly fixed and natural hierarchies of the Old South.

The sheriff's notice was not reprinted anywhere else, probably because it was an advertisement rather than an editorial or news item. But we might also wonder if other editors resisted turning it into a news feature for other reasons. Perhaps the gender flipping was too strange. A person might "wander" up to the boundary between humans and apes in the South, but no white man in 1854 was likely to entertain publicly such gender fluidity in any race; the sexes were supposedly fixed by God and Nature, complete with the hierarchy that put male editors on top. For northern editors, the world had changed since their fascination with the Wild Woman of the Navidad in 1850. Not only had race and slavery now been overtly introduced into the story, but also the Fugitive Slave Law had proven to be unpopular in practice. Running fugitive-slave ads for their entertainment value might seem like a perilous undertaking in the mid-1850s. Furthermore, the passage of the Kansas-Nebraska Act early in 1854 had made sectional politics much more pronounced. For whatever reason, the Navidad story fell out of favor as a news item. But that was a good thing. It was a sign that some northerners were beginning to split off from a national consensus on racial and gender hierarchies.

Southern and northern reactions to wild-women sightings continued to diverge in the aftermath of the Navidad event. In 1856, distinctions emerged during conversations about the Wild Woman of Cincinnati, with Republicans and some Know Nothings taking interest in her as a person and patient, while Democrats envisioned her as capable of acting and deception. When a new story of feral womanhood emerged from rural Alabama in 1857, the northern and southern press reactions continued to splinter. Southern editors embraced the tale, but the spectacular collapse of the Wild Woman of Cincinnati show and the growing divisions over slavery seem to have engendered a healthy skepticism among northern editors. These men, especially in the cities of the Northeast, became increasingly unwilling to credit wild-woman reports. Historian Michael Newton writes that "nothing separates us so much from the past as our inability to believe in wonders," and by this point, some northeasterners had reached that state of doubt.[71] The fact that the Alabama Wild Woman of 1857 was accompanied by an implausible beast no doubt fueled that skepticism.

This tale had its origins in Marengo County, Alabama. Never more than three paragraphs long, the story told of a hunting party that had spotted "a medium sized woman, fair and quite naked, with the exception of moccasins." Like all wild people, she proved fleet of foot. "She runs with great velocity," the editor reported, "leaping on all fours over every impediment like an antelope." In many ways, this was a classic feral-woman story, including the necessary detail that she was "fair," thereby highlighting the abnormality of her wildness. The editor even included a report of the disappearance, fifteen years earlier during a flood, of "a little girl, daughter of a French woman residing on the banks of the Tumbigbee river." This detail gave the now-adult woman a guaranteed European ancestry.[72] Also, her nudity was a classic touch for a feral-woman tale, even if it stretched credulity for the cold nights of the hill country of Alabama in early March. Her moccasins were a delightful detail.

But the person who invented the story added an even more improbable feature that gave the whole tale a symbolic meaning that shored up the white South's threatened racial and gender hierarchies. With northerners debating racial egalitarianism and greater rights for women in society and wives in marriage, white southern men struggled to defend their own primacy. The Alabama tale was one minor manifestation of their ideological struggle for continued mastery.

The Alabama Wild Woman, it turns out, had a protector. Whenever she was sighted, reports insisted, she was seen in the company of "a large ram, of remarkable whiteness." The ram helped her escape all captors, as she held on to its wool "when running up the hills and springing over rocks. The ram appeared very much attached to this wild and singular creature, and protects her." The story claimed that the small French girl had had "a pet lamb," so presumably this formidable and loyal creature had served as the girl's protector for the past fifteen years. While the editor declared it "a mystery" how the two had "existed fifteen years in the woods, away from all intercourse in the world," the matter made sense symbolically.[73] Only a strong white male could protect vulnerable white womanhood from the world.

But in the world of the Old South, no white woman could be allowed to exist independently for long. Left on her own, she might escape from male control and formulate her own opinions. It is not surprising, therefore, that the initial story was followed by a sequel only a few days later. This update declared that the earlier report "had occasioned no little excitement" in Marengo County. Men there had mobilized "a 'party of huntsmen' a few days since" that had gone in pursuit. They had seized the Alabama Wild Woman north of the town of Linden "after a chase of two days." The sexual politics of male mastery were made clear by the editor, who wrote that the woman's capture "has created a great excitement among the b'hoys, the right of property being protested."[74] In other words, the "b'hoys" were contesting among one another for who would own the woman and her body. Wild no more, the young woman would now be someone's "property." The ram was not mentioned in the sequel, probably since he was no longer needed due to the surplus of other white male protectors now available.

The Wild Woman of Alabama proved to be immensely popular with southern editors.[75] Fewer northern editors reprinted the Alabama story than had printed versions of the Wild Woman of the Navidad or of Cincinnati.[76] The relative absence of northern interest in this southern story, with its heavy overlay of white patriarchy, is notable because it was not caused by apathy toward wild-woman news generally. Indeed, when such a story erupted out of Beach, Canada, in 1859, northern editors mustered more enthusiasm. That report, lacking any connection to the defense of slavery, managed to interest eight northern editors but only one southern newspaperman.[77] Slavery and its intersections with a wild-woman story clearly affected a tale's appeal to both northern and southern editors. That disparity highlights how sectional matters drove their way into even news reports about feral people. The North and South had become distinct cultures by 1860.

Many of the northern editors who reprinted the Wild Woman of Alabama story openly ridiculed it along with those who believed it. After running the initial report of the moccasin-wearing young French woman and her great white ram, a Lowell, Massachusetts, editor slyly pulled the rug out from under the story: "The question now is, can this wild woman of Marengo county be the same, and the pet lamb grown into a patriarch, with wool enough to cover all the people's eyes?"[78] It is surely significant that the Lowell newspaper endorsed Republican candidates; the party was filled with women and men who resisted patriarchal abuses of power. The very word "patriarch" would have been enough to raise red flags among the paper's readers, and the editor was right to see the white ram as a stand-in for male rule.[79]

Northern ridicule of the Alabama Wild Woman and her patriarchal white ram was not an entirely new phenomenon. A small number of northern publications had mocked the Wild Woman of Cincinnati the previous year. Especially in the big-city media, Cincinnati's version had sparked comic skepticism.

Quite early in June 1856, a Boston paper greeted the Wild Woman of Cincinnati report with doubts: "We fear the story is a hoax, like that of the Aztec children, exhibited here a few years ago by one Morris, and more recently in Europe."[80] A New York City editor gave the original *Cincinnati Commercial* story only a one-paragraph summary before concluding, "the narrative may be true, but it reads like a fish story."[81] By the end of the summer and now armed with the Shreveport story purporting to unmask the people behind a fraud, the same New York editor played up the whole incident for laughs, commenting, "only a few months ago, [Anne Eliza Paul] was living as a wife with the said Northcote, her captor, and consequently must have gone wild in a great hurry and with wonderful vigor, to have reached her present degree of savageness." Neither Williams nor Paul escaped his ridicule. Williams was mocked as having "the quick perception of true genius," while Paul was described as "no less than his wife, without the trivial preliminary called marriage." Behind these barbs lay an assumed cultural superiority over the hoaxers, which empowered the writers to call something a fraud without having even seen it. These northern newspapermen also assumed the cultural authority to mock people taken in by the exhibit.[82] That mockery went beyond the Democrats' rather casual acceptance of the fraud once it was supposedly unveiled. To turn it into comedy required an additional layer of cultural detachment.

The refinement of the wild woman into cultural satire reached its purest level with the appearance of a story in the *Saturday Evening Post* in late June 1856. The column claimed to give "Advice to Watering Place Landlords and Country Board Dispensers." Among the best ways "to make your house attractive" to paying guests during the summer season, it suggested, "was to bring out your Natural Curiosities." If you have a big snake to show off, for example, add length to it and claim that its eyes are red. Festoon your supposed lover's leap with "an Indian tradition" and perhaps try to "dig out a Hermit's Cave" somewhere on the property. Amid this gallery of fake wonders and false advertising copy, a wild woman would fit right in: "if you could possibly have a wild woman, or an entirely unknown animal in the woods around you, it would fill your house the whole summer. A wild woman would cost about a dollar and a half per day, and found in whiskey and tobacco." Faking a fascinatingly terrifying wild beast "may be got up cheaper" since all you would have to do is to pay someone to make "the tracks every night" and mark "its devastating course with the blood of chickens." If anyone were smart enough to follow this advice, the writer concluded, "you may begin to set out your hen coops on your lawn, and advertise them as cottages to let to families at forty dollars per week—board included."[83]

What is notable about this satire, reprinted from a second New York City publication, is the target of its wit. While others aimed at the hoaxers, such as the trio from Shreveport, for their deceptive ways, these writers and editors made fun of the broader public who were taken in by these flimsy humbugs. In this they resembled the Lowell editor who dismissed the white ram as ridiculous but wondered if it might still have "wool enough to cover all the people's eyes." Just how gullible would people, even northern people, prove to be? The staff at the *Saturday Evening Post* built their joke around the idea that advertising was a house of lies that would take in a crowd of fools. The humor came from the sense of cultural superiority that readers got from being in on that joke. That this humor only came out of the northeastern cities of New York, Boston, and Lowell suggests a sectional difference between part of the North and the rest of the country about what was possible in the natural world, not to mention the basic cultural question of what (and who) was funny.

CONCLUSIONS

Cincinnati served as a crossroads of the North and South. In many ways, the Wild Woman of Cincinnati proves the point that the two sections shared a great deal. The production was a truly national event. Southerners (at least by their self-presentation) put on the show, and northerners constituted its primary audience. It drew national media attention, and Northcott had expressed his hope to take the show to points east. We could add that people came to the Queen City during its run from all over the country to nominate Democrat James Buchanan for president, a person who then won votes all over the nation. People paid in national currency to see the exhibition.

But if we look at the Wild Woman show more deeply, sectional variations emerge. While all newspapers reacted similarly to the exhibition's initial appearance, partisan differences in coverage emerged by the time Judge Burgoyne's probate court met. Know Nothing editors, unlike Democrats, sometimes wrote about the Wild Woman as a victim who deserved sympathy. More importantly, supporters of the Republican Party, which existed almost exclusively in the North, reacted differently than their Democratic counterparts. Republican editors occasionally wrote dismissively of the Wild Woman as a humbug, but many in the reformist party saw her as incapacitated by tragedy and in need of medical treatment. Whereas Democrats found it easy to visualize a woman as knowingly deceptive, Republicans envisioned women as morally pure and likely to be victimized by male power. In these ways, the parties justified their gendered platforms. For Democrats, male power and privilege needed to be preserved since women were fallible and untrustworthy. Republicans who saw the need to reform their culture and adjust the legal props of patriarchy turned the Wild Woman of Cincinnati into a model of innocent womanhood harmed by unchecked male power. They also turned to government for agencies like the police, the courts, and the state asylum to curtail abusive male behaviors.

The history of other feral women in the United States over the antebellum years confirms that there were sectional differences regarding both partisan gender ideologies and tolerance for slavery and racism. Southerners and northerners both enjoyed a feral-woman story, and early versions of wild-woman tales from Texas drew readers from across the country. There was, it seems, a national consensus that white women who survived on their own in nature deserved attention. But this consensus frayed even in the early 1850s. Reports of the Wild Woman of the Navidad initially excited attention from around the nation but kept it only as long as editors could assure their readers that she was not of African ancestry. As long as she was Mexican or white, this wild woman was interesting and newsworthy. But northern editors proved increasingly unwilling to reprint these stories as she morphed into an escaped slave, and no one turned the sheriff's fugitive-slave advertisement into a news feature even when he made the runaway into a fascinating mix of genders. By the time Alabamians boasted of a naked wild woman of their own, the northern reaction was indifference laced with cynicism. Journalists in the North's biggest cities even mocked people who trusted stories about wild women, red-eyed snakes, and unknown, bloodthirsty beasts.

Scholarship that has found similarities between the North and South has focused on economic practices and a national culture of white supremacy. In these matters, they have an argument worth attention, though skepticism about the capitalist nature of slavery and its labor practices is warranted. Yet there were also significant differences that must not be forgotten. The North witnessed the growth of a well-financed biracial abolitionist movement that vocally and sometimes effectively fought for racial equality and an end to slavery. It also had an organized and ideologically sophisticated woman's rights movement. Neither movement ever convened in southern states. Unlike women in the southern states, who were effectively silenced on matters of woman's rights, some women in the North spoke firmly in public on controversial political topics, including questioning the patriarchal laws that governed American society. The presence of powerful female reformers must not be underestimated in any attempt to consider similarities between the two sections' cultures and politics. Such large political and social movements challenging sexual and racial inequality constituted a sex-tional politics that divided the country. The way the two sections of the country reacted to the Wild Woman of Cincinnati and other examples of feral women is a demonstration of how these sex-tional politics could play out even in parts of the culture that would seem far removed from the political issues of the day.

4

WOMEN AND POWER IN ANTEBELLUM AMERICA

To this point, we have focused on what men saw and thought when they looked at the Wild Woman. The focus now shifts to consider how women reacted to the show, how the Wild Woman might have experienced her exhibition, and the larger question of how much power and authority women had in Cincinnati and the United States in 1856.

Scholars have learned much about American women in the 1850s, allowing for the placement of the Wild Woman in the context of what other women thought and did at the time of the show. In addition, the many silences that surrounded the Wild Woman as she stood on exhibit and then endured institutionalization in Dayton require interpretation. This contextual reconstruction helps forge answers for important questions in antebellum women's history: How much power did women have in this society? What were their sources of empowerment? It also exposes the consequences of women's disempowerment and their exclusion by men from social and political authority. While some women accessed sources of power in the mid-nineteenth century, to what extent was the Wild Woman able to benefit from those with such authority?

The answer depends in part on how the actual woman at its center experienced the Wild Woman episode. Analyzing the available evidence allows us to discover the likelihood of the Wild Woman being an actor in a hoax, a traumatized or otherwise incapacitated woman, or an actual feral human. Each of these categories has its own implications for the nature of her experience and agency. While it is possible to construct a viable historical scenario in which the Wild Woman was an empowered individual who enjoyed her time in Cincinnati and shared fully in the fruits of her exhibition, the more likely possibilities are more troubling.

Yet in all of this, there remains a striking lack of evidence about the Wild Woman herself. It is worth repeating that we do not even know her actual name. The Southern Ohio Asylum never released it, and she never provided her name to the court, the press, or her jailors. Without knowing her name, any census data or vital records that may exist remain unavailable to us. She did not leave any letters or a diary. Nevertheless, the Wild Woman and her actions still tell us a great deal about women in antebellum America.

THE WILD WOMAN AND SOCIAL EMPOWERMENT

Historians have identified several sources of empowerment for nineteenth-century American women. These avenues to power were more available to some than to others, depending on factors such as race, class, legal status (free or enslaved), religion, ethnicity, and marital status. Nevertheless, they point to ways in which a discrete number of women controlled their own lives and influenced those around them. While some individuals have always been able to draw strength from their own characters, historians have identified several public and institutional structures that enabled antebellum women to influence society. These included churches, where women made up a majority of converts and congregants in these decades. Girls also attended single-sex academies with advanced curriculums in roughly equal numbers to boys. But the young women who were graduated from these challenging schools found many careers closed to them as well as strong social expectations that they limit their lives exclusively to marriage and reproductive work. Nevertheless, many forged careers as writers, editors, educators, and social activists. Work as leaders of civic organizations, religious associations, and charities, some of which came with salaries but most of which did not, also enabled women to shape the world around them. Finally, they found ways to change government policies, access public funding for the charities they led, and campaign for candidates of their choice, all without the benefit of the vote. Assessing how much these paths to power helped the Wild Woman, or how they failed to assist her, indicates the degree of gender equality in antebellum America.

The most striking conclusion about the Wild Woman is how isolated she was from almost all of the routes that women took to gain control over their private and public worlds. Even if most female Cincinnatians believed the Wild Woman was either a feral or incapacitated person in need of help, would they be able to help her? Did they have the power to intervene on her behalf and give her assistance?

For over six weeks, even the most powerful women in Cincinnati proved unable or unwilling to help their feral sister. Reading the sources around the Wild Woman for evidence of influential women is an exercise in noticing silences. As an example, women's historians have reconstructed the ways female Americans of all races and regions built, joined, and helped run churches. Examples abound. Early American Baptist churches were governed in part by committees of church members, which often included women.[1] Black Methodist women in Revolutionary Virginia, even ones who were enslaved, enjoyed full church membership and encouraged their ministers to investigate poor conduct by slaveholders and take antislavery theological stances.[2] By the mid-nineteenth century, religious women worked closely in public capacities to raise money for churches, missionaries, and Bible and religious-tract distribution.[3] Perhaps more than anything else, organized religion served as a springboard from which women jumped into public life. As men moved into the selfish worlds of business and politics, women gained an (albeit limited) authority to act as moral anchors for their society. This cultural authority allowed some to declare certain conducts as impermissible, and they bonded together as groups to alter such behaviors.

It is rather surprising then to find not a single minister or church mentioned in the entire history of the Wild Woman. To the best of our knowledge, no clergy visited her or pondered her circumstances, her faith, or her salvation. None rushed to her aid or preached about her. No one asked what her religious background might be. No committee of church women seem to have called on her or offered her aid. One religious newspaper in New York City even ran the *Cincinnati Commercial*'s entire first report, including the puerile sentence about her being "scantily but neatly clad, standing with a stout rope around her waist, and attached to a bed post."[4] For his part, Captain Northcott claimed to be interested in returning the Wild Woman to civilization and mental health, but he appears to have never drawn on the financial or emotional resources of the city's churches. It is possible that clergymen and their female allies attempted to assist the Wild Woman only to be rebuffed by Northcott (and the Wild Woman, too, if she was in on the ploy). Or perhaps they proved to be so ineffectual that their efforts failed to appear in the newspapers. But whatever the cause of the silence, the ministry and its female congregants failed the Wild Woman, leaving her isolated and without assistance during her exhibition. That is surprising and points to a possible inability of female congregants to push their reach into the mostly male business district of Cincinnati and its entertainment world.

Likewise, female academies also failed to help the Wild Woman. Recent scholarship by historian Mary Kelley has proven the extensive reach, influence, and quality of these single-sex schools in the decades before the Civil War. Functioning much as private colleges do now, the women's academies took in boarding students from far away as well as local day students. The female students enrolled in rigorous classes in subjects strikingly similar to what male students took at their schools. Girls attended in the same numbers as boys, and they paid roughly equal tuitions. This occurred, Kelley finds, all across the country in every region.[5]

The strength of female academies in Cincinnati demonstrates the power of this educational movement. Even as the Wild Woman show was open in the city, three local schools staged their graduation exercises. Each was an important cultural and social event that attracted attention from the public and the newspapers. Glendale Female College's commencement address might seem like a small affair, with a graduating class of only eight students, but it still warranted advance notice in the *Cincinnati Daily Times*. On the day of commencement, two special trains departed for Glendale, one at 8 A.M. for people going to the graduation ceremony, and one at 6 P.M. for those attending a celebratory evening concert at the college.[6]

The students at Glendale Female College would have seen graduation week as a challenge and as an opportunity to display their hard-earned talents. They were still taking exams on Monday and Tuesday, and Wednesday's commencement ceremony included them reading their compositions and performing "vocal and instrumental music" for attendees.[7] The *Times* also gave extensive coverage of the commencement exercises held at nearby Wesleyan Female College, reporting on the essays read during the final day of the students' academic careers. The college's guests heard women speak on topics ranging from "The Wealth of the World—Its Original Minds" to "Right Conquers Wrong, and Glory Follows Pain." Wesleyan's graduation day lasted from dawn through the evening exercises, with more presentations by students of their original work.

Historian Kelley writes that the women who graduated from these academies learned to think of themselves as intellectually capable, skilled individuals who could make contributions to society. She writes that, "in terms of preparing themselves for a role in civil society, daily recitation and its culmination in the compositions, addresses, and orations delivered at public examinations were equally tangible demonstrations of self-mastery."[8] Such was certainly the case in Cincinnati. The young women would have read newspaper coverage of the graduations that listed their names next to their compositions and performances as well as among the list of graduates. In addition, their essays were treated with a critical eye that took their ideas and performances seriously. Martha L. Hawkes and Isabella Porter, for example, presented "able compositions, and spoke well for the culture of the minds of their authors."[9] The composition of Mary M. Reilly, by contrast, "contained good thoughts," but the reporter took his assignment seriously enough to add that the "solemn and studied tone in which it was read" detracted from its effectiveness.[10] The main speaker at the Cincinnati Female Seminary closed his remarks by saying to the young women: "You are to go into the world. Go armed with the complete armor of righteousness."[11] Women's historians can trace the careers of female graduates nationwide as they took their charge "to go into the world" to heart. While many lived exclusively private lives after their school days, others formed or led church organizations, charities, reform groups, other women's academies, or wrote fiction and nonfiction that changed their culture.[12]

But these academies, their faculty, and their students had no known effect on the Wild Woman during her exhibition. We have no record of anyone from the academies attempting to help her. Northcott had claimed on his arrival in the city that he was "conducting her to Columbus, or some other suitable place, to be educated."[13] But even though he was surrounded by women's academies, he never seized the opportunity to place her at one of these schools. Had Northcott been serious about trying to coax the Wild Woman back into American society, he would have done well to tap these institutions and their educational expertise. Again, however, he failed to ask for such aid. This suggests that the showman wanted control over the Wild Woman and the profits that come with that power. It also means that she was cut off from the women who had the educational knowledge and institutional settings that could have benefited a feral woman most.

Women in the antebellum decades also gained a powerful place as leaders and members of charities. Often religious leaders and women's academy graduates, they controlled substantial budgets, sometimes drawn in part from money appropriated by state or local governments grateful for the work that their benevolent organizations did. The women's organizations also benefited from being legally incorporated by governments, allowing them (even though married women usually were barred by law from such basic financial functions as owning property) to control investments and to sign contracts.[14] By 1856, women occupied powerful, state-sanctioned positions in the leadership of these charitable groups.

Most women's civic groups performed charity work. Some of the earliest and largest took care of the poor, widows, and orphans.[15] Others had religious goals. By the 1830s, Black and white women in the North began to branch out, forming associations with more overtly reformist missions such as the elimination of slavery, prostitution, or alcohol. Others worked to assist fugitive slaves.[16] Some of these associations became increasingly radical, and the start of woman's rights conventions, well under way by 1856, suggests how assertive some women had become, at least in the North.[17]

But none of these groups, to our knowledge, intervened in the Wild Woman show. Perhaps they did not see her case as falling within their particular social mission. Perhaps she was too old to be an orphan or not obviously widowed. She was not poor enough to warrant charitable relief, at least in a traditional sense. A female antislavery association would have hesitated before stepping in since Northcott claimed she was white and no one ever questioned that identification. Although tied up and on display, she was not obviously a prostitute to be saved by a Female Moral Reform Association. Neither the most powerful nor the most radical women in Cincinnati proved able to aid such a unique case as the Wild Woman. While women had education, civic organizations, and religious authority, none intervened on behalf of a woman who was promoted as a feral very much in need of help. This is a sad commentary on the state of women's place in antebellum society.

Conservative thinkers would have taken a different approach to the question of women's power. They located a woman's safety and authority exclusively in her private home and her family. But here, too, the Wild Woman found no allies. Neither her family nor her home offered her respite. Her family materialized only after she had recovered and gained her release from the asylum, even then only in questionable secondhand reports of their existence. As far as having a home of her own within which to shelter from the dangers of public life, there was no protection for the Wild Woman. We do not know where she resided while in Cincinnati, but she seems to have lived in the business district. The *Cincinnati Columbian* introduced

"Mr. Canon" in its courthouse coverage as the man "over whose store the woman had been kept." While she played with his children there, he testified that "she would shrink from himself."[18] In order not to be seen free of charge on the way to work, she may have lived in the same building as her exhibition spaces. One such place was Bacon's Mercantile College, which occupied a four-story building on a corner lot. The college served only male students, advertising itself to "young men desiring to acquire a thorough Commercial Education."[19] It was, in other words, an exclusively male setting about as divorced from a home and family as possible. Conservatives are fond of saying that families, especially fathers and husbands, are the protectors of women. These people offered the Wild Woman no security or help.

Even though many female groups, and all men, failed to help the Wild Woman, there were people who sensed that she needed help and did something about it. The women who lived in Walnut Hills dispatched a representative to Judge Burgoyne "stating that suspicions were entertained that the female on exhibition in this city as 'a wild woman,' ... was insane, and suggesting that some measures should be taken to investigate the matter."[20] What is especially notable here is that these women acted in coordination with their local government to get something done.

We do not often think of women in the 1850s as having political power, given that they were barred from voting and holding elected office. But the success of the Walnut Hills women is not entirely surprising. In addition to their strength in churches, academies, and civic organizations, female activists in the 1850s allied themselves with political parties. This was especially true of antislavery women, who publicly participated in Republican Party parades, rallies, and speeches. Their valuable support during elections translated into an ability to wield power in state and local governments.[21] This was not their first attempt at improving their society. In the 1830s and 1840s, activist women had tried to change people's bad or immoral behaviors through persuasive arguments and by offering good examples. When these failed to effect change, they turned to government coercion as a more potent tool. By the 1850s, women sought to have laws passed curtailing drunkenness, slavery, and prostitution. These activists found male allies in the Republican and Know Nothing Parties.[22] In states with reformist majorities, such as Vermont, free-state Kansas, and Wisconsin, women's right to vote (if only in local schoolboard elections) was seriously discussed during the 1850s.[23]

Turning to the Cincinnati government for help in rescuing the Wild Woman may not have been the first option for the Walnut Hills women, but it is hardly surprising that they worked through political channels to accomplish their goal. Even without the vote, many women in the 1850s knew how to maneuver their way through the halls of municipal government. They were the precursors of those who would inaugurate Progressive Era legislation and regulation in cities and states in the 1880s and 1890s regarding child labor, women's industrial work, sweatshops, clean water, and sanitation.

The trend toward women's involvement in municipal government, so clearly visible throughout the North, was underway in Cincinnati in the 1850s. Writing about the Queen City in the 1840s and 1850s, historian Alan I. Marcus finds a powerful "governmental campaign to free the municipality of the social evils."[24] The city did this with "abruptly developed social services" starting in the 1840s.[25] These reforms brought about a systematic redesign of municipal services. Jed Dannenbaum's analysis of the changing dynamics of the temperance campaign in Cincinnati also sees the 1850s as a turning point for reform there. He finds women taking important roles in engineering this social change. Before 1850, Dannenbaum writes, "women had been willing to remain subordinate to men in the areas of public activity and organizational leadership within the temperance movement."[26] But things had changed by 1856, when "temperance tactics shifted from the advocacy of moral suasion to that of prohibition."[27] Passing laws against alcohol sales seemed likely to exclude women from any meaningful part in the movement, but they "quickly began to demand an equal role in traditionally male spheres of action."[28] Women were among those who took Cincinnati's temperance movement out of voluntarism and into political compulsion.

It is worth pausing to consider who the women of Walnut Hills might have been. The *Cincinnati Daily Enquirer* did not name the individuals who had urged Judge Burgoyne to action. We cannot even be sure that the staff knew who had made the overture or even if they were correct about where the women lived. Burgoyne himself lived in Cincinnati at 593 Sycamore Street, relatively far removed from Walnut Hills, a town that did not get incorporated into the city until after the Civil War.[29] "Walnut Hills" could have been used by the Know Nothing editor as (a potentially inaccurate) shorthand for a kind of activist women who the paper's readers would have understood as Republican in orientation—those who tended toward abolitionism and possibly woman's rights. Understanding the reputation for activism that Walnut Hills women had earned by 1856 provides a fuller picture of who the *Enquirer* was blaming for mobilizing the powers of municipal government to enact change.

Walnut Hills was the home of Lane Seminary, an evangelical Protestant institution that had emerged as a hotbed of abolitionist activism in the early 1830s. A band of radical abolitionist students, including Theodore Weld, had been frustrated in their very public attempt to win the entire seminary over to Garrisonianism and decamped to Oberlin in 1834. But Lane and its host town, Walnut Hills, remained antislavery even after its most radical students left. Its reform-minded faculty and students, in the words of historian Joan Hedrick, continued to foster "hopes for a better world," and they did not shy away from their self-imposed duty to fight for it. Newspaper reports from 1843 and 1852 linked Walnut Hills to specific attempts by enslaved people to gain their freedom by traveling north. Both stories gained extensive coverage outside of the Cincinnati region. The 1843 escape, which failed, devolved into a long-contested court case. The 1852 escape was linked to Walnut Hills resident Harriet Beecher Stowe, whose authorship of *Uncle Tom's Cabin* sealed the town's image as an antislavery community.[30] If people knew anything about Walnut Hills, it was that women there were evangelical activists and likely to aid enslaved people seeking freedom.

Locals would also know that many of the women living in Walnut Hills looked favorably on the Republican Party in 1856. We can see their partisan alignment from later in 1856, when the Republicans staged a twilight procession of its supporters through Cincinnati. The torchlit parade featured a quasi-military feel that foreshadowed the "Wide Awake" clubs of the 1860 campaign. In this case, the procession was headed by the Washington Dragoons and the Steuben Guards Artillery. But for all of this military dash and masculine bravado, there was also a female presence that other parties did not choose to emulate. Many Republican rallies in 1856 featured a float with thirty-one young women in white as allegorical representations of the states, with one in black mourning for bleeding Kansas. The Tenth Ward's Republicans maintained this tradition by filling their part of the parade with "several cars" that "were filled with pretty girls, representing the states." Those in Cincinnati went even further, dispersing women throughout their parade. The Young Men's National Republican Association trotted by on horseback, and with them "rode a number of beautiful young ladies." It is important to note that the *Cincinnati Daily Gazette* also noticed women in the parade from "the Walnut Hills delegation." This section of the procession, it reported, contained people both "in carriages and on horseback. In some of the carriages were ladies, and among these one or two of the most venerable ladies of this county."[31] Walnut Hills women turned out as visible members of the Republican Party coalition during the presidential campaign that culminated shortly after the Wild Woman was released from Dayton.

There are two especially notable elements to the *Gazette* story about this procession through the streets of Cincinnati. The first is that almost all women who participated in Republican parades across the North in 1856 were described as young and attractive. The appearance, therefore, of some of the "most venerable ladies of the county" would have stood out. These were older women who were there because of their informed and considered political beliefs. These Walnut Hills residents would have made their political beliefs known long before the October parade, and they had the social capital to force their way into the Republicans' self-presentation even though they were not part of the usual script.

The second notable feature was the degree of hatred and violence that these women inspired by their willingness to enact their politics. The Republican parade meet with violent opposition as it progressed through Cincinnati. Women, at least as reported by the *Gazette,* bore the brunt of the violence. The paper said that Know Nothings "frightened the horses, uttered the most gross obscenity to the women, and threw stones and other missiles into the crowd. . . . At least twenty ladies were knocked down by stones thrown at the procession. Two were badly hurt on the south-east corner of Vine and Fourth streets." Among the casualties were a Mrs. Mitchell, who "had an eye put out" and a Mrs. Stevens, whose head was "badly bruised." One "little girl" was also "struck in the face" and "badly hurt," while another suffered a broken arm. No specific mention was made of the venerable persons from Walnut Hills who rode in the parade, but "many ladies who were in the carriages in the procession were struck with sticks."[32] Republican men were also hurt during the twilight march through the city, but it is very clear that femininity offered no protection to these partisan women. Instead, their willingness to participate may have provoked an additional dose of violence from men who thought women had no place in political affairs.

And yet, many female reformers clearly believed that they belonged in the halls of city government in the 1850s. While at least one historian has minimized the power accrued by such "partisan enablers" as the women who participated in the Cincinnati Republican parade, their engagement with partisan politics during the 1850s may have been the key that unlocked the doors of city hall, or at least Judge Burgoyne's courtroom. According to historians Ronald Zboray and Mary Saracino Zboray, antislavery women in the 1850s identified themselves with the Republican Party. They followed the campaigns, knew the issues, and understood themselves as members of the party just as much as the men around them. Surely their allegiances could not have been lost on men, and their activism in public and private could readily translate into influence (if not direct power).[33]

Antislavery women's conviction that they had a place in politics may have been the flash point for the violence seen on Cincinnati streets in October 1856. Certainly, the *Cincinnati Daily Enquirer* was taking a swipe at Judge Burgoyne, as well as male Republicans generally, by stating that he had acted at the behest of women. Both physically attacking female activists and belittling their male allies would have been traditional tactics for anxious patriarchs looking to protect their superior status. But for the women living in Walnut Hills, going to Burgoyne's office would have been a familiar walk down a well-marked path.[34] At last, one of women's new sources of power paid off, and their years of cultivating ties to reformers in local government would bring action. Hardly powerless or complacent in antebellum society, financially secure women had found a way, after over a month and a half, to close the Wild Woman show.

We should also note that the women who moved through political channels were, almost certainly, also graduates of women's academies, members of churches, and leaders of charitable or religious groups. Some may even have attended the national Woman's Rights Convention in Cincinnati in late 1855. To say that those routes to female empowerment failed to aid the Wild Woman is to say that those institutions did not intervene (or were barred from doing so). But they could not directly aid her. Nevertheless, the Walnut Hills women who did intervene no doubt had a sense of self, an awareness of their social mission, and an authority predicated on these sources of empowerment. Without the changes over the past several decades, it is impossible to see women setting off to mobilize their government to act on behalf of the disempowered woman on exhibit.

How should we think about their closure of the exhibition? The answer to that question matters. If it was important for the show to end, then it matters that women had managed to amass the cultural authority and governmental influence necessary to bring about that action. To answer that question, though, requires understanding what the show meant for the woman in the spotlight. Trying to determine how the Wild Woman experienced the exhibit will involve answering the most commonly asked question of all: was she authentic, deeply traumatized, or a humbug? If she was either an incapacitated victim of Northcott's greedy exhibition or a feral person in need of help, then the empowerment of women and their allies in local government was a humanitarian necessity.

FERAL, TRAUMATIZED, OR A HOAX?

Ever since Captain Northcott began talking with reporters in late May about the Wild Woman he claimed to have caught, Americans fixated on the same question they always asked of such human-zoo shows: was she a real wild woman or was it all a humbug? But rather than attempting to determine once and for all the question of her authenticity, asking who the Wild Woman was will let us explore how much power women had in antebellum America and how necessary that empowerment was for women's happiness. It will show us how vital it was that the women of Walnut Hills were able to close the exhibit through their influence with Judge Burgoyne. The matter at hand is this: How miserable was the Wild Woman's life in June and July 1856? In other words, how much did she need to be rescued?

There are three distinct possibilities for the Wild Woman's identity, each with its own meaning. First, what were the implications for the Wild Woman if she was performing a role and did so willingly (and quite well). Second, what does it mean if the doctors, Judge Burgoyne, and the Walnut Hills women were right in thinking of her as so mentally disabled that she was unable to grant her consent to her own exhibition. Lastly, while it is unlikely that she was really a feral woman, many people in Cincinnati believed that that was her true background, and it is worth considering what that means in terms of the place of women in society in 1856.

THE WILD WOMAN AS ACTOR

Cincinnati newspapers reported that many believed the Wild Woman was a humbug as early as her probate-court hearing. By the end of the summer, most people said that it had all been a humbug. They were pushed to that conclusion in part by the Shreveport story that went so far as to give names to the people who had supposedly pulled off the hoax. I usually lean toward this answer, but then I catch myself and suspect that I am guilty of wishful thinking, for this is, without a doubt, the best-case scenario for the woman at the heart of the show.

Being a knowing participant in the production would have guaranteed the Wild Woman the best experience of the three possibilities for who she was. If she consciously performed the role in tandem with her fellow performers, Northcott and Walters, then she was to some degree a free agent who might have shared evenly in the profits from her labor. In this scenario, she might have enjoyed giving the performance and thrilled at having pulled it off. She might have laughed afterward at what she had heard as Cincinnatians debated her supposed background and condition as she had performed before them. Even the role itself could have been liberating, with its loose clothing and freedom from any social expectations that she entertain or flirt with her audience. She may have even created the role and written the script.

If we think of the Wild Woman as a self-employed entrepreneur or as a paid worker, then we need to consider that women's historians often regard wage work as a potential source of empowerment for women.[35] Not all such scholars agree with that perspective, arguing that "women's" work was very poorly paid (think sewing and piecework) or paid at barely half the rate that male workers received for the same job (think teaching). But if the Wild Woman entered this job voluntarily, she might have split the earnings fairly with her two partners. If she was indeed the mistress of Joe Williams, the Shreveport carpenter, then she may have claimed a good portion of the show's gate for her own household. Being the star of a show and earning either a wage or part of the profits could be a real step up from being a woman stuck on a male-dominated family farm.

But was this the case? There is some evidence that the Wild Woman was part of a team of hoaxers who succeeded in separating the foolish from their quarters. First, if Walters is to be believed, Northcott and the Wild Woman had a long chat the night before she was due in court and his own disappearance. The picture of them in the Cincinnati jail whispering by moonlight evokes images of lovers planning their eventual reunion at a prearranged place. Second, there is the janitor who told people he had heard the Wild Woman and the ticket seller having a laugh after they thought everyone had gone home. This, too, conjures up the happy image of the Wild Woman laughing all the way to the bank with the proceeds of her work. And then there are all the Cincinnatians and a couple of doctors who, after giving the matter a hard look and some consideration, thought that the exhibition was a hoax. Perhaps the Wild Woman was, when all is said and done, having a good time in the Queen City.

Might she, after all, really have been Ann Eliza Paul, the Shreveport woman who could not pull off acting like a tawny bear when wrapped up in its fur but who looked strange and attractive enough to be a plausible and entertaining wild woman? A considerable body of evidence suggests that this was the case. Perhaps the most persuasive comes from a Cincinnati doctor, George Blackman, who wrote in 1857 that he was convinced the Wild Woman had humbugged her way through the city. Without stating his source or even if he had interviewed the woman herself, Blackman wrote that when she was in the Dayton asylum, she gave "a full confession that the story of her capture was an invention; that her appearance of wildness and *fear of man* were assumed; that her scanty apparel was designed to add to the effect; and that the whole was a scheme to make money."[36] Scholar Erik Anderson, who has studied the Wild Woman episode, concludes that "it thus seems possible that Northcote and the Wild Woman were Williams and Paul."[37] Anderson even found the pair living in the same household in the 1850 census listings for Shreveport. The record identifies Williams as the head of household, a thirty-two-year-old carpenter who had been born in North Carolina. "Ann Paul" was then a nineteen-year-old from Missouri (a detail that was claimed by the woman who was released from the Dayton asylum). This would have made them about thirty-eight and twenty-five in 1856, ages that seem consistent with the descriptions we have of her. But it was not a romantic love nest, at least not in 1850. Williams and his supposed mistress shared the house at that time with two other men, William Sterrett and J. T. Donnegan, both carpenters, who at ages twenty-three and twenty-four may have been either employees of Williams or just friends.[38] Tantalizingly, Donnegan had been born in Ohio, but whether he had any connections in Cincinnati is impossible to know. Still, the connection between Louisiana and the show in Cincinnati could all have been coincidental and dreamed up by an entrepreneurial or misinformed Shreveport editor.

There is one further clue, however, that offers at least a whiff of support for the idea that Williams and Paul could have been the centerpieces of the

Wild Woman act. It could even provide, to wishful thinkers, a happy ending for the Wild Woman. According to Louisiana marriage records, Ann Eliza Paul married Joe Williams in Caddo on November 19, 1859.[39] Using this as our endpoint for the couple's relationship during the 1850s, we could start with them sharing a house with two men, possibly employees, in Shreveport. Over the next six years, they could have begun a sexual relationship that resulted in reports that she was his "mistress." By 1856, they had experimented with the tawny bear outfit before settling into rehearsals for the Wild Woman act. Later, as the show verged on collapse—at this point, if hoping for a happy story, we might curse the meddling Walnut Hills women for thwarting our ambitious, romantic pair—the two lovers lay down together in the Cincinnati jail to plan their reunion. Upon her release from the asylum a few months later, the couple met up again, counted their money, paid off Walters, and settled down over the next three years to eventual wedded bliss with a fabulous story to tell their children. In this version of events, which has the makings of a good movie or novel, the Walnut Hills women need not have bothered saving the Wild Woman because she was profiting financially and personally from her own ingenuity and hard work.

But there are problems with telling the story of Williams and Paul as the heroes in a romantic tale of two lovers almost making it big in the world. The first is that the evidence is entirely secondhand at best. We have only Dr. Blackman's word that the Wild Woman confessed to having impersonated a feral woman and donned scanty clothing to attract interest in the show. But did she confess to him? Even if she did tell the doctor that version of events, she may just have been telling him what he wanted to hear in order to win a quicker release from the asylum. A sane con artist, after all, is not insane and therefore more than ready for her release. Also, Dr. Blackman gives every appearance in print of being an opinionated man who would not have been able to hide his thoughts if he did talk to the Wild Woman. She could have quickly sized up what he wanted to hear from her. As for the other available evidence, the Shreveport story could easily have been merely wrong guesswork (upon wondering why no one had seen Williams and Paul lately) or fabricated. As for Walters's testimony that Northcott and the Wild Woman enjoyed a whispered conversation on the jail floor before he disappeared, there is every reason to doubt her versions of events entirely. All of which is to say that while we have some reasons to think that the Wild

Woman was a talented actor and may have been Ann Eliza Paul, at best the evidence is inconclusive.

The other problems with writing the Wild Woman show as a happy, enriching romantic caper center around the question of whether Paul would have been an even partner in her own exhibition. This could go either way, depending on the interpersonal dynamics of her relationship with Williams. Paul would have enjoyed greater legal rights as his mistress than as his wife, owing to the restrictions American law placed on wives' legal ownership of their own wages, property, and bodies. But still, what should we think about the fact that she was a mistress and not a wife? Did the fact that they waited years to get married (perhaps several, depending on when their relationship began) point to Williams refusing to wed his lover, thus pointing to him as the dominant partner? Alternatively, did she instead adamantly refuse to marry him, choosing her own legal freedom over the subservient status of wives in nineteenth-century America? Historian Sara E. Lampert's study of popular female entertainers in the period finds their empowerment, even though filling halls with paying customers, to be curtailed by "their place within patriarchal structures." She writes that "presumptions of patriarchal authority within marriage made it far more difficult for wives to challenge or subvert a husband's decisions about the family's career trajectory."[40] Being a mistress instead of a wife might have granted Paul more independence and power than most actresses enjoyed. Perhaps their relationship was an equal one, with two iconoclastic people sharing the sense that it was marriage, not a feral-person show, that was the true sham. There are no answers here, but we need to be cautious before reconstructing them as modern-day, heroic con artists or romantic outlaws. In the nineteenth century, men held most of the cards, and women rarely were equal partners.

Most importantly, just because Paul may have been Williams's lover does not guarantee that she was free of mental illness in 1856 and able to grant her consent to her exhibition. Paul may have been very much in need of help. And there is one more problem, a tough barrier for anyone who wants to turn the Wild Woman (whether Paul or another actor) into a happy tale of a woman's empowerment. There is no way to get around the fact that Paul (or another woman) was the only person in the show's cast to end up incarcerated, if only in an insane asylum. While the Cincinnati criminal courts had no claim on the Wild Woman or her confederates, Paul still ended up behind locked doors. Her incarceration had everything to do with the ways her society systematically denied her rights and power. She entered the courtroom unable to refuse compliance with the judge's order of confinement. Most famously this situation also happened to Mary Todd Lincoln, committed by her son Robert and a legal system that listened to him, not her.[41] In Burgoyne's courtroom, all of the doctors were men, as were the judge and the prosecuting attorney. (Remember, there was no defense attorney.) As a woman alone, and a mute one at that, she had only Walters to speak for her, and she was no help at all. The Wild Woman, be it Paul or someone else, had to follow a court ruling in which she literally had had no say. A man might well have been treated differently.

It is unclear how much an actor in a hoax would have resented being forced to stay in the Dayton asylum from the middle of July to early September. Asylums were not the horrific places of cruelty and confinement that they had been, and she was able, eventually, to go for walks with the matron into town. But she was undeniably detained while her two coconspirators were at liberty and happily spending the money she had earned.

It must also be pointed out that her forced undressing in court, surrounded as she was by so many men and only one other woman, would have been a strikingly humiliating, frightening, and possibly traumatic experience. The struggle that occurred during the first attempt to remove her clothes would have left her bruised and winded. To have that attack followed almost immediately by a second assault that resulted in her being knocked unconscious by chloroform, only to then regain consciousness in a courtroom (perhaps still undressed) and have to deal with disorientation while doctors, Walters, and Burgoyne talked about her and her fate, must have been initially confusing and then deeply disheartening. By the end of the day, being stuck back in a jail cell with Walters (who had hardly come to her aid) and forced to talk with a reporter and the jailors would have put the final layer of misery on an awful, degrading, and painful ordeal. The extent of her disempowerment during the hearing and her subsequent incarceration is hard to exaggerate. That she was placed in that position in part by means of the social power wielded by the women in Walnut Hills would have offered no comfort at all. It is also a useful if unpleasant reminder that sometimes one group of women can use their power, knowingly or unwittingly, to oppress other women.

THE WILD WOMAN AS UNWILLING CAPTIVE

What would the Wild Woman have seen if she had been an unwilling participant in Northcott's show? What would have been her experience had she been either a feral woman who had been captured and held by force or a woman so incapacitated by mental illness that she could not express herself verbally or function well enough to seek help on her own terms? If either of these were the case, the Wild Woman would have known social isolation, fear, and confusion. All of the horrors that the legal and medical communities inflicted on the Wild Woman discussed earlier, while bad enough for a willing actor who understood what was happening, would have been all the more terrifying to someone whose mental faculties were compromised or who was entering an unknown "civilization" and its conventions after living alone in the wilderness. In both of these cases, the people of Cincinnati seem to have provided little or no help to her until the Walnut Hills women and Judge Burgoyne intervened for her treatment and recovery.

The evidence that the Wild Woman was impaired due to some traumatic event comes mostly from the doctors who examined her. They saw enough in her behavior to warrant such a diagnosis, and Judge Burgoyne decided that there was enough of a likelihood of their being correct to commit her. Her symptoms are impossible to evaluate from a chronological distance, and the behavioral descriptions we have of her are vague and not entirely consistent. For example, the *Cincinnati Commercial* wrote that "she stood at the foot of the bed, partially hiding behind it and rocking slowly, but with nervous uneasiness, from one foot to the other, and staring fixedly upon us."[42] The Wild Woman's "rocking slowly" could be indicative of mental distress, but it is hardly conclusive. In addition, the *Commercial* was the only newspaper to include that detail. The Wild Woman's timidity and eye motions, which made such powerful impressions on observers in 1856, lose their meanings at this distance. The state of her mental health seems impossible to know.

In the introduction, I dismissed the idea that the Wild Woman was genuinely feral and that Northcott's story was truthful. That still seems a logical conclusion, even as historian Michael Newton reminds us that strange things do happen. An expert on feral children in Western culture, Newton admits that "it is now impossible to know the veracity of the stories" he writes about.[43] While it is impossible to decide conclusively whether the Wild Woman was a true feral, the salient point to remember is that many people in 1856 seriously entertained the thought that her immediate background lay in the wilds of the Wachita Mountains. Most lost confidence in the show's veracity when the city shuttered it, but skeptics did not control the discussions prior to the arrival of the police. If they had, Northcott would have had to leave town. How people reacted to a woman they considered to be a helpless and scared feral is significant in assessing the importance of the Walnut Hills women's political empowerment.

Even if we cannot tell if the Wild Woman was traumatized or feral, what matters is that most people in Cincinnati thought that she was one or the other and therefore unable to grant her consent to her own exhibition. It is alarming, given that reality, that so little was done to help her. If insane or feral, she was obviously in great distress. Often cowering and seemingly always scared, she radiated a need for help. The talk of the town for weeks, the Wild Woman remained Northcott's captive, his "pet." Her exhibition would have been a very long torment for someone without the mental capacity or social background to process why a line of strangers kept coming into her room to stare at her and talk about her for eleven hours a day. There would have been little security or privacy and no explanation for this threatening set of circumstances.

Northcott claimed that doctors had advised him to exhibit the Wild Woman in an effort to acclimate her to being around people.[44] Given her behavior, that appears to have been a hard, even cruel, path to recovery. Why or how would meeting paying strangers help her get used to human interaction? Hard questions should have been asked of Northcott: Who were those consulting doctors? How have you spent the money you have collected to help her heal? Why have you not asked for donations for her care instead of putting her on view before the public? How much have you collected? What are your plans? If anyone asked Northcott such questions, there is no record of it.

It is hard to escape the conclusion that Northcott was left to do whatever he wanted to do with the Wild Woman in Cincinnati for almost two months. While that would make sense if everyone in the city had believed that the show was a humbug staged by the three principals, it seems inexcusable since much of the public thought of her as a feral or traumatized person. The key to understanding this passive, heartless behavior by the public lies in how they interpreted the relationship between Northcott and the Wild Woman.

Put simply, some (or even most) Cincinnatians thought of the Wild Woman as Northcott's property. As a *Cincinnati Daily Times* reporter wrote, even as late as her trial, "Capt. Northcote, the 'owner' of the female, was called, but did not appear to defend himself."[45] There it is: Northcott was her "owner." Two different dynamics legitimized his tacit claim to the Wild Woman as his property. One (unstated) premise for ownership would have been that he had hunted her as one would a wild animal. His time, hunting prowess, and victory against her in hand-to-hand combat had made her his prize. His ownership rested on seeing her as one would a wild horse; the Wild Woman was there to be taken and commanded by the first man able to do so. This was clear when the capture of a wild woman in Alabama "created a great excitement among the b'hoys, the right of property being protested."[46]

The second justification for Northcott's ownership of the Wild Woman rested on the legal power that husbands had over wives, or fathers over daughters. In any American household, law gave power to men instead of women. The male head of household ruled over all of the "dependents" living in the home, including his wife, children, workers or apprentices, and slaves or indentured servants. This power to give orders held true even though the work of the "dependents" was necessary to the family's survival. Northcott's status as the Wild Woman's "owner" therefore rested on classing her as either a wild animal to be caught or as his "dependent," when in fact he needed her at least as much as she needed him. While equally wrong, both foundations for his presumed ownership of the Wild Woman explain how the public could accept Northcott's claim to control her as though she were his pet. Both premises highlight the extent of patriarchal authority and the magnitude of the antipatriarchal reforms sought by the woman's rights movement and their male and female allies in the Republican Party. Remaking America as a more egalitarian and fair society would not be easy, nor is that work done now.

That many Cincinnatians thought that Northcott owned, or at least deserved to control, the Wild Woman's body to the point of staging it for display tells us that most men held women in low regard in 1856. For all of the power that some had amassed through hard work with churches or civic organizations, Northcott was able to claim to have thrown a lasso around a woman and dragged her across America with a rope around her waist until he could charge people to gawk at her. In doing so, he faced hardly a whiff of opposition during at least the first month of the show. That is a statement of just how powerless some women could be in the 1850s.

TWO MORE FERAL OHIOANS

We can see the extent of patriarchal power again by examining what happened after Ohioans discovered two feral people in their state in 1856. Neither went on to become famous. To the best of our knowledge, neither case ever earned more than a single paragraph of copy, with at most a handful of other newspapers reprinting the original story. Northcott made sure that everyone knew about his show, but no one managed to hawk tickets to see these two people. Neither initial report earned a follow-up story from any journalist, even though the second case is unsettling. What interests us here is how a male feral Ohioan was treated differently than a female person who police thought might be a wild girl.

The first story ran originally in the *Dayton Gazette* and was picked up in June by the *Cincinnati Daily Times,* where interest in feral humanity was running high due to the appearance of the Wild Woman a few weeks earlier. It begins with "some gentlemen" traveling through the countryside near Oakland, Ohio: "They saw, in the fields, near the road, what appeared to be a man, entirely naked. They left the vehicle, and made chase. The naked object made tracks for the woods, and was only caught after a hard run. It turned out to be a man perfectly wild, either naturally or by insanity, and in a state of absolute nudity." The "wild man," as he was called in the headline of the Cincinnati paper, was coaxed into the wagon, but when "one of the party attempted to draw over the captive's nether limbs a pair of old pantaloons that had been procured for the purpose," he rebelled. "This he resisted with the utmost desperation," the paper reported. The wild man escaped during the struggle but was unable to reach the woods before he was apprehended a second time. The story ends with a reassuring finality. The captive was eventually clothed and brought into town, "where he has taken up lodgings with landlord Emley, until his case can be investigated."[47] Emley seems to have been trusted to take care of this man and clear up all of the possible loose ends regarding his identity, his place in the world, and his health.

The second feral episode is less comforting because it lacks any hint of such a tidy resolution. In this case, the supposedly feral person was an African American girl, discovered in Cincinnati as she was being carried through the city completely covered by a large shawl. The story is worth reading in its entirety:

About ten o'clock this morning, two policemen discovered an Italian carrying a suspicious looking bundle on his shoulder through the streets, a bundle which looked as if it was a human being wrapped up in a shawl. As in duty bound they stopped the Italian for the purpose of inquiry. The man not only refused to give information, but would not permit the officers to touch the bundle. In fact he acted so strangely that they arrested him, and marched him and the package off to the watch-house. On the way he confessed that he had a wild woman on his shoulder, and an examination at the watch-house, exposed a deformed negro girl dressed up for exhibition. The police seemed puzzled what to do with the case.[48]

From its mysterious start to its uncertain end, this story raises more questions than it answers. Stopped because he had "a suspicious looking bundle," the Italian was then detained. We cannot say for sure why he was detained, though it is easy to envision the girl verbally or physically protesting her imprisonment. Why did the man think he could carry her through the city in the broad daylight of ten in the morning? Most importantly, what happened to the child?

There are, unfortunately, no answers to these questions. Instead, historians have only this single, isolated news report. The most salient point is that a white man, the Italian, seemed to think that he had the right to wrap a girl in a shawl and carry her across the city with the stated intent of putting her on exhibit somewhere. Perhaps more astonishingly, the police seemed unclear about what to do with the man and the girl he had with him; they "seemed puzzled what to do with the case." Even though Ohio was a free state, the officers seemed reluctant to question the man's right to the "negro" girl. This is a deeply troubling statement that questions what the term "free state" meant in practice.

The officers' confusion is an echo of the idea that somehow Northcott could be the "owner" of the Wild Woman, that she could be his "pet." Did they hesitate to free the girl and arrest "the Italian" for kidnapping because the person in the shawl was of African descent? Possibly, though the story makes no mention of him claiming that she was his property. Most likely, the officers' indecision was based on her age, her sex, and her physical disability in addition to her race. The child was legally and culturally disadvantaged; to be a minor, a person of color, a female, and physically disabled was to have four strikes against you in antebellum culture. The only thing that may have made the policemen take the two as far as the watch house was that the man had several strikes against him as an Italian and likely a Roman Catholic who spoke English as a second language. One can easily imagine a more polished and native-born man talking his way past the police without being detained.

We can try to sympathize with the officers' confusion as they tried to figure out the truth of what was happening and the social and legal positions of the two people they had detained. But by the time they had made it to the station, some experienced senior officer had presumably taken charge and had had time to think about it; after all, enough time had passed for someone to notify the reporter. And still the police were puzzled? We must express our indignation at their lack of moral sense. No man should be allowed to place another person in a bundle and carry her through a city dressed up as a "wild woman" and ready for exhibition. The man was engaging in what we now identify as human trafficking, and the girl should have been returned to her family, or, failing that as a realistic option, given over to an orphanage. There was, in fact, a "colored orphan asylum" in Cincinnati in 1856.[49] That she was a "deformed negro girl" does not lessen her right as a person, an Ohioan, and an American to live a peaceful life. Rather, it should entitle her to our fullest consideration. That such humanitarian concern did not automatically serve as the first and foremost consideration of the police is troubling and speaks to the deeply hierarchical view of society that many nineteenth-century Americans possessed.

The extreme situation of this girl helps clarify what was happening to the Wild Woman of Cincinnati at the same time. She had also shown up in Cincinnati as a captive. While not literally slung over Northcott's shoulder, the Wild Woman had been presented (and understood) as his property, just as the Italian seemed to think he possessed the girl. The rope around the woman's waist was the equivalent of the girl's bundle of fabric. Of course, there were also differences. The Wild Woman and the wild girl were of different races and ages, and Northcott seems to have been a slicker and more imposing man than the Italian. But the similarities in the two cases are striking when considering how the city received the news of the two captives' arrivals. Cincinnatians and others reacted the same way in both cases; they saw a captive female human being and did not know what to do. They were puzzled enough to do little or nothing in both cases, at least initially.

Women's status as property, as dependents, as objects to be looked at, and as people whose labor was to be appropriated was hard to overcome. The two wild people who shared Ohio with the Wild Woman of Cincinnati prove that point; a "wild man" was dropped off to have his status investigated and resolved. A "wild girl" left the police who discovered her "puzzled [as] what to do with the case."

In the end, the only people to question the idea that men owned women were other women, the ones of Walnut Hills. These activists would eventually liberate the Wild Woman from the rope and the exhibition hall, from her status as a prisoner. We do not know if anyone freed the African American girl, whose story disappeared from the news as quickly as it had arrived. But both cases suggest that men, when left to their own devices, were all too willing to enjoy looking at women who were tied up before they went on to do other things. The Wild Woman and the wild girl are proof that it is absolutely essential for women of all races to have the social and political power to fight for their own rights, equality, and freedom. No one else will do it for them.

The Wild Woman of Cincinnati attracted a large amount of attention across the United States for a brief period in 1856. While the production did not shape the course of the nation's history, the way people thought about the Wild Woman helps us see answers to important questions. Republicans and Democrats wrote about her in very different ways, using her as a blank screen on which to project their ideas about who women were and what the power dynamics between the sexes should be. In the process, they teach us that antebellum politics was based, in part, on how the parties talked about gender and the social and political issues that arise regarding men, women, and the relationships between them. With the regional Republicans taking one stand and the Democrats, strongest in the South but allied with likeminded men in the North, taking another, we can see that the two sections of the country differed in their gender ideologies. While it is true that some northerners, especially Democrats, shared a common response to the Wild Woman with southerners, Republicans diverged from the conservative consensus that she was a hoax who could be ignored once the thrill of looking at her was gone. Instead, Republicans joined with activist women in thinking that men were likely to abuse women and that it was the role of government to help their victims. That was a vitally important step on the unfinished journey to equal rights for the sexes. The fact that women led the way in liberating the Wild Woman from her imprisonment, enlisting Judge Burgoyne, a Republican, in the matter, shows that they had political influence long before they had the right to vote. While it is important that women had other venues in which to exercise power, it was their ability to tap into the power of government that enabled them to have real influence on this event. The ability to access government's reach and protection remains at least as vital for women now as it was in the 1850s.

NOTES

Introduction

1. *Cincinnati Daily Enquirer*, May 24, June 21, 1856.
2. Ibid., May 21, June 13, 1856.
3. Steven J. Ross, *Workers on the Edge: Work, Leisure, and Politics in Industrializing Cincinnati, 1788–1890* (New York: Columbia University Press, 1985), 164.
4. *Cincinnati Daily Enquirer*, May 23, 1856.
5. *Cincinnati Daily Gazette*, June 14, 1856.
6. *Cincinnati Daily Enquirer*, May 25, 1856.
7. *Cincinnati Daily Gazette*, June 19, 23, 1856.
8. *Cincinnati Daily Enquirer*, May 25, 1856.
9. *Covington (KY) Journal*, June 28, 1856.
10. Stephen Mihm, *A Nation of Counterfeiters: Capitalists, Con Men, and the Making of the United States* (Cambridge, MA: Harvard University Press, 2007).
11. James Fairhead, *The Captain and "the Cannibal": An Epic Story of Exploration, Kidnapping, and the Broadway Stage* (New Haven, CT: Yale University Press, 2015), 95.
12. *Sandusky (OH) Register*, May 26, 1856, copied from *Cincinnati Commercial*, n.d.
13. *Chicago Times*, June 5, 1856, copied from *Cincinnati Commercial*, n.d.
14. Ibid.
15. Ibid.
16. *New York Herald*, July 14, 1856.
17. *New York Daily Tribune*, July 16, 1856, copied from the *Cincinnati Daily Gazette*, n.d.

1. The Capture and Exhibition of a Woman

1. The opening date of the Wild Woman show is not known, which makes it impossible to determine exactly how long the show ran.
2. *Cincinnati Daily Gazette*, June 24, 1856.
3. Ibid., July 8, 1856.
4. *New York Tribune*, July 16, 1856, copied from the *Cincinnati Daily Gazette*, n.d.
5. *Cincinnati Daily Gazette*, July 8, 1856.
6. Ibid.

7. Matthew Goodman, *The Sun and the Moon: The Remarkable True Account of Hoaxers, Showmen, Dueling Journalists, and Lunar Man-Bats in Nineteenth-Century New York* (New York: Basic Books, 2008), 263.

8. Ibid., 263–64. See also Neil Harris, *Humbug: The Art of P. T. Barnum* (Chicago: University of Chicago Press, 1973), 79; James W. Cook, *The Arts of Deception: Playing with Fraud in the Age of Barnum* (Cambridge, MA: Harvard University Press, 2001), 14, 74; and P. T. Barnum, *The Humbugs of the World* (London: John Camden Hotten, 1866), 8–9.

9. Benjamin Reiss, *The Showman and the Slave: Race, Death, and Memory in Barnum's America* (Cambridge, MA: Harvard University Press, 2001). See also A. H. Saxon, *P. T. Barnum: The Legend and the Man* (New York: Columbia University Press, 1989), 68–74; Cook, *Arts of Deception*, 1–29; and Stephen Mihm, ed., *The Life of P. T. Barnum, Written by Himself, with Related Documents* (Boston: Bedford / St. Martin's, 2018), 46–52, 57–60.

10. Susie King Taylor, *Reminiscences of My Life in Camp: An African American Woman's Civil War Memoir* (Athens: University of Georgia Press, 2006), 1.

11. *Cincinnati Daily Times*, June 26, July 5, 7, 8, 1856; *Cincinnati Daily Gazette*, July 3, 8, 1856.

12. The ten newspapers reporting the 1843 story were the *Baltimore Sun*, January 30, 1843; *Philadelphia Public Ledger*, January 31, 1843; *Daily Madisonian (Washington, DC)*, February 4, 1843, copied from the *Pittsburgh Chronicle*, n.d.; *Pensacola Gazette*, February 11, 1843; *Plattsburgh (NY) Republican*, February 11, 1843; *Albany Evening Journal*, February 15, 1843; *Boston Recorder*, February 23, 1843; *Augusta (ME) Age*, February 24, 1843; and *Brattleboro Vermont Phoenix*, February 24, 1843.

13. *New York Commercial Advertiser* July 9, 1845, copied from the *Caddo Gazette (Shreveport, LA)*, n.d. Other newspapers that ran the story include the *New York Spectator*, July 12, 1845; *Boston Courier*, July 14, 1845; *Middletown (CT) Constitution*, July 16, 1845; *Barre (MA) Patriot*, July 18, 1845; *Brattleboro Vermont Phoenix*, July 18, 1845; *Richmond Enquirer*, July 19, 1845; *St. Albans (VT) Messenger*, July 23, 1845; *Hartford (CT) Times*, July 26, 1845; and the *Milwaukee Daily Sentinel*, August 20, 1845.

14. *New York Herald*, July 27, 1845, copied from the *Baltimore Clipper*, n.d.; *Philadelphia Public Ledger*, July 28, 1845; *Newark Centinel of Freedom*, July 29, 1845.

15. *Weekly Indiana State Sentinel* (Indianapolis), May 22, 1856.

16. *Chicago Times*, June 5, 1856, copied from the *Cincinnati Commercial*, n.d.

17. Cook, *Arts of Deception*, 17.

18. W. S. Gilbert, *The Mikado*, Act II.

19. For Twain's early journalistic career and his "hoaxes," see Gary Scharnhorst, *The Life of Mark Twain: The Early Years, 1835–1871* (Columbia: University of Missouri Press, 2018), 178–84, 215–20; Roy Morris Jr., *Lighting Out for the Territory: How Samuel Clemens Headed West and Became Mark Twain* (New York: Simon and Schuster, 2010), 16–7, 107–08, 121–23; and Ron Powers, *Mark Twain: A Life* (New York: Free Press, 2005), 111–13, 124–28.

20. *Chicago Times*, June 5, 1856, copied from the *Cincinnati Commercial*, n.d.

21. *Little Rock (AR) True Democrat*, May 6, 1856, announced the forthcoming departure of the *Hickman* on the tenth.

22. *Chicago Times*, June 5, 1856, copied from the *Cincinnati Commercial*, n.d.

23. Ibid.

24. Ibid.

25. Ibid.

26. Ibid.

27. Ibid.

28. For Cincinnati and Ohio, see Nikki M. Taylor, *Frontiers of Freedom: Cincinnati's Black Community, 1802–1868* (Athens: Ohio University Press, 2005), 117–77; and Henry Louis Taylor Jr. and Vicky Dula, "The Black Residential Experience and Community Formation in Antebellum Cincinnati," in *Race and the City: Work, Community, and Protest in Cincinnati, 1820–1970*, ed. Henry Louis Taylor Jr. (Urbana: University of Illinois Press, 1993): 96–125. For a broader context, see James Oliver Horton and Lois E. Horton, *In Hope of Liberty: Culture, Community and Protest Among Northern Free Blacks, 1700–1860* (New York: Oxford University Press, 1997), 102–7.

29. James W. Cook writes that the audience for Barnum's Joice Heth was "almost entirely white." There is no reason to think that the Wild Woman show was different. Cook, *Arts of Deception*, 24.

30. Kevin Young, *Bunk: The Rise of Hoaxes, Humbug, Plagiarists, Phonies, Post-Facts, and Fake News* (Minneapolis: Graywolf, 2018), 41. See also Young's analysis of the Cottingley fairies, ibid., 54–61. Barnum began trying to find a "Circassian Beauty" in 1856.

31. Laurel Clark Shire, *The Threshold of Manifest Destiny: Gender and National Expansion in Florida* (Philadelphia: University of Pennsylvania Press, 2016), 2.

32. Isabella Bird, *The Englishwoman in America* (London: John Murray, 1856), 118.

33. For the interplay between patriarchal family structures and practices and reproductive patterns, see John Mack Faragher, *Sugar Creek: Life on the Illinois Prairie* (New Haven, CT: Yale University Press, 1986). Overviews of changing models of masculinity in the 1800s include Michael Kimmel, *Manhood in America: A Cultural History* (New York: Free Press, 1996); E. Anthony Rotundo, "Learning about Manhood: Gender Ideals and the Middle-Class Family in Nineteenth-Century America," in *Manliness and Morality: Middle-Class Masculinity in Britain and America, 1800–1940*, ed. J. A. Mangan and James Walvin (New York: St. Martin's, 1987), 35–51; and E. Anthony Rotundo, *American Manhood: Transformations in Masculinity from the Revolution to the Modern Era* (New York: Basic Books, 1993). The number of children per household dropped by half over the course of the nineteenth century. See Janet Farrell Brodie, *Contraception and Abortion in Nineteenth-Century America* (Ithaca, NY: Cornell University Press, 1994), 2.

34. For biographies analyzing how ideologies of masculinity shaped individual men, see especially Sarah Watts, *Rough Rider in the White House: Theodore Roosevelt and the Politics of Desire* (Chicago: University of Chicago Press, 2003; and Stacey M. Robertson, *Parker Pillsbury: Radical Abolitionist, Male Feminist* (Ithaca, NY: Cornell University Press, 2000).

35. Steven J. Ross uses "the age of manufacturing" as an organizing framework for his study. See Ross, *Workers on the Edge*, vii.

36. Alisse Portnoy, *Their Right to Speak: Women's Activism in the Indian and Slave Debates* (Cambridge, MA: Harvard University Press, 2005); Susan Zaeske, *Signatures of Citizenship: Petitioning, Antislavery, and Women's Political Identity* (Chapel Hill: University of North Carolina Press, 2003); and Deborah Bingham Van Broekhoven, "'Let Your Names Be Enrolled': Method and Ideology in Women's Antislavery Petitioning," in *The Abolitionist Sisterhood:*

Women's Political Culture in Antebellum America, ed. Jean Fagan Yellin and John C. Van Horne (Ithaca, NY: Cornell University Press, 1994): 179–99.

37. *Chicago Times,* June 5, 1856, copied from the *Cincinnati Commercial,* n.d.

38. Ibid.

39. No records exist of the thoughts of a paying customer, so we are here dependent on inferences and logic.

40. Lawrence W. Levine, *Highbrow/Lowbrow: The Emergence of Cultural Hierarchy in America* (Cambridge, MA: Harvard University Press, 1988).

41. Ross, *Workers on the Edge,* 163–92 (quote, 165).

42. Fairhead, *Captain and "the Cannibal."*

43. Ibid., 90.

44. Ibid., 71.

45. Bruce Mills, ed., *Letters from New-York: A Portrait of New York on the Cusp of its Transformation into a Modern City* (Athens: University of Georgia Press, 1998), 161–67. For Child, see Carolyn L. Karcher, *The First Woman in the Republic: A Cultural Biography of Lydia Maria Child* (Durham: Duke University Press, 1994).

46. Dell Upton, "Inventing the Metropolis: Civilization and Urbanity in Antebellum New York," in *Art and the Empire City: New York, 1825–1861,* ed. Catherine Hoover Voorsanger and John K. Howat (New Haven, CT: Yale University Press, 2000), 3–45, quotation on 26. See also the cultural analysis in Allison Pingree, "America's 'United Siamese Brothers': Chang and Eng and Nineteenth-Century Ideologies of Democracy and Domesticity," in *Monster Theory: Reading Culture,* ed. Jeffrey Jerome Cohen (Minneapolis: University of Minnesota Press, 1996), 92–114.

47. Helen R. Deese, ed., *Daughter of Boston: The Extraordinary Diary of a Nineteenth-Century Woman* (Boston: Beacon Press, 2005), 107–08. For a fuller analysis of how Powers's supporters guided the sculpture's reception, see Wendy Jean Katz, *Regionalism and Reform: Art and Class Formation in Antebellum Cincinnati* (Columbus: Ohio State University Press, 2002), 137–71.

48. *Cincinnati Daily Enquirer,* July 4, 1856.

49. *Chicago Times,* June 5, 1856, copied from the *Cincinnati Commercial,* n.d.

50. *Cincinnati Daily Gazette,* June 30, 1856.

51. *Chicago Times,* June 5, 1856, copied from the *Cincinnati Commercial,* n.d.

52. *Greenville (SC) Southern Enterprise,* June 5, 1856, copied from the *Cincinnati Daily Enquirer,* n.d.

53. *Chicago Times,* June 5, 1856, copied from the *Cincinnati Commercial,* n.d.

54. Laura Mulvey, "Visual Pleasure and Narrative Cinema," *Screen* 16, no. 3 (1975): 6–18.

55. *Chicago Times,* June 5, 1856, copied from the *Cincinnati Commercial,* n.d.

56. The *Cincinnati Daily Gazette* wrote about the Wild Woman on June 30, 1856.

57. For Mary Rogers, see Amy Gilman Srebnick, *The Mysterious Death of Mary Rogers: Sex and Culture in Nineteenth-Century New York* (New York: Oxford University Press, 1995), 51–57; and Daniel Stashower, *The Beautiful Cigar Girl: Mary Rogers, Edgar Allen Poe, and the Invention of Murder* (New York: Dutton, 2006). For the daguerreotypist, see Lawrence T. McDonnell, *Performing Disunion: The Coming of the Civil War in Charleston, South Carolina* (New York: Cambridge University Press, 2018), 72. Northcott also picked up on the larger trend of people putting themselves on display. Examples of this trend range from Sojourner Truth's sales of her own photographic image to Sam Patch, the famous waterfall jumper, who did "meet and greets"

at a Niagara Falls museum. See Nell Irvin Painter, "Representing Truth: Sojourner Truth's Knowing and Becoming Known," *Journal of American History* 81, no. 2 (September 1994): 461–92; and Paul E. Johnson, *Sam Patch, the Famous Jumper* (New York: Hill & Wang, 2003), 115.

58. Sara E. Lampert, *Starring Women: Celebrity, Patriarchy, and American Theater, 1790–1850* (Urbana: University of Illinois Press, 2020), 143 (quotes). See also ibid., 130–34, 142–46, 150–51, 160–68.

59. For Heth, see Young, *Bunk*, 33. For Morrell, see Fairhead, *Captain and "the Cannibal,"* 96.

60. *Dallas Herald,* June 28, 1856.

61. *Cincinnati Daily Gazette,* June 30, 1856.

62. For European context, especially for the early 1800s, see Michael Newton, *Savage Girls and Wild Boys: A History of Feral Children* (New York: Picador, 2002), 98–181.

63. *Cincinnati Daily Times,* June 26, 1856.

64. *Cincinnati Daily Gazette,* June 30, 1856.

65. *Weekly Indiana State Sentinel* (Indianapolis), May 22, 1856. Oddly, some of the same sentences appear in a later story in the *Cincinnati Daily Enquirer*, even though that writer claimed to have seen her on the boat. *Greenville (SC) Southern Enterprise,* June 5, 1856, copied from the *Cincinnati Daily Enquirer*, n.d.

66. *Chicago Times,* June 5, 1856, copied from the *Cincinnati Commercial*, n.d.

67. Ibid.

68. *Weekly Indiana State Sentinel* (Indianapolis), May 22, 1856.

69. *Chicago Times,* June 5, 1856, copied from the *Cincinnati Commercial*, n.d. (italics mine).

70. Ibid.

71. *Cincinnati Daily Gazette,* June 30, 1856.

72. Alice Galon, *The Wild Woman; or, The Wrecked Heart, Being the True Autobiography of the "Wild Woman," Who Was Recently Exhibited at Cincinnati, and Was Rescued from Her Persecutors by the Citizens of that City, and Sent to the Insane Asylum at Dayton, Ohio* (Cincinnati: Barclay, 1857).

73. Holly Kent, "Wearing Black, Wearing Bows: Union Women and the Politics of Dress in the US Fashion Press, 1861–1865," *Women's History Review* 26, no. 4 (2017): 559.

74. Daniel E. Sutherland, ed., *A Very Violent Rebel: The Civil War Diary of Ellen Renshaw House* (Knoxville: University of Tennessee Press, 1996), 183.

75. Newton, *Savage Girls and Wild Boys,* 235.

76. A month into the Wild Woman's stay in Cincinnati, the *Gazette* reported, "She is led into the room by a rope some six feet in length, and fastened securely about her waist." *Cincinnati Daily Gazette,* June 30, 1856.

2. Closing the Show and Trying a Woman in Court

1. *Cincinnati Daily Gazette,* June 30, 1856.
2. Ibid., July 8, 1856.
3. *Cincinnati Daily Enquirer,* July 10, 1856.
4. Ibid.
5. *Worcester (MA) National Aegis,* July 23, 1856. A different retelling reported that she said: "Lord o' mercy! what are they going to do?" *Newark Centinel of Freedom,* July 22, 1856.

6. *Cincinnati Daily Gazette,* July 10, 1856.

7. *Cincinnati Daily Enquirer,* July 10, 1856.

8. *Cincinnati Daily Gazette,* July 10, 1856. The new law was Ohio General Assembly, "AN ACT to Provide for the Uniform Government and the Better Regulation of the Lunatic Asylums of the State and the Care of Idiots and the Insane. Legislative Acts Passed and Joint Resolutions Adopted by the General Assembly Ohio" (Secretary of State, April 1856), 81–96. See Erik D. Anderson, "Feral Bodies, Feral Nature: Wild Men in America" (PhD diss., Brown University, 2010), 104–5.

9. *Cincinnati Daily Enquirer,* July 10, 1856.

10. Ibid., July 11, 1856.

11. Ibid.

12. *New York Daily Tribune,* July 16, 1856; *New York Herald,* July 14, 1856, copied from the *Cincinnati Columbian,* July 11, 1856.

13. *New York Daily Tribune,* July 16, 1856, copied from the *Cincinnati Daily Gazette,* n.d.

14. The three Cincinnati newspapers present were the *Daily Gazette,* the *Columbian,* and the *Daily Times.* The papers almost certainly shared a common stenographer's record of the day's proceedings since the accounts of testimony are similar. But each provided different opening and concluding paragraphs about the Wild Woman and how she acted and reacted to the events around her. Since the Daily *Gazette* is no longer extant, quotations drawn from it are from the *New York Daily Tribune,* a fellow Republican Party newspaper, which copied its account. The *Cincinnati Daily Enquirer* and the *Daily Gazette* seem to have shared all coverage.

15. *New York Daily Tribune,* July 16, 1856, copied from the *Cincinnati Daily Gazette,* n.d.

16. *Cincinnati Daily Times,* July 10, 1856.

17. *New York Herald,* July 14, 1856, copied from *Cincinnati Columbian,* July 11, 1856.

18. *New York Daily Tribune,* July 16, 1856, copied from *Cincinnati Daily Gazette,* n.d.

19. Ibid.

20. Ibid.

21. Ibid.

22. *New York Herald,* July 14, 1856, copied from the *Cincinnati Columbian,* July 11, 1856.

23. *Cincinnati Daily Times,* July 10, 1856.

24. Ibid.

25. Ibid.

26. George Blackman, "Reviews and Notices: Medico-Legal Examination on the Case of Charles B. Huntington," *Western Lancet* 3 (March 1857): 223.

27. *New York Herald,* July 14, 1856, copied from the *Cincinnati Columbian,* July 11, 1856. Newspapers usually identified the doctors only by their last names, occasionally adding initials. Likely full names are drawn from *Williams' Cincinnati Directory, City Guide and Business Mirror; for Cincinnati in 1856* (Cincinnati: C. S. Williams, 1856). I have also consulted the 1853 edition of this book.

28. *History of Cincinnati and Hamilton County, Ohio: Their Past and Present* (Cincinnati: S. B. Nelson, 1894), 238.

29. Alan I. Marcus, *Plague of Strangers: Social Groups and the Origins of City Services in Cincinnati, 1819–1870* (Columbus: Ohio State University Press, 1991), 183.

30. *New York Herald*, July 14, 1856, copied from the *Cincinnati Columbian*, July 11, 1856. The *Cincinnati Daily Gazette* omitted this speech from its account.

31. *New York Daily Tribune*, July 16, 1856, copied from the *Cincinnati Daily Gazette*, n.d. Dr. Williams could have been either Elkanah Williams or A. F. Williams, both doctors in the city in 1856. *Williams' Cincinnati Directory* (1856).

32. *New York Herald*, July 14, 1856, copied from the *Cincinnati Columbian*, July 11, 1856.

33. I. Loudon, "Puerperal Insanity in the 19th Century," *Journal of the Royal Society of Medicine* 81, no. 2 (February 1988): 76.

34. Murphy's testimony from *New York Herald*, July 14, 1856, copied from the *Cincinnati Columbian*, July 11, 1856.

35. Cox's testimony from ibid.

36. *New York Daily Tribune*, July 16, 1856, copied from the *Cincinnati Daily Gazette*, n.d.

37. *New York Herald*, July 14, 1856, copied from the *Cincinnati Columbian*, July 11, 1856.

38. *New York Daily Tribune*, July 16, 1856, copied from the *Cincinnati Daily Gazette*, n.d.

39. Blackman, "Reviews and Notices," 223.

40. *New York Herald*, July 14, 1856, copied from the *Cincinnati Columbian*, July 11, 1856.

41. *New York Daily Tribune*, July 16, 1856, copied from the *Cincinnati Daily Gazette*, n.d.

42. It is unclear exactly when Walters spoke during the trial. The two accounts have her speaking at different times in relation to the doctors' testimonies. Her inconsistencies are more glaring when reading the *Cincinnati Columbian*'s report, which presents her testimony in one solid block. The *Cincinnati Daily Gazette*'s account has her answering questions at two different points in the trial. My reading of the events in the courtroom is based on the *Daily Gazette*'s rendering of when she spoke, not only because it makes her inconsistencies more understandable but also because it presents her testimony in question-and-answer format, which the *Columbian* does not. That she would have been answering questions rather than delivering a long monologue (as in the *Columbian*'s account) is backed up when she concluded her remarks (even in the *Columbian*'s version) by sarcastically commenting, "I hope you have got it all down; you have asked me plenty." *New York Herald*, July 14, 1856, copied from the *Cincinnati Columbian*, July 11, 1856.

43. All quotations from *New York Daily Tribune*, July 16, 1856, copied from the *Cincinnati Daily Gazette*, n.d.

44. Ibid.

45. Ibid.

46. *New York Herald*, July 14, 1856, copied from the *Cincinnati Columbian*, July 11, 1856.

47. Ibid.

48. Thomas J. Brown, *Dorothea Dix: New England Reformer* (Cambridge, MA: Harvard University Press, 1998), 172.

49. *New York Daily Tribune*, July 16, 1856, copied from the *Cincinnati Daily Gazette*, n.d.

50. Ibid.

51. Ibid.

52. Ibid.

53. Ibid.; *Cincinnati Daily Times*, July 10, 1856, 1, 3.

54. *New York Daily Tribune*, July 16, 1856, copied from the *Cincinnati Daily Gazette*, n.d.

55. *Arkansas State Gazette and Democrat* (Little Rock) and *Little Rock (AR) True Democrat*, issues from mid-April through May 1856. The riverboat *Hickman*, on which the Wild Woman show arrived in Cincinnati, left Little Rock on May 11. See *Arkansas State Gazette and Democrat* (Little Rock), May 17, 1856.

56. *New York Herald*, July 14, 1856, copied from the *Cincinnati Columbian*, July 11, 1856.

57. Ibid.

58. *Cincinnati Daily Times*, July 11, 1856.

59. *Cincinnati Daily Enquirer*, July 15, 1856.

60. *New York Herald*, July 14, 1856, copied from the *Cincinnati Columbian*, July 11, 1856.

61. *New York Daily Tribune*, July 16, 1856, copied from the *Cincinnati Daily Gazette*, n.d.

62. Ibid.

63. *Cincinnati Daily Times*, July 10, 1856.

64. Ibid., July 14, 1856.

65. *Cincinnati Daily Enquirer*, July 13, 1856. Another paper reported that "a large crowd was in attendance." *Cincinnati Daily Times*, July 14, 1856.

66. *Cincinnati Daily Enquirer*, July 13, 1856.

67. Ibid.

68. Brown, *Dorothea Dix*, 114.

69. Kathleen De Grave, *Swindler, Spy, Rebel: The Confidence Woman in Nineteenth-Century America* (Columbia: University of Missouri Press, 1995), 33.

70. *Cincinnati Daily Enquirer*, July 13, 1856.

71. David J. Rothman, *The Discovery of Asylum: Social Order and Disorder in the New Republic* (Boston: Little, Brown, 1971), 109–54 (specific list of causes on 111). Dorothea Dix blamed the apparent increase in mental illness on similar causes, including excessive liberty, competition, and ambition in American society during these years. David Gollaher, *Voice for the Mad: The Life of Dorothea Dix* (New York: Free Press, 1995), 171, 284–85.

72. Brenna Holland, "Mad Speculation and Mary Girard: Gender, Capitalism, and the Cultural Economy of Madness in the Revolutionary Atlantic," *Journal of the Early Republic* 39 no. 4 (Winter 2019): 650, 649. See also Andrew Scull, *Madness in Civilization: A Cultural History of Insanity from the Bible to Freud, from the Madhouse to Modern Medicine* (Princeton, NJ: Princeton University Press, 2015); Lynn Gamwell and Nancy Tomes, *Madness in America: Cultural and Medical Perceptions of Mental Illness before 1914* (Ithaca, NY: Cornell University Press, 1995); and Mary Ann Jimenez, *Changing Faces of Madness: Early American Attitudes and Treatment of the Insane* (Hanover, NH: University Press of New England, 1987).

73. *Baltimore Sun,* January 30, 1843; *Philadelphia Public Ledger,* January 31, 1843; *Daily Madisonian* (Washington, DC), February 4, 1843, reprinted from *Pittsburgh Chronicle*, n.d.; *Pensacola Gazette,* February 11, 1843; *Plattsburgh (NY) Republican,* February 11, 1843; *Brother Jonathan* (New York City), February 11, 1843; *Albany Evening Journal,* February 15, 1843; *Boston Recorder,* February 23, 1843; *Augusta (ME) Age,* February 24, 1843; *Vermont Phoenix* (Brattleboro), February 24, 1843; *American Masonic Register,* March 4, 1843; *Lutheran Standard* (New Philadelphia, OH), March 15, 1843; *Waynesboro (PA) Circulator,* June 3, 1843; and *Milford (MA) Practical Christian,* June 10, 1843. These thirteen papers are only the ones appearing in the digitized newspaper databases; many others not included may have picked up the story as well.

74. *Daily Madisonian* (Washington, DC), February 4, 1843.

75. Ibid.

76. Catharine Maria Sedgwick, *A New-England Tale; or, Sketches of New-England Character and Manners* (1822; repr., New York: Oxford University Press, 1995), 84.

77. Ibid., 87–88.

78. Ibid., 86.

79. Ibid.

80. Ibid., 16.

81. Ibid., 17.

82. Joan D. Hedrick, *Harriet Beecher Stowe: A Life* (New York: Oxford University Press, 1994).

83. John L. Brooke, *"There Is a North": Fugitive Slaves, Political Crisis, and Cultural Transformation in the Coming of the Civil War* (Amherst: University of Massachusetts Press, 2019), 188, 196.

84. Ibid., 221. For theatrical productions of *Uncle Tom's Cabin* in Cincinnati, see ibid., 188, 196.

85. Harriet Beecher Stowe, *Uncle Tom's Cabin; or, Life among the Lowly* (1852; repr., New York: Penguin, 1981), 520.

86. Ibid., 521.

87. Ibid., 560.

88. Ibid., 522.

89. Ibid.

90. Ibid., 526.

91. Ibid.

92. Ibid., 501.

93. Ibid., 525.

94. Ibid., 568.

95. Ibid. Consider also Cassy's "keen, sneering glitter in her eyes." Ibid., 569.

96. Ibid., 518.

97. Cassy's recovery is also seen in her eyes, as would be the case with the Wild Woman later. On the path to freedom and befriended by a girl her own daughter's age, Cassy turns out to have "magnificent eyes, now soft with tears." Ibid., 580.

98. Galon, *Wild Woman*, 68, 79, 80.

99. Ibid., 80.

100. *Cincinnati Daily Enquirer*, July 15, 1856.

3. Sex-tionalism and the Gender Ideologies of the Political Parties

1. This is the dominant analytical lens for antebellum political history. Recent excellent examples include, but are not limited to, Jonathan H. Earle, *Jacksonian Antislavery and the Politics of Free Soil, 1824–1854* (Chapel Hill: University of North Carolina Press, 2004); Lynn Hudson Parsons, *The Birth of Modern Politics: Andrew Jackson, John Quincy Adams, and the Election of 1828* (New York: Oxford University Press, 2009); Allen C. Guelzo, *Lincoln and Douglas: The Debates That Defined America* (New York: Simon and Schuster, 2008); Richard J. Ellis, *Old Tip vs. the Sly Fox: The 1840 Election and the Making of a Partisan Nation* (Lawrence: Uni-

versity Press of Kansas, 2020); and John W. Quist and Michael J. Birkner, eds., *James Buchanan and the Coming of the Civil War* (Gainesville: University Press of Florida, 2013).

2. Books that analyze partisan racial ideologies include Jean H. Baker, *Affairs of Party: The Political Culture of Northern Democrats in the Mid-Nineteenth Century* (Ithaca, NY: Cornell University Press, 1983), 177–258; Joshua A. Lynn, *Preserving the White Man's Republic: Jacksonian Democracy, Race, and the Transformation of American Conservatism* (Charlottesville: University of Virginia Press, 2019); Mark E. Neely Jr., *Lincoln and the Democrats: The Politics of Opposition in the Civil War* (New York: Cambridge University Press, 2017), 45–135; Michael Todd Landis, *Northern Men with Southern Loyalties: The Democratic Party and the Sectional Crisis* (Ithaca, NY: Cornell University Press, 2014); Eric Foner, *Free Soil, Free Labor, Free Men: The Ideology of the Republican Party before the Civil War* (New York: Oxford University Press, 1970), 261–300; Foner, *The Fiery Trial: Abraham Lincoln and American Slavery* (New York: W. W. Norton, 2010); and Bruce Laurie, *Beyond Garrison: Antislavery and Social Reform* (New York: Cambridge University Press, 2005), 84–124, 231–71. Ethnic and religious factors are analyzed in William E. Gienapp, *The Origins of the Republican Party, 1852–1856* (New York: Oxford University Press, 1987); Lee Benson, *The Concept of Jacksonian Democracy: New York as a Test Case* (Princeton, NJ: Princeton University Press, 1961); Ronald P. Formisano, *The Birth of Mass Political Parties: Michigan, 1827–1861* (Princeton, NJ: Princeton University Press, 1971), 3–14, 137–94; and William G. Shade, "Pennsylvania Politics in the Jacksonian Period: A Case Study, Northampton County, 1824–1844," *Pennsylvania History* 39, no. 3 (Summer 1972): 313–33. Joel H. Silbey writes, for example, that "parties and ethnoreligious values melded together in the minds of the electorate, as did parties and distinct economic policies." Silbey, *The American Political Nation, 1838–1893* (Stanford, CA: Stanford University Press, 1991), 162–75 (quote, 175). For a historiographic discussion of the limits these historians placed on ethnic and religious factors in elections, see Ronald P. Formisano, "The Invention of the Ethnocultural Interpretation," *American Historical Review* 99 (April 1994): 453–77.

3. Excellent histories that emphasize gender issues in politics and elections include, but are not limited to, Norma Basch, "Marriage, Morals, and Politics in the Election of 1828," *Journal of American History* 80 (December 1993): 890–918; Kristen Tegtmeier Oertel, *Bleeding Borders: Race, Gender, and Violence in Pre–Civil War Kansas* (Baton Rouge: Louisiana State University Press, 2009), 58–108; Lynn, *Preserving the White Man's Republic,* 119–45; Stephanie McCurry, "The Two Faces of Republicanism: Gender and Pro-Slavery Politics in Antebellum South Carolina," *Journal of American History* 78 (March 1992): 1245–64, and Brie Swenson Arnold, "'To Inflame the Mind of the North': Slavery Politics and the Sexualized Violence of Bleeding Kansas," *Kansas History* 38, no. 1 (Spring 2015): 22–39.

4. Politically independent newspapers that covered the Wild Woman included the *Richmond Daily Dispatch,* July 21, 1856, and the *Nebraska Advertiser* (Brownville), August 9, 1856.

5. Very brief summaries of the story appeared in the *Charleston (SC) Courier,* May 27, 1856, and the *Baltimore Sun,* May 24, 1856. The *Washington (DC) Evening Star* gave it seven paragraphs on May 26, 1856.

6. *Chicago Times,* June 5, 1856; *Dallas Herald,* June 28, 1856; *Nashville Daily Union and American,* May 31, 1856; *Opelousas (LA) Patriot,* June 14, 1856; *Washington (PA) Reporter,* June 11, 1856; *Clearfield (PA) Raftsman's Journal,* June 18, 1856; *Carroll (OH) Free Press,* June 5, 1856.

7. For Republicans, see *Irasburgh (VT) Orleans Independent Standard,* May 30, 1856; *Montpelier (VT) Green Mountain Freeman,* July 17, 1856; *Newark Centinel of Freedom,* May 27, 1856; Know Nothings in *Alexandria (VA) Gazette,* May 26, 1856; *Winchester (TN) Appeal,* June 21, 1856; Democratic papers were *Bedford (PA) Gazette,* June 6, 1856; *Pittsfield (MA) Sun,* July 10, 1856; *New Albany (IN) Daily Ledger,* May 22, 1856.

8. *Cincinnati Daily Enquirer,* July 15, 16, 18, 29, August 8, 15, 23, September 9, 1856. For example, see the August 8 item, included here in full: "One of our reporters is informed by Deputy Sheriff Shattuck, who visited Dayton a few days since, that the physician of the Lunatic Asylum in that city reports the condition of the wild woman as improving; that she is regularly and gradually gaining back physically and mentally; that some statements of an interesting character have been already obtained from her, and that when a more complete history can be obtained the particulars will be then laid before the public—though the Doctor declines to make piecemeal disclosures, which might subject him to the daily importunities of the curious."

9. The lone Democratic newspaper in the databases to run the shorter version of the story was the *Dallas Herald,* August 2, 1856. As discussed later, this contrasts with one Know Nothing, five Republican, and one abolitionist paper.

10. *Weekly Indiana State Sentinel (Indianapolis),* August 7, 1856. The *Sentinel* seems to have copied a *New Orleans Courier* story, which in turn had reprinted it from Shreveport's *Caddo Gazette.*

11. For convergence, see Adam I. P. Smith, *The Stormy Present: Conservatism and the Problem of Slavery in Northern Politics, 1846-1865* (Chapel Hill: University of North Carolina Press, 2017), 100-33; and Michael E. Woods, *Arguing until Doomsday: Stephen Douglas, Jefferson Davis, and the Struggle for American Democracy* (Chapel Hill: University of North Carolina Press, 2020).

12. *Dallas Herald,* August 2, 1856; *Daily Ohio Statesman (Columbus),* August 5, 1856.

13. Democratic editors in New York City profited by reporting on brothel culture as early as the 1830s. They also created a celebrity culture around Mary Rogers, a young woman whose looks were used to attract customers. See Patricia Cline Cohen, *The Murder of Helen Jewett* (New York: Vintage Books, 1998); Srebnick, *Mysterious Death of Mary Rogers;* and Stashower, *Beautiful Cigar Girl.* See also Democratic connections to the "Flash Press," which reported on brothels, prostitution, and sexual misconduct. Patricia Cline Cohen, Timothy J. Gilfoyle, and Helen Lefkowitz Horowitz, *The Flash Press: Sporting Male Weeklies in 1840s New York* (Chicago: University of Chicago Press, 2008); Helen Lefkowitz Horowitz, *Rereading Sex: Battles over Sexual Knowledge and Suppression in Nineteenth-Century America* (New York: Alfred A. Knopf, 2002); Helen Lefkowitz Horowitz, ed., *Attitudes toward Sex in Antebellum America: A Brief History with Documents* (Boston: Bedford / St. Martin's, 2006); and Donna Dennis, *Licentious Gotham: Erotic Publishing and Its Prosecution in Nineteenth-Century New York* (Cambridge, MA: Harvard University Press, 2009).

14. *Cincinnati Daily Enquirer,* July 29, 1856.

15. For Democratic politics and gender roles, see Michael D. Pierson, "'Guard the Foundation Well': Antebellum New York Democrats and the Defense of Patriarchy," *Gender and History* 7 no. 1 (April 1995): 25-40; Joshua A. Lynn, "A Manly Doughface: James Buchanan and the Sectional Politics of Gender," *Journal of the Civil War Era* 8 no. 4 (December 2018): 591-620; Thomas J. Balcerski, "Beards, Bachelors, and Brides: The Surprisingly Spicy Politics of

the Presidential Election of 1856," *Common-Place: The Journal of Early American Life* 16, no. 4 (September 2016), http://commonplace.online/article/beards-bachelors-and-brides/; and Stephanie McCurry, *Masters of Small Worlds: Yeoman Households, Gender Relations, and the Political Culture of the Antebellum South Carolina Low Country* (New York: Oxford University Press, 1995).

16. *Trenton (NJ) State Gazette,* August 7, 1856.

17. Trial report, *Washington (DC) Sentinel,* July 17, 1856; trial report, *Alexandria (VA) Gazette,* July 17, 1856.

18. *Shreveport (LA) Southwestern,* July 30, 1856.

19. *Evansville (IA) Daily Journal,* July 17, 1856.

20. *Athens (TN) Post,* August 8, 1856. It makes no sense for a person to write such a stutter as "I, I afraid." It seems to have been a bastardization of an earlier story from the *Cincinnati Daily Enquirer,* July 16, 1856. That story reported on her trip to Dayton with two deputy sheriffs. On the way, she refused to say her name to the officers. When asked to write her name, she "wrote a very handsomely formed J., but immediately scratched it over, declined to write further, and when the request was renewed by the officers she wrote in a very legible hand, 'I afraid.'" Somehow, the "J" became an "I," and her double refusal to give her name turned into a stutter, all wrapped up in fear. See also *North American and United States Gazette* (Philadelphia), July 18, 1856, which introduced its own variables into the story.

21. John R. Mulkern, *The Know-Nothing Party in Massachusetts: The Rise and Fall of a People's Movement* (Boston: Northeastern University Press, 1990), 111; Jean Gould Hales, "'Co-Laborers in the Cause': Women in the Ante-Bellum Nativist Movement," *Civil War History* 25, no. 2 (June 1979): 124. See also Janet L. Coryell, *Neither Heroine Nor Fool: Anna Ella Carroll of Maryland* (Kent, OH: Kent State University Press, 1990), 1–46.

22. Mark Voss-Hubbard, *Beyond Party: Cultures of Antipartisanship in Northern Politics before the Civil War* (Baltimore: Johns Hopkins University Press, 2002), 115. One element of Know Nothing politics that would have discouraged women's participation was its use of violence on Election Day and throughout the year. See Mark E. Neely Jr., "Apotheosis of a Ruffian: The Murder of Bill Pool and American Political Culture," in *A Political Nation: New Directions in Mid-Nineteenth-Century American Political History,* ed. Gary W. Gallagher and Rachel A. Sheldon (Charlottesville: University of Virginia Press, 2012), 36–63.

23. Jean H. Baker, *Ambivalent Americans: The Know Nothing Party in Maryland* (Baltimore: Johns Hopkins University Press, 1977); Frank Towers, *The Urban South and the Coming of the Civil War* (Baltimore: Johns Hopkins University Press, 2004).

24. Hales, "'Co-Laborers in the Cause,'" 119.

25. *Janesville (WI) Free Press,* September 4, 1856; *Milwaukee Daily Sentinel,* August 19, 1856; *Lowell (MA) Daily Citizen,* August 13, 1856; *Clearfield (PA) Raftsman's Journal,* August 20, 1856; *Newark Centinel of Freedom,* July 22, 1856; *Worcester (MA) National Aegis,* July 23, 1856; *Burlington (IA) Weekly Hawk-Eye and Telegraph,* July 23, August 27, 1856. See also the abolitionist *New-Lisbon (OH) Anti-Slavery Bugle,* August 9, 1856.

26. The "I, I afraid" story appeared in *Washington (PA) Reporter,* July 23, 1856, and the *Wheeling (VA) Daily Intelligencer,* July 19, 1856. The Wheeling paper made no political endorsements in 1856, having been Whig in 1852, but moved to the Republicans by 1860. *New York Herald,* July 20, 1856.

27. *Cincinnati Daily Gazette,* June 24, 1856.

28. Ibid., June 30, 1856. The *Cincinnati Daily Gazette* may have run the notice because it had accepted advertising revenue from Northcott. See first ad for the Wild Woman in *Cincinnati Daily Gazette,* July 8, 1856. It is also possible, however, that its reporter visited because the show had moved to a new location "opposite the Gazette office, on the South East corner of Fourth and Vine." Ibid.

29. The exception, as noted earlier, was the *Cincinnati Daily Enquirer,* the largest paper in the city.

30. The most notable characteristic of the Democratic story was its factual tone, free of editorializing. It stated that she had been cured and discharged from the asylum before adding: "She has recovered her power of language and states that she is a native of Missouri, 23 years of age, and is mother of two children. Her father removed to western Texas while yet young, whither she has been sent to join her children." *Washington (PA) Review and Examiner,* October 11, 1856. The Cincinnati Know Nothing paper lost interest in her after this very short report published two days after her trip to Dayton: "The wild woman came to her senses, while being conducted to the Lunatic Asylum day before yesterday. She refused to talk, but by motions promised to give an expose of the whole affair, in a few days." *Cincinnati Daily Times,* July 16, 1856. With that, the Know Nothings lost sight of her.

31. *Newark Centinel of Freedom,* August 19, 1856.

32. *Terre Haute Wabash Express,* September 10, 1856.

33. *Montpelier (VT) Green-Mountain Freeman,* September 18, 1856; *Honolulu Pacific Commercial Advertiser,* December 11, 1856 (quotes). The Honolulu paper ran a slightly longer version of the story.

34. *Columbus Ohio State Journal,* January 21, 1857.

35. *Newark Centinel of Freedom,* August 19, 1856.

36. *Montpelier (VT) Green-Mountain Freeman,* September 18, 1856; *Honolulu Pacific Commercial Advertiser,* December 11, 1856 (quotes).

37. *Washington (PA) Review and Examiner,* October 11, 1856.

38. *Cincinnati Daily Enquirer,* August 23, 1856. McIlhenny was described in the late 1800s as "formerly a Whig, but upon organization of the Republican party he espoused its principles, and has since been a liberal Republican." *A Biographical Cyclopaedia and Portrait Gallery of Distinguished Men, with an Historical Sketch, of the State of Ohio* (Cincinnati: John C. Yorston, 1879), 222.

39. *Cincinnati Daily Enquirer,* September 9, 1856.

40. Michael D. Pierson, *Free Hearts and Free Homes: Gender and American Antislavery Politics* (Chapel Hill: University of North Carolina Press, 2003), 115–33; Pamela Herr, *Jessie Benton Fremont: A Biography* (Norman: University of Oklahoma Press, 1987), 243–74.

41. For women's roles in the 1856 Republican Party, see Pierson, *Free Hearts and Free Homes,* 139–64; Ronald J. Zboray and Mary Saracino Zboray, *Voices without Votes: Women and Politics in Antebellum New England* (Durham: New Hampshire University Press, 2010), 179–96; Arnold, "'To Inflame the Mind of the North'"; Nicole Etcheson, "'Labouring for the Freedom of This Territory': Free-State Kansas Women in the 1850s," *Kansas History* 21, no. 2 (Summer 1998): 68–87; Oertel, *Bleeding Borders;* Kristen A. Tegtmeier, "The Ladies of Lawrence Are Arming! The Gendered Nature of Sectional Violence in Early Kansas," in *Antislavery Violence:*

Sectional, Racial, and Cultural Conflict in Antebellum America, ed. John R. McKivigan and Stanley Harrold (Knoxville: University of Tennessee Press, 1999), 215–35; and Michael D. Pierson, "'Prairies on Fire': The Organization of the 1856 Mass Republican Rally in Beloit, Wisconsin," *Civil War History* 48, no. 2 (June 2002): 101–22.

42. For abolitionists and their critique of slavery's familial and sexual practices, see Ronald G. Walters, *The Antislavery Appeal: American Abolitionism after 1830* (Baltimore: Johns Hopkins University Press. 1976); Ronald G. Walters, "The Erotic South: Civilization and Sexuality in American Abolitionism," *American Quarterly* 25, no. 2 (May 1973): 177–201; Karen Sanchez-Eppler, *Touching Liberty: Abolitionism, Feminism and the Politics of the Body* (Berkeley: University of California Press, 1993); Marc M. Arkin, "The Federalist Trope: Power and Passion in Abolitionist Rhetoric," *Journal of American History* 88, no. 1 (June 2001): 75–98; and Kristin Hoganson, "Garrisonian Abolitionists and the Rhetoric of Gender, 1850–1860," *American Quarterly* 45, no. 4 (December 1993): 558–95.

43. Holly M. Kent, *Her Voice Will Be on the Side of Right: Gender and Power in Women's Antebellum Antislavery Fiction* (Kent, OH: Kent State University Press, 2017), 137.

44. Steven Weisenburger, *Modern Medea: A Family Story of Slavery and Child-Murder from the Old South* (New York: Hill and Wang, 1998), 3–86.

45. Lucy Stone speech, in Mark Reinhardt, *Who Speaks for Margaret Garner? The True Story That Inspired Toni Morrison's Beloved* (Minneapolis: University of Minnesota Press, 2010), 112. See also Sally G. McMillen, *Lucy Stone: An Unapologetic Life* (New York: Oxford University Press, 2015), 133. For an analysis of the meanings of Stone's reference to skin color, see especially Nikki M. Taylor, *Driven toward Madness: The Fugitive Slave Margaret Garner and Tragedy on the Ohio* (Athens: Ohio University Press, 2016), 92–109.

46. Weisenburger, *Modern Medea;* Taylor, *Driven toward Madness;* Reinhardt, *Who Speaks for Margaret Garner?;* Julius Yanuck, "The Garner Fugitive Slave Case," *Mississippi Valley Historical Review* 40, no. 1 (June 1953): 47–66.

47. James Oliver Horton and Stacy Flaherty, "Black Leadership in Antebellum Cincinnati," in *Race and the City: Work, Community, and Protest in Cincinnati, 1820–1970*, ed. Henry Louis Taylor Jr. (Urbana: University of Illinois Press, 1993), 70–95 (quote, 76).

48. For southern migrations to the Midwest, see Nicole Etcheson, *The Emerging Midwest: Upland Southerners and the Political Culture of the Old Northwest* (Bloomington: Indiana University Press, 1996).

49. Bridget Ford, *Bonds of Union: Religion, Race, and Politics in a Civil War Borderland* (Chapel Hill: University of North Carolina Press, 2016), 85.

50. Anne E. Marshall, *Creating a Confederate Kentucky: The Lost Cause and Civil War Memory in a Border State* (Chapel Hill: University of North Carolina Press, 2010); Christopher Phillips, *The Rivers Ran Backward: The Civil War and the Remaking of the American Middle Border* (New York: Oxford University Press, 2016). For Indiana and Kentucky communities as being similar until the Civil War drove them apart, see Stephen I. Rockenbach, *War upon Our Border: Two Ohio Valley Communities Navigate the Civil War* (Charlottesville: University of Virginia Press, 2016).

51. Edward L. Ayers and Sarah S. Rubin, *Valley of the Shadow: Two Communities in the American Civil War; the Eve of War* (New York: W. W. Norton, 2000); L. Diane Barnes, *Artisan Workers in the Upper South: Petersburg, Virginia, 1820–1865* (Baton Rouge: Louisiana State Uni-

versity Press, 2008), 24. For how slavery limited Virginia's urban capitalist development, see John Majewski, "Freeing the Lavish Hand of Nature: Environment and Economy in Nineteenth-Century Hampton Roads," in *Confederate Cities: The Urban South During the Civil War Era*, ed. Andrew L. Slap and Frank Towers (Chicago: University of Chicago Press, 2015), 261–85.

52. For slavery and the founding of New England, see Wendy Warren, *New England Bound: Slavery and Colonization in Early New England* (New York: Liveright, 2016); Catherine Adams and Elizabeth H. Pleck, *Black Women in Colonial and Revolutionary New England* (New York: Oxford University Press, 2010); Christy Clark-Pujara, *Dark Work: The Business of Slavery in Rhode Island* (New York: New York University Press, 2016); and Jared Ross Hardesty, *Unfreedom: Slavery and Dependence in Eighteenth-Century Boston* (New York: New York University Press, 2016). For northern involvement in the international slave trade in the 1850s, see Anthony J. Connors, *Went to the Devil: A Yankee Whaler in the Slave Trade* (Amherst, MA: Bright Leaf, 2019). For the Old Northwest, including the enslavement of Native Americans, see Tiya Miles, *The Dawn of Detroit: A Chronicle of Slavery and Freedom in the City on the Straits* (New York: New Press, 2017); M. Scott Heerman, *The Alchemy of Slavery: Human Bondage and Emancipation in the Illinois Country, 1730–1865* (Philadelphia: University of Pennsylvania Press, 2018); James Simeone, *Democracy and Slavery in Frontier Illinois: The Bottomland Republic* (DeKalb: Northern Illinois University Press, 2000); Stephen Middleton, *The Black Laws: Race and the Legal Process in Early Ohio* (Athens: Ohio University Press, 2005); and Christopher P. Lehman, *Slavery in the Upper Mississippi Valley, 1787–1865: A History of Human Bondage in Illinois, Iowa, Minnesota, and Wisconsin* (Jefferson, NC: McFarland, 2011). The most recent treatment of Civil War–era northern racism is Paul D. Escott, *The Worst Passions of Human Nature: White Supremacy in the Civil War North* (Charlottesville: University of Virginia Press, 2020). For kidnapping, see Jonathan Daniel Wells, *The Kidnapping Club: Wall Street, Slavery, and Resistance on the Eve of the Civil War* (New York: Bold Type Books, 2020); Jonathan Daniel Wells, *Blind No More: African American Resistance, Free Soil Politics, and the Coming of the Civil War* (Athens: University of Georgia Press, 2021), 14–42, 83–88; and Lucy Maddox, *The Parker Sisters: A Border Kidnapping* (Philadelphia: Temple University Press, 2016). For a persuasive argument that northern resistance rendered the Fugitive Slave Law unenforceable throughout most of the North in the late 1850s, see Robert H. Churchill, "When the Slave Catchers Came to Town: Cultures of Violence along the Underground Railroad," *Journal of American History* 105, no. 3 (December 2018): 514–37.

53. Matthew Salafia, *Slavery's Borderland: Freedom and Bondage along the Ohio River* (Philadelphia: University of Pennsylvania Press, 2013), 6.

54. Edward L. Ayers, *In the Presence of Mine Enemies: War in the Heart of America, 1859–1863* (New York: W. W. Norton, 2003), xx. The literature on the relationship between capitalism and slavery is vast. Recent works that serve as a starting point for further reading include those that find a strong correlation between the two, including Edward E. Baptist, *The Half Has Never Been Told: Slavery and the Making of American Capitalism* (New York: Basic Books, 2014); and Sven Becket and Seth Rockman, eds., *Slavery's Capitalism: A New History of American Economic Development* (Philadelphia: University of Pennsylvania Press, 2016). Their approaches have recently been criticized in works that include James L. Huston, "Slavery, Capitalism, and the Interpretations of the Antebellum United States: The Problem of Definition," *Civil War History* 65, no. 2 (June 2019): 119–56; and Erik Mathisen, "The Second Slavery, Capitalism, and

Emancipation in Civil War America," *Journal of the Civil War Era* 8 no. 4 (December 2018): 677–99. See also Thomas Bender, ed., *The Antislavery Debate: Capitalism and Abolitionism as a Problem in Historical Interpretation* (Berkeley: University of California Press, 1992); H. Reuben Neptune, "Throwin' Scholarly Shade: Eric Williams in the New Histories of Capitalism and Slavery," *Journal of the Early Republic* 39 no. 2 (Summer 2019): 299–326; and Christopher Morris, "With 'the Economics-of-Slavery Culture Wars,' It's Déjà vu All Over Again," *Journal of the Civil War Era* 10, no. 4 (December 2020): 524–57. For a nicely balanced interpretation, see William Dusinberre, *Slavemaster President: The Double Career of James Polk* (New York: Oxford University Press, 2003), 55–70.

55. For armed conflict between abolitionists and proslavery forces, see Stanley Harrold, *Border War: Fighting over Slavery before the Civil War* (Chapel Hill: University of North Carolina Press, 2010); and Stanley Harrold, *Subversives: Antislavery Community in Washington, D.C., 1828–1865* (Baton Rouge: Louisiana State University Press, 2003); as well as numerous studies of the Underground Railroad. For cultural differences, see James M. McPherson, *Battle Cry of Freedom: The Civil War Era* (New York: Oxford University Press, 1988), 6–46.

56. On education, see Mary Kelley, *Learning to Stand and Speak: Women, Education, and Public Life in America's Republic* (Chapel Hill: University of North Carolina Press, 2006); and Jonathan Daniel Wells, *Women Writers and Journalists in the Nineteenth-Century South* (New York: Cambridge University Press, 2011). For politics, see Elizabeth R. Varon, *We Mean to Be Counted: White Women and Politics in Antebellum Virginia* (Chapel Hill: University of North Carolina Press, 1998); Zboray and Zboray, *Voices without Votes;* Elizabeth J. Clapp, *A Notorious Woman: Anne Royall in Jacksonian America* (Charlottesville: University of Virginia Press, 2016); and Susan Graham, "'A Warm Politition and Devotedly Attached to the Democratic Party': Catharine Read Williams, Politics, and Literature in Antebellum America," *Journal of the Early Republic* 30, no. 2 (Summer 2010): 253–78. For evangelical and benevolent women, see John W. Quist, *Restless Visionaries: The Social Roots of Antebellum Reform in Alabama and Michigan* (Baton Rouge: Louisiana State University Press, 1998), 81–89, 142–45, 195–99; Anne M. Boylan, *The Origins of Women's Activism: New York and Boston, 1797–1840* (Chapel Hill: University of North Carolina Press, 2002); and Christine Leigh Heyrman, *Doomed Romance: Broken Hearts, Lost Souls, and Sexual Tumult in Nineteenth-Century America* (New York: Alfred A. Knopf, 2021).

57. Bocock, *Congressional Globe*, 34th Cong., 1st Sess., 820; Jayne Crumpler DeFiore, "'COME and Bring the Ladies': Tennessee Women and the Politics of Opportunity during the Presidential Campaigns of 1840 and 1844," *Tennessee Historical Quarterly* 51 (Winter 1992): 209. For 1844, see Varon, *We Mean to Be Counted*, 88–93. See also Harriet Prewett's reliance on a man to edit the political section of her newspaper in Christopher J. Olsen, "'Molly Pitcher' of the Mississippi Whigs: The Editorial Career of Mrs. Harriet N. Prewett," *Journal of Mississippi History* 58 (Fall 1996): 237–54. Varon, *We Mean to be Counted*, 119, 119–23. For Hicks as symbol of southern women's outspokenness, see Wells, *Women Writers and Journalists*, 19–21, 114–16.

58. Wells, *Women Writers and Journalists*, 112.

59. Anne M. Boylan, "Women and Politics in the Era before Seneca Falls," *Journal of the Early Republic* 10 (Fall 1990), 377, 378.

60. Richard S. Newman, *The Transformation of American Abolitionism: Fighting Slavery in the Early Republic* (Chapel Hill: University of North Carolina Press, 2002), 131–75.

61. *National Anti-Slavery Standard* (New York City), October 13, 1860. For women on floats and female antislavery novelists, see Pierson, *Free Hearts and Free Homes,* 115–90; and Michael J. McManus, *Political Abolitionism in Wisconsin, 1840–1861* (Kent, OH: Kent State University Press, 1998), 150–51.

62. Cook, *Arts of Deception,* 110–17.

63. There was also an earlier report that played out in 1845. That story seems to have started in the *Caddo Gazette,* which curiously may also, eleven years later, have been the source for the story that three Shreveport residents—Williams, Paul, and Bond—had staged the Cincinnati show. In 1845, its story was reprinted in the *New York Commercial Advertiser* and then widely reprinted across the country. The New York journalists wrote:

> The Caddo Gazette gives an account of a woman who has lived in the woods near there for the last three months. Her husband died in Mississippi, and she came to her present whereabout on foot. She sleeps in the woods, yet no one knows where, as she never makes her appearance during the day. The Gazette says she frequently comes to the house of Mr. Polk, at a late hour of the night, when they give her what she desires to eat, and after she has satisfied her appetite she retires again to the woods. She manifests, we are told, much fear of being taken, particularly by the sheriff. She came on one occasion to the house of Mr. Polk, and carded and spun a portion of cotton thread to mend her clothes. She is the mother of several children, and has a brother in North Carolina who is wealthy, and who, it is believed, would gladly rescue her from her wretched condition.

New York Commercial Advertiser, July 9, 1845. See also *New York Spectator,* July 12, 1845; *Boston Courier,* July 14, 1845; *Middletown (CT) Constitution,* July 16, 1845; *Barre (MA) Patriot,* July 18, 1845; *Brattleboro Vermont Phoenix,* July 18, 1845; *Richmond Enquirer,* July 19, 1845; *St. Albans (VT) Messenger,* July 23, 1845; *Hartford (CT) Times,* July 26, 1845; and *Milwaukee Daily Sentinel,* August 20, 1845.

64. *Texian Advocate* (Victoria, TX), November 9, 1848. The story was reprinted in at least fifteen American newspapers: *Alexandria (LA) Gazette,* March 20, 1849; *Trenton (NJ) State Gazette,* March 20, 1849; *Albany Evening Journal,* March 21, 1849; *Worcester (MA) National Aegis,* March 21, 1849; *Baltimore Sun,* March 21, 1849; *Richmond Whig,* March 23, 1849; *Boston Saturday Rambler,* March 24, 1849; *New York Organ and Temperance Safeguard,* March 24, 1849; *St. Louis Daily Missouri Republican,* March 30, 1849; *Brattleboro (VT) Semi-Weekly Eagle,* April 2, 1849; *New Hampshire Patriot and State Gazette* (Concord), April 12, 1849; *Wabash Courier* (Terre Haute, IN), April 14, 1849; *Mississippi Free Trader* (Natchez), April 18, 1849; *Vermont Journal* (Windsor), April 20, 1849; and *St. Albans (VT) Messenger,* April 26, 1849. For the fullest treatment of the wild people of the Navidad, see Anderson, "Feral Bodies, Feral Nature," 16–91.

65. *Texian Advocate* (Victoria, TX), November 9, 1848.

66. *Houston Democratic Telegraph and Texas Register,* January 17, 1850.

67. *Houston Democratic Telegraph and Texas Register,* January 17, 1850, alluding to the *Texian Advocate (Victoria, TX),* n.d., (referred to as the *Victoria Advocate); Mississippi Free Trader* (Natchez), January 30, 1850; *Alexandria (VA) Gazette,* February 8, 1850.

68. *New London (CT) Daily Chronicle,* February 7, 1850; *Philadelphia Public Ledger,* Febru-

ary 7, 1850; *New Hampshire Gazette* (Portsmouth), February 12, 1850; *Daily Sanduskian* (Sandusky, OH), February 12, 1850; New York, *Spirit of the Times* (New York City), February 16, 1850, referring to *Philadelphia Presbyterian,* n.d.; *New-York Organ: A Family Companion,* February 16, 1850; *Daily Ohio Statesman (Columbus),* February 16, 1850 and again on March 1, 1850; *Salem (MA) Observer,* February 16, 1850; *Middletown (CT) Constitution,* February 20, 1850; *Hudson River Chronicle* (Ossining, NY), February 26, 1850; *Brattleboro (VT) Semi-Weekly Eagle,* February 28, 1850; *Bellows Falls (VT) Gazette,* March 7, 1850; and *Brattleboro Vermont Phoenix,* March 29, 1850.

69. Longer versions appeared in these southern newspapers: *New Orleans Daily Crescent,* February 27, 1851; *Savannah (GA) Daily Republican,* March 7, 1851; *Washington (DC) Daily National Intelligencer,* March 10, 1851; *Washington (DC) Southern Press,* March 10, 1851; *Edgefield (SC) Advertiser,* March 13, 1851; *Alexandria Gazette and Virginia Advertiser,* March 14, 1851; *Athens (TN) Post,* March 14, 1851; *Semi-Weekly Camden (SC) Journal,* March 14, 1851; *Fayetteville North-Carolinian,* March 15, 1851; *Bowling Green (MO) Democratic Banner,* March 17, 1851; *Staunton (VA) Spectator,* March 19, 1851; *Spirit of Jefferson* (Charles Town, VA), March 25, 1851; *Glasgow (MO) Weekly Times,* March 27, 1851. Northern presses that published the longer version included *New York Spectator,* March 7, 1851; *New York Evening Post,* March 10, 1851; *New York Daily Tribune,* March 10, 1851; *Albany Journal,* March 11, 1851; *American Union* (Boston), March 15, 1851; *Portsmouth (OH) Inquirer,* March 17, 1851; *Montpelier (VT) Green-Mountain Freeman,* March 27, 1851; and *Plymouth (IN) Pilot,* April 16, 1851. One-sentence notices appeared in *Boston Daily Atlas,* March 7, 1851; *New York Evening Post,* March 7, 1851; *Baltimore Sun,* March 7, 1851; *New York Daily Tribune,* March 7, 1851; *Salem (MA) Observer,* March 8, 1851; *Boston Courier,* March 10, 1851; *Spirit of Democracy* (Woodsfield, OH), March 12, 1851; and *North Carolina Standard* (Raleigh), March 15, 1851.

70. *Texas State Gazette* (Austin), June 24, August 5, 1854.

71. Newton, *Savage Girls and Wild Boys,* 16.

72. Quotations from a two-paragraph version in *Charleston (SC) Mercury,* March 10, 1857. A three-paragraph version that inserts details from the *Linden (AL) Jeffersonian* about the hunting party's brush with the wild woman appears in *North American and United States Gazette* (Philadelphia), March 12, 1857.

73. *Charleston (SC) Mercury,* March 10, 1857.

74. Ibid., March 11, 1857.

75. In addition to the *Charleston Mercury,* the story appeared in *Charlotte (NC) Western Democrat,* March 21, 1857; *Houma (LA) Ceres,* March 21, 1857; *Shepherdstown (VA) Register,* March 21, 1857; *Greenville (SC) Southern Enterprise,* March 19, 1857; *Delaware Weekly Republican* (Wilmington), March 26, 1857; *Abbeville (SC) Banner,* March 19, 1857; *Harrisonburg (LA) Independent,* September 23, 1857; *Daily Nashville (TN) Patriot,* February 26, 1857; *Athens (TN) Post,* February 27, 1857; and *Carolina Spartan* (Spartanburg, SC), March 19, 1857.

76. *North American and United States Gazette* (Philadelphia), March 12, 1857; *Connecticut Courant* (Hartford), March 21, 1857; *Lowell (MA) Daily Citizen and News,* March 16, 1857; *Columbia Democrat and Bloomsburg General Advertiser* (Bloomsburg, PA), April 18, 1857; *Preble County Democrat* (Eaton, OH), April 16, 1857; and *Biddeford (ME) Union and Eastern Journal,* April 3, 1857.

77. See *Albany Evening Journal,* July 27, 1859; *New York Daily Tribune,* July 27, 1859; *North*

American and United States Gazette (Philadelphia), July 28, 1859; *Daily Ohio Statesman (Columbus)*, July 30, 1859; *Freedom's Champion* (Atchison City, KS), August 6, 1859; *Connecticut Courant* (Hartford), August 6, 1859; *New York Ledger*, August 20, 1859; and *Porter's Spirit of the Times* (New York City), August 20, 1859. The lone southern newspaper was the *Easton (MD) Gazette*, August 6, 1859.

78. *Lowell (MA) Daily Citizen and News,* March 16, 1857; *Biddeford (ME) Union and Eastern Journal,* April 3, 1857.

79. Michael D. Pierson, "'Slavery Cannot Be Covered Up with Broadcloth or a Bandanna': The Evolution of White Abolitionist Attacks on the 'Patriarchal Institution,'" *Journal of the Early Republic* 25, no. 3 (Fall 2005): 383–416.

80. *American Union* (Boston), June 7, 1856.

81. *Brother Jonathan* (New York City), May 31, 1856.

82. Ibid., August 9, 1856.

83. *Saturday Evening Post,* June 28, 1856, copied from *New York Picayune*, n.d.

4. Women and Power in Antebellum America

1. Susan Juster, *Disorderly Women: Sexual Politics and Evangelicalism in Revolutionary New England* (Ithaca, NY: Cornell University Press, 1994).

2. Cynthia Lynn Lyerly, "Religion, Gender, and Identity: Black Methodist Women in a Slave Society, 1770–1810," in *Discovering the Women in Slavery: Emancipating Perspectives on the American Past,* ed. Patricia Morton (Athens: University of Georgia Press, 1996), 202–26.

3. Scholarly work on women's engagement with American churches is vast. It includes Jon F. Sensbach, *Rebecca's Revival: Creating Black Christianity in the Atlantic World* (Cambridge, MA: Harvard University Press, 2005); Ann Braude, *Radical Spirits: Spiritualism and Women's Rights in Nineteenth-Century America* (Boston: Beacon, 1989); Heyrman, *Doomed Romance;* Ashley E. Moreshead, "'Beyond All Ambitious Motives': Missionary Memoirs and the Cultivation of Early American Evangelical Heroines," *Journal of the Early Republic* 38, no. 1 (Spring 2018): 37–60; Richard Francis, *Ann the Word: The Story of Ann Lee, Female Messiah, Mother of the Shakers, the Woman Clothed with the Sun* (New York: Penguin, 2000); Nancy F. Cott, *The Bonds of Womanhood: "Woman's Sphere" in New England, 1780–1835* (New Haven, CT: Yale University Press, 1977), 126–59; and Nancy A. Hewitt, *Woman's Activism and Social Change: Rochester, New York, 1822–1872* (Ithaca, NY: Cornell University Press, 1984).

4. *Christian Ambassador* (New York City), June 28, 1856.

5. Kelley, *Learning to Stand and Speak.*

6. *Cincinnati Daily Times,* June 18, 1856.

7. Ibid.

8. For graduation exercises and women's academies, see Kelley, *Learning to Stand and Speak,* 92–99 (quote, 94).

9. *Cincinnati Daily Times,* June 20, 1856.

10. Ibid.

11. Ibid.

12. Kelley, *Learning to Stand and Speak,* 112–53. This was true even before the antebellum period. Mary Beth Norton finds a sharp uptick in the percentage of women born in the years

1780–1809 who received an "advanced education" and then earned inclusion in the multivolume reference work *Notable American Women*. Mary Beth Norton, *Liberty's Daughters: The Revolutionary Experience of American Women, 1750–1800* (Boston: Little, Brown, 1980), 272–93, esp. 287–89.

13. Boston, *Flag of Our Union*, June 14, 1856.

14. For charters, see Lori D. Ginzberg, *Women and the Work of Benevolence: Morality, Politics, and Class in the Nineteenth-Century United States* (New Haven, CT: Yale University Press, 1990), 48–53. For government aid, see ibid., 73–74, 78–79, 123–24.

15. Boylan, *Origins of Women's Activism*.

16. There is a large literature on women and the antislavery movement, including Julie Roy Jeffrey, *The Great Silent Army of Abolitionism: Ordinary Women in the Antislavery Movement* (Chapel Hill: University of North Carolina Press, 1998); Shirley J. Yee, *Black Women Abolitionists: A Study in Activism, 1828–1860* (Knoxville: University of Tennessee Press, 1992); Stacey M. Robertson, *Hearts Beating for Liberty: Women Abolitionists in the Old Northwest* (Chapel Hill: University of North Carolina Press, 2010); Beth A. Salerno, *Sister Societies: Women's Antislavery Organizations in Antebellum America* (DeKalb: Northern Illinois University Press, 2005); Yellin and Van Horne, *Abolitionist Sisterhood;* Debra Gold Hansen, *Strained Sisterhood: Gender and Class in the Boston Female Anti-Slavery Society* (Amherst: University of Massachusetts Press, 1993); Deborah Bingham Van Broekhoven, *The Devotion of These Women: Rhode Island in the Antislavery Network* (Amherst: University of Massachusetts Press, 2002); and Zaeske, *Signatures of Citizenship*. For anti-prostitution campaigns, see Carroll Smith-Rosenberg, "Beauty, the Beast, and the Militant Woman: A Case Study in Sex Roles and Social Stress in Jacksonian America," *American Quarterly* 23, no. 4 (October 1971): 562–84; and Daniel S. Wright, *The First of Causes to Our Sex: The Female Moral Reform Movement in the Antebellum Northeast, 1834–1848* (New York: Routledge, 2006).

17. For antebellum woman's rights movement, see Sylvia D. Hoffert, *When Hens Crow: The Woman's Rights Movement in Antebellum America* (Bloomington: Indiana University Press, 1995); Judith Wellman, *The Road to Seneca Falls: Elizabeth Cady Stanton and the First Woman's Rights Convention* (Urbana: University of Illinois Press, 2004); Sally G. McMillen, *Seneca Falls and the Origins of the Women's Rights Movement* (New York: Oxford University Press, 2008); Lori D. Ginzberg, *Untidy Origins: A Story of Woman's Rights in Antebellum New York* (Chapel Hill: University of North Carolina Press, 2005); Sherry H. Penney and James D. Livingston, *A Very Dangerous Woman: Martha Wright and Women's Rights* (Amherst: University of Massachusetts Press, 2004); and Lisa Tetrault, *The Myth of Seneca Falls: Memory and the Women's Suffrage Movement* (Chapel Hill: University of North Carolina Press, 2014).

18. *New York Herald*, July 14, 1856, copied from *Cincinnati Columbian*, July 11, 1856.

19. Richard Swainson Fisher, *The Progress of the Republic* (Washington, DC: W. M. Morrison, 1856), 275. The school also had a branch in Madison, Wisconsin. Aside from a central location, its students themselves were also a potential market for Northcott. For the exhibition at Bacon's, see *New York Daily Tribune*, July 16, 1856.

20. *Cincinnati Daily Enquirer*, July 10, 1856.

21. For reform women's engagement with government, see Alison M. Parker, *Articulating Rights: Nineteenth-Century American Women on Race, Reform and the State* (DeKalb: Northern Illinois University Press, 2010); and Alison M. Parker and Stephanie Cole, eds., *Women and the*

Unstable State in Nineteenth-Century America (College Station: Texas A&M University Press, 2000). For women and the Republican Party, see Zboray and Zboray, *Voices without Votes,* 179–217; and Pierson, *Free Hearts and Free Homes,* 115–90.

22. The Know Nothings have been increasingly seen as reformist in local politics and even woman's rights, despite their xenophobic and anti-Catholic rhetoric and legislation. See Tyler Anbinder, *Nativism and Slavery: The Northern Know Nothings and the Politics of the 1850s* (New York: Oxford University Press, 1992); Voss-Hubbard, *Beyond Party;* Mulkern, *Know-Nothing Party in Massachusetts;* and Hales, "'Co-Laborers in the Cause.'"

23. Marilyn S. Blackwell and Kristen T. Oertel, *Frontier Feminist: Clarina Howard Nichols and the Politics of Motherhood* (Lawrence: University Press of Kansas, 2010); McManus, *Political Abolitionism in Wisconsin,* 150–51.

24. Marcus, *Plague of Strangers,* 91.

25. Ibid., xxi.

26. Jed Dannenbaum, *Drink and Disorder: Temperance Reform in Cincinnati from the Washingtonian Revival to the WCTU* (Urbana: University of Illinois Press, 1984), 181.

27. Ibid., 182.

28. Ibid.

29. *Williams' Cincinnati Directory, City Guide, and Business Mirror for 1857* (Cincinnati: C. S. Williams, 1857), 51.

30. Hedrick, *Harriet Beecher Stowe,* 172; *New York Daily Tribune,* July 24, 1843; *Richmond Daily Whig,* July 28, 1843; *Salem (OH) Anti-Slavery Bugle,* December 11, 1852.

31. *Burlington (IA) Weekly Hawk-Eye and Telegraph,* October 15, 1856, copied from *Cincinnati Daily Gazette,* October 8, 1856.

32. Ibid.

33. Jean H. Baker, "Public Women and Partisan Politics, 1840–1860," in *A Political Nation: New Directions in Mid-Nineteenth-Century American Political History,* ed., Gary W. Gallagher and Rachel Sheldon (Charlottesville: University of Virginia Press, 2012), 64–81; Zboray and Zboray, *Voices without Votes,* 179–96. We might flip Baker's diminishing term "partisan enabler" to an empowering meaning; the women's partisanship bought them a voice in local governments.

34. Hedrick, *Harriet Beecher Stowe,* 172. There was also probably a class-based attack implied in the *Cincinnati Daily Enquirer* report that the women were from Walnut Hills. One newspaperman reported that Cincinnati "has climbed the beautiful hill-sides toward Walnut Hill, Mount Auburn and Brighton," rural places that offered pleasant views and space. Another report identified a man who was spending the amazing sum of $75,000 to build a "family mansion on Walnut Hills, near Cincinnati, in the vicinity of Lane Seminary." For urban Cincinnatians, Walnut Hills was a leafy suburb of large houses, long vistas, and freedom from noise and nasty smells. *New York Daily Tribune,* June 18, 1855; *Gallipolis (OH) Journal,* February 26, 1852.

35. This argument is made most persuasively by historians of female textile-mill workers in the earlier decades of the Industrial Revolution in New England. See Paul E. Johnson, "The Modernization of Mayo Greenleaf Patch: Land, Family, and Marginality in New England, 1766–1818," *New England Quarterly* 55, no. 4 (December 1982): 488–516; and Thomas Dublin, *Women at Work: The Transformation of Work and Community in Lowell, Massachusetts, 1826–1860* (New York: Columbia University Press, 1979).

36. Blackman, "Reviews and Notices," 225.

37. Anderson, "Feral Bodies, Feral Nature," 117.

38. 1850 US Manuscript Census, Shreveport, Caddo Parish, Louisiana, M432, National Archives and Records Administration, Washington, DC, microfilm, frame 230, p. 341B.

39. Marriage in Caddo, November 19, 1859, "Louisiana, U.S., Compiled Marriage Index, 1718–1925," Ancestry.com, 2004, https://www.ancestry.com/search/collections/7837/ (subscription required).

40. Lampert, *Starring Women*, 4, 66.

41. Jean H. Baker, *Mary Todd Lincoln: A Biography* (New York: W. W. Norton, 1987), 315–50.

42. *Chicago Times*, June 5, 1856, copied from *Cincinnati Commercial*, n.d.

43. Newton, *Savage Girls and Wild Boys*, 235.

44. *Cincinnati Daily Gazette*, July 8, 1856.

45. *Cincinnati Daily Times*, July 14, 1856.

46. *Charleston (SC) Mercury*, March 11, 1857.

47. *Cincinnati Daily Times*, June 12, 1856, copied from *Dayton (OH) Gazette*, n.d.

48. *Cincinnati Daily Times*, July 14, 1856.

49. Taylor, *Frontiers of Freedom*, 117, 128.

BIBLIOGRAPHY

PRIMARY SOURCES

Newspapers: Microfilm

Arkansas State Gazette and Democrat (Little Rock), 1856
Cincinnati Daily Enquirer, 1856
Cincinnati Daily Gazette, 1856
Cincinnati Daily Times, 1856
Covington (KY) Journal, 1856
Little Rock (AR) True Democrat, 1856

Newspapers: Digital Collections

Chronicling America. Library of Congress (1840–60). https://chroniclingamerica.loc.gov/.
Early American Newspapers. Readex Corporation (1840–60). https://www.readex.com/products/early-american-newspapers-series (subscription required).
Historical Periodicals Collection, Series 4. American Antiquarian Society (1840–60). https://www.americanantiquarian.org/newspapers-periodicals (subscription required).

Articles, Books, and Other Primary Sources

1850 US Manuscript Census. Shreveport, Caddo Parish, Louisiana. M432. National Archives and Records Administration, Washington, DC. Microfilm.
Barnum, P. T. *The Humbugs of the World*. London: John Camden Hotten, 1866.
Bird, Isabella. *The Englishwoman in America*. London: John Murray, 1856.
Blackman, George. "Reviews and Notices: Medico-Legal Examination of the Case of Charles B. Huntington." *Western Lancet* 3 (March 1857): 218–25.

Deese, Helen R., ed. *Daughter of Boston: The Extraordinary Diary of a Nineteenth-Century Woman.* Boston: Beacon, 2005.

Fisher, Richard Swainson. *The Progress of the Republic.* Washington, DC: W. M. Morrison, 1856.

Galon, Alice. *The Wild Woman; or, The Wrecked Heart, Being the True Autobiography of the "Wild Woman," Who Was Recently Exhibited at Cincinnati, and Was Rescued from Her Persecutors by the Citizens of that City, and Sent to the Insane Asylum at Dayton, Ohio.* Cincinnati: Barclay, 1857.

"Louisiana, U.S., Compiled Marriage Index, 1718–1925." Ancestry.com, 2004. https://www.ancestry.com/search/collections/7837/ (subscription required).

Mihm, Stephen, ed. *The Life of P. T. Barnum, Written by Himself, with Related Documents.* Boston: Bedford / St. Martin's, 2018.

Mills, Bruce, ed. *Letters from New-York: A Portrait of New York on the Cusp of Its Transformation into a Modern City.* Athens: University of Georgia Press, 1998.

Ohio General Assembly. "AN ACT to Provide for the Uniform Government and the Better Regulation of the Lunatic Asylums of the State and the Care of Idiots and the Insane. Legislative Acts Passed and Joint Resolutions Adopted by the General Assembly Ohio." Secretary of State, April 1856, 81–96.

Sedgwick, Catharine Maria. *A New-England Tale; or, Sketches of New-England Character and Manners.* 1822. Reprint, New York: Oxford University Press, 1995.

Stowe, Harriet Beecher. *Uncle Tom's Cabin; or, Life among the Lowly.* 1852. Reprint, New York: Penguin, 1981.

Sutherland, Daniel E., ed. *A Very Violent Rebel: The Civil War Diary of Ellen Renshaw House.* Knoxville: University of Tennessee Press, 1996.

Taylor, Susie King. *Reminiscences of My Life in Camp: An African American Woman's Civil War Memoir.* Athens: University of Georgia Press, 2006.

Twain, Mark. "The Private History of a Campaign That Failed." In *Mark Twain's Civil War,* edited by David Rachels, 47–78. Lexington: University Press of Kentucky, 2007.

Williams' Cincinnati Directory, City Guide and Business Mirror; for Cincinnati in 1856. Cincinnati: C. S. Williams, 1856.

SECONDARY SOURCES

Articles, Books, Dissertations, and Websites

Adams, Catherine, and Elizabeth H. Pleck. *Black Women in Colonial and Revolutionary New England.* New York: Oxford University Press, 2010.

Anbinder, Tyler. *Nativism and Slavery: The Northern Know Nothings and the Politics of the 1850s.* New York: Oxford University Press, 1992.

Anderson, Erik D. "Feral Bodies, Feral Nature: Wild Men in America." PhD dissertation, Brown University, 2010.

Arkin, Marc M. "The Federalist Trope: Power and Passion in Abolitionist Rhetoric." *Journal of American History* 88, no. 1 (June 2001): 75–98.

Arnold, Brie Swenson. "'To Inflame the Mind of the North': Slavery Politics and the Sexualized Violence of Bleeding Kansas." *Kansas History* 38, no. 1 (Spring 2015): 22–39.

Ayers, Edward L. *In the Presence of Mine Enemies: War in the Heart of America, 1859–1863*. New York: W. W. Norton, 2003.

Ayers, Edward L., and Sarah S. Rubin. *Valley of the Shadow: Two Communities in the American Civil War; the Eve of War*. New York: W. W. Norton, 2000.

Baker, Jean H. *Affairs of Party: The Political Culture of Northern Democrats in the Mid-Nineteenth Century*. Ithaca, NY: Cornell University Press, 1983.

———. *Ambivalent Americans: The Know Nothing Party in Maryland*. Baltimore: Johns Hopkins University Press, 1977.

———. *Mary Todd Lincoln: A Biography*. New York: W. W. Norton, 1987.

———. "Public Women and Partisan Politics, 1840–1860." In *A Political Nation: New Directions in Mid-Nineteenth-Century American Political History*, edited by Gary W. Gallagher and Rachel A. Sheldon, 64–81. Charlottesville: University of Virginia Press, 2012.

Balcerski, Thomas J. "Beards, Bachelors, and Brides: The Surprisingly Spicy Politics of the Presidential Election of 1856." *Common-Place: The Journal of Early American Life* 16, no. 4 (September 2016). http://commonplace.online/article/beards-bachelors-and-brides/.

Baptist, Edward E. *The Half Has Never Been Told: Slavery and the Making of American Capitalism*. New York: Basic Books, 2014.

Barnes, L. Diane. *Artisan Workers in the Upper South: Petersburg, Virginia, 1820–1865*. Baton Rouge: Louisiana State University Press, 2008.

Basch, Norma. "Marriage, Morals, and Politics in the Election of 1828." *Journal of American History* 80 (December 1993): 890–918.

Becket, Sven, and Seth Rockman, eds., *Slavery's Capitalism: A New History of American Economic Development*. Philadelphia: University of Pennsylvania Press, 2016.

Bender, Thomas, ed. *The Antislavery Debate: Capitalism and Abolitionism as a Problem in Historical Interpretation*. Berkeley: University of California Press, 1992.

Benson, Lee. *The Concept of Jacksonian Democracy: New York as a Test Case*. Princeton, NJ: Princeton University Press, 1961.

A Biographical Cyclopaedia and Portrait Gallery of Distinguished Men, with an Historical Sketch, of the State of Ohio. Cincinnati: John C. Yorston, 1879.

Blackwell, Marilyn S., and Kristen T. Oertel. *Frontier Feminist: Clarina Howard Nichols and the Politics of Motherhood*. Lawrence: University Press of Kansas, 2010.

Boylan, Anne M. *The Origins of Women's Activism: New York and Boston, 1797–1840.* Chapel Hill: University of North Carolina Press, 2002.

———. "Women and Politics in the Era before Seneca Falls." *Journal of the Early Republic* 10, no. 3 (Fall 1990): 363–82.

Braude, Ann. *Radical Spirits: Spiritualism and Women's Rights in Nineteenth-Century America.* Boston: Beacon, 1989.

Brodie, Janet Farrell. *Contraception and Abortion in Nineteenth-Century America.* Ithaca, NY: Cornell University Press, 1994.

Brooke, John L. *"There Is a North": Fugitive Slaves, Political Crisis, and Cultural Transformation in the Coming of the Civil War.* Amherst: University of Massachusetts Press, 2019.

Brown, Thomas J. *Dorothea Dix: New England Reformer.* Cambridge, MA: Harvard University Press, 1998.

Churchill, Robert H. "When the Slave Catchers Came to Town: Cultures of Violence Along the Underground Railroad," *Journal of American History* 105, no. 3 (December 2018): 514–37.

Clapp, Elizabeth J. *A Notorious Woman: Anne Royall in Jacksonian America.* Charlottesville: University of Virginia Press, 2016.

Clark-Pujara, Christy. *Dark Work: The Business of Slavery in Rhode Island.* New York: New York University Press, 2016.

Cohen, Patricia Cline. *The Murder of Helen Jewett.* New York: Vintage Books, 1998.

Cohen, Patricia Cline, Timothy J. Gilfoyle, and Helen Lefkowitz Horowitz. *The Flash Press: Sporting Male Weeklies in 1840s New York.* Chicago: University of Chicago Press, 2008.

Connors, Anthony J. *Went to the Devil: A Yankee Whaler in the Slave Trade.* Amherst, MA: Bright Leaf, 2019.

Cook, James W. *The Arts of Deception: Playing with Fraud in the Age of Barnum.* Cambridge, MA: Harvard University Press, 2001.

Coryell, Janet L. *Neither Heroine Nor Fool: Anna Ella Carroll of Maryland.* Kent, OH: Kent State University Press, 1990.

Cott, Nancy F. *The Bonds of Womanhood: "Woman's Sphere" in New England, 1780–1835.* New Haven, CT: Yale University Press, 1977.

Dannenbaum, Jed. *Drink and Disorder: Temperance Reform in Cincinnati from the Washingtonian Revival to the WCTU.* Urbana: University of Illinois Press, 1984.

DeFiore, Jayne Crumpler. "'COME and Bring the Ladies': Tennessee Women and the Politics of Opportunity during the Presidential Campaigns of 1840 and 1844." *Tennessee Historical Quarterly* 51 (Winter 1992): 197–212.

Dennis, Donna. *Licentious Gotham: Erotic Publishing and Its Prosecution in Nineteenth-Century New York.* Cambridge, MA: Harvard University Press, 2009.

Dublin, Thomas. *Women at Work: The Transformation of Work and Community in Lowell, Massachusetts, 1826–1860.* New York: Columbia University Press, 1979.

Dusinberre, William. *Slavemaster President: The Double Career of James Polk*. New York: Oxford University Press, 2003.
Earle, Jonathan H. *Jacksonian Antislavery and the Politics of Free Soil, 1824–1854*. Chapel Hill: University of North Carolina Press, 2004.
Ellis, Richard J. *Old Tip vs. the Sly Fox: The 1840 Election and the Making of a Partisan Nation*. Lawrence: University Press of Kansas, 2020.
Escott, Paul D. *The Worst Passions of Human Nature: White Supremacy in the Civil War North*. Charlottesville: University of Virginia Press, 2020.
Etcheson, Nicole. *The Emerging Midwest: Upland Southerners and the Political Culture of the Old Northwest*. Bloomington: Indiana University Press, 1996.
———. "'Labouring for the Freedom of This Territory': Free-State Kansas Women in the 1850s." *Kansas History* 21, no. 2 (June 1998): 68–87.
Fairhead, James. *The Captain and "the Cannibal": An Epic Story of Exploration, Kidnapping, and the Broadway Stage*. New Haven, CT: Yale University Press, 2015.
Faragher, John Mack. *Sugar Creek: Life on the Illinois Prairie*. New Haven, CT: Yale University Press, 1986.
Foner, Eric. *The Fiery Trial: Abraham Lincoln and American Slavery*. New York: W. W. Norton, 2010.
———. *Free Soil, Free Labor, Free Men: The Ideology of the Republican Party before the Civil War*. New York: Oxford University Press, 1970.
Ford, Bridget. *Bonds of Union: Religion, Race, and Politics in a Civil War Borderland*. Chapel Hill: University of North Carolina Press, 2016.
Formisano, Ronald P. *The Birth of Mass Political Parties: Michigan, 1827–1861*. Princeton, NJ: Princeton University Press, 1971.
———. "The Invention of the Ethnocultural Interpretation." *American Historical Review* 99 (April 1994): 453–77.
Francis, Richard. *Ann the Word: The Story of Ann Lee, Female Messiah, Mother of the Shakers, the Woman Clothed with the Sun*. New York: Penguin, 2000.
Gamwell, Lynn, and Nancy Tomes, *Madness in America: Cultural and Medical Perceptions of Mental Illness before 1914*. Ithaca, NY: Cornell University Press, 1995.
Gienapp, William E. *The Origins of the Republican Party, 1852–1856*. New York: Oxford University Press, 1987.
Ginzberg, Lori D. *Untidy Origins: A Story of Woman's Rights in Antebellum New York*. Chapel Hill: University of North Carolina Press, 2005.
———. *Women and the Work of Benevolence: Morality, Politics, and Class in the Nineteenth-Century United States*. New Haven, CT: Yale University Press, 1990.
Gollaher, David. *Voice for the Mad: The Life of Dorothea Dix*. New York: Free Press, 1995.
Goodman, Matthew. *The Sun and the Moon: The Remarkable True Account of Hoaxers, Showmen, Dueling Journalists, and Lunar Man-Bats in Nineteenth-Century New York*. New York: Basic Books, 2008.

Graham, Susan. "'A Warm Politition and Devotedly Attached to the Democratic Party': Catharine Read Williams, Politics, and Literature in Antebellum America." *Journal of the Early Republic* 30, no. 2 (Summer 2010): 253–78.

Grave, Kathleen de. *Swindler, Spy, Rebel: The Confidence Woman in Nineteenth-Century America.* Columbia: University of Missouri Press, 1995.

Guelzo, Allen C. *Lincoln and Douglas: The Debates That Defined America.* New York: Simon and Schuster, 2008.

Hales, Jean Gould. "'Co-Laborers in the Cause': Women in the Ante-Bellum Nativist Movement." *Civil War History* 25, no. 2 (June 1979): 119–38.

Hansen, Debra Gold. *Strained Sisterhood: Gender and Class in the Boston Female Anti-Slavery Society.* Amherst: University of Massachusetts Press, 1993.

Hardesty, Jared Ross. *Unfreedom: Slavery and Dependence in Eighteenth-Century Boston.* New York: New York University Press, 2016.

Harris, Neil. *Humbug: The Art of P. T. Barnum.* Chicago: University of Chicago Press, 1973.

Harrold, Stanley. *Border War: Fighting over Slavery before the Civil War.* Chapel Hill: University of North Carolina Press, 2010.

———. *Subversives: Antislavery Community in Washington, D.C., 1828–1865.* Baton Rouge: Louisiana State University Press, 2003.

Hedrick, Joan D. *Harriet Beecher Stowe: A Life.* New York: Oxford University Press, 1994.

Heerman, M. Scott. *The Alchemy of Slavery: Human Bondage and Emancipation in the Illinois Country, 1730–1865.* Philadelphia: University of Pennsylvania Press, 2018.

Herr, Pamela. *Jessie Benton Frémont: A Biography.* Norman: University of Oklahoma Press, 1987.

Hewitt, Nancy A. *Woman's Activism and Social Change: Rochester, New York, 1822–1872.* Ithaca, NY: Cornell University Press, 1984.

Heyrman, Christine Leigh. *Doomed Romance: Broken Hearts, Lost Souls, and Sexual Tumult in Nineteenth-Century America.* New York: Alfred A. Knopf, 2021.

History of Cincinnati and Hamilton County, Ohio: Their Past and Present. Cincinnati: S. B. Nelson, 1894.

Hoffert, Sylvia D. *When Hens Crow: The Woman's Rights Movement in Antebellum America.* Bloomington: Indiana University Press, 1995.

Hoganson, Kristin. "Garrisonian Abolitionists and the Rhetoric of Gender, 1850–1860." *American Quarterly* 45, no. 4 (December 1993): 558–95.

Holland, Brenna. "Mad Speculation and Mary Girard: Gender, Capitalism, and the Cultural Economy of Madness in the Revolutionary Atlantic." *Journal of the Early Republic* 39, no. 4 (Winter 2019): 647–76.

Horowitz, Helen Lefkowitz, ed. *Attitudes toward Sex in Antebellum America: A Brief History with Documents.* Boston: Bedford / St. Martin's, 2006.

———. *Rereading Sex: Battles over Sexual Knowledge and Suppression in Nineteenth-Century America.* New York: Alfred A. Knopf, 2002.

Horton, James Oliver, and Lois E. Horton. *In Hope of Liberty: Culture, Community and Protest among Northern Free Blacks, 1700–1860.* New York: Oxford University Press, 1997.

Horton, James Oliver, and Stacy Flaherty, "Black Leadership in Antebellum Cincinnati." In *Race and the City: Work, Community, and Protest in Cincinnati, 1820–1970,* edited by Henry Louis Taylor Jr., 70–95. Urbana: University of Illinois Press, 1993.

Huston, James L. "Slavery, Capitalism, and the Interpretations of the Antebellum United States: The Problem of Definition." *Civil War History* 65, no. 2 (June 2019): 119–56.

Jeffrey, Julie Roy. *The Great Silent Army of Abolitionism: Ordinary Women in the Antislavery Movement.* Chapel Hill: University of North Carolina Press, 1998.

Jimenez, Mary Ann. *Changing Faces of Madness: Early American Attitudes and Treatment of the Insane.* Hanover, NH: University Press of New England, 1987.

Johnson, Paul E. "The Modernization of Mayo Greenleaf Patch: Land, Family, and Marginality in New England, 1766–1818." *New England Quarterly* 55, no. 4 (December 1982): 488–516.

———. *Sam Patch, the Famous Jumper.* New York: Hill and Wang, 2003.

Juster, Susan. *Disorderly Women: Sexual Politics and Evangelicalism in Revolutionary New England.* Ithaca, NY: Cornell University Press, 1994.

Karcher, Carolyn L. *The First Woman in the Republic: A Cultural Biography of Lydia Maria Child.* Durham, NC: Duke University Press, 1994.

Katz, Wendy Jean. *Regionalism and Reform: Art and Class Formation in Antebellum Cincinnati.* Columbus: Ohio State University Press, 2002.

Kelley, Mary. *Learning to Stand and Speak: Women, Education, and Public Life in America's Republic.* Chapel Hill: University of North Carolina Press, 2006.

Kent, Holly M. *Her Voice Will Be on the Side of Right: Gender and Power in Women's Antebellum Antislavery Fiction.* Kent, OH: Kent State University Press, 2017.

———. "Wearing Black, Wearing Bows: Union Women and the Politics of Dress in the US Fashion Press, 1861–1865." *Women's History Review* 26, no. 4 (August 2017): 555–67.

Kimmel, Michael. *Manhood in America: A Cultural History.* New York: Free Press, 1996.

Lampert, Sara E. *Starring Women: Celebrity, Patriarchy, and American Theater, 1790–1850.* Urbana: University of Illinois Press, 2020.

Landis, Michael Todd. *Northern Men with Southern Loyalties: The Democratic Party and the Sectional Crisis.* Ithaca, NY: Cornell University Press, 2014.

Laurie, Bruce. *Beyond Garrison: Antislavery and Social Reform.* New York: Cambridge University Press, 2005.

Lehman, Christopher P. *Slavery in the Upper Mississippi Valley, 1787–1865: A History of Human Bondage in Illinois, Iowa, Minnesota, and Wisconsin.* Jefferson, NC: McFarland, 2011.

Levine, Lawrence W. *Highbrow/Lowbrow: The Emergence of Cultural Hierarchy in America.* Cambridge, MA: Harvard University Press, 1988.

Loudon, I. "Puerperal Insanity in the 19th Century." *Journal of the Royal Society of Medicine* 81, no. 2 (February 1988): 76–9.

Lyerly, Cynthia Lynn. "Religion, Gender, and Identity: Black Methodist Women in a Slave Society, 1770–1810." In *Discovering the Women in Slavery: Emancipating Perspectives on the American Past,* edited by Patricia Morton, 202–26. Athens: University of Georgia Press, 1996.

Lynn, Joshua A. "A Manly Doughface: James Buchanan and the Sectional Politics of Gender." *Journal of the Civil War Era* 8, no. 4 (December 2018): 591–620.

———. *Preserving the White Man's Republic: Jacksonian Democracy, Race, and the Transformation of American Conservatism.* Charlottesville: University of Virginia Press, 2019.

Maddox, Lucy. *The Parker Sisters: A Border Kidnapping.* Philadelphia: Temple University Press, 2016.

Majewski, John. "Freeing the Lavish Hand of Nature: Environment and Economy in Nineteenth-Century Hampton Roads." In *Confederate Cities: The Urban South during the Civil War Era,* edited by Andrew L. Slap and Frank Towers, 261–85. Chicago: University of Chicago Press, 2015.

Marcus, Alan I. *Plague of Strangers: Social Groups and the Origins of City Services in Cincinnati, 1819–1870.* Columbus: Ohio State University Press, 1991.

Marshall, Anne E. *Creating a Confederate Kentucky: The Lost Cause and Civil War Memory in a Border State.* Chapel Hill: University of North Carolina Press, 2010.

Mathisen, Erik. "The Second Slavery, Capitalism, and Emancipation in Civil War America." *Journal of the Civil War Era* 8 no. 4 (December 2018): 677–99.

McCurry, Stephanie. *Masters of Small Worlds: Yeoman Households, Gender Relations, and the Political Culture of the Antebellum South Carolina Low Country.* New York: Oxford University Press, 1995.

———. "The Two Faces of Republicanism: Gender and Pro-Slavery Politics in Antebellum South Carolina." *Journal of American History* 78 (March 1992): 1245–64.

McDonnell, Lawrence T. *Performing Disunion: The Coming of the Civil War in Charleston, South Carolina.* New York: Cambridge University Press, 2018.

McManus, Michael J. *Political Abolitionism in Wisconsin, 1840–1861.* Kent, OH: Kent State University Press, 1998.

McMillen, Sally G. *Lucy Stone: An Unapologetic Life.* New York: Oxford University Press, 2015.

———. *Seneca Falls and the Origins of the Women's Rights Movement.* New York: Oxford University Press, 2008.

McPherson, James M. *Battle Cry of Freedom: The Civil War Era*. New York: Oxford University Press, 1988.

Middleton, Stephen. *The Black Laws: Race and the Legal Process in Early Ohio*. Athens: Ohio University Press, 2005.

Mihm, Stephen. *A Nation of Counterfeiters: Capitalists, Con Men, and the Making of the United States*. Cambridge, MA: Harvard University Press, 2007.

Miles, Tiya. *The Dawn of Detroit: A Chronicle of Slavery and Freedom in the City on the Straits*. New York: New Press, 2017.

Moreshead, Ashley E. "'Beyond All Ambitious Motives': Missionary Memoirs and the Cultivation of Early American Evangelical Heroines." *Journal of the Early Republic* 38, no. 1 (Spring 2018): 37–60.

Morris, Christopher. "With 'the Economics-of-Slavery Culture Wars,' It's Déjà vu All Over Again." *Journal of the Civil War Era* 10, no. 4 (December 2020): 524–57.

Morris, Jr., Roy. *Lighting Out for the Territory: How Samuel Clemens Headed West and Became Mark Twain*. New York: Simon and Schuster, 2010.

Mulkern, John R. *The Know-Nothing Party in Massachusetts: The Rise and Fall of a People's Movement*. Boston: Northeastern University Press, 1990.

Mulvey, Laura. "Visual Pleasure and Narrative Cinema." *Screen* 16, no. 3 (1975): 6–18.

Neely, Mark E., Jr. "Apotheosis of a Ruffian: The Murder of Bill Pool and American Political Culture." In *A Political Nation: New Directions in Mid-Nineteenth-Century American Political History*, edited by Gary W. Gallagher and Rachel A. Sheldon, 36–63. Charlottesville: University of Virginia Press, 2012.

———. *Lincoln and the Democrats: The Politics of Opposition in the Civil War*. New York: Cambridge University Press, 2017.

Neptune, H. Reuben. "Throwin' Scholarly Shade: Eric Williams in the New Histories of Capitalism and Slavery." *Journal of the Early Republic* 39 no. 2 (Summer 2019): 299–326.

Newman, Richard S. *The Transformation of American Abolitionism: Fighting Slavery in the Early Republic*. Chapel Hill: University of North Carolina Press, 2002.

Newton, Michael. *Savage Girls and Wild Boys: A History of Feral Children*. New York: Picador, 2002.

Norton, Mary Beth. *Liberty's Daughters: The Revolutionary Experience of American Women, 1750–1800*. Boston: Little, Brown, 1980.

Oertel, Kristen Tegtmeier. *Bleeding Borders: Race, Gender, and Violence in Pre-Civil War Kansas*. Baton Rouge: Louisiana State University Press, 2009.

Olsen, Christopher J. "'Molly Pitcher' of the Mississippi Whigs: The Editorial Career of Mrs. Harriet N. Prewett." *Journal of Mississippi History* 58 (Fall 1996): 237–54.

Painter, Nell Irvin. "Representing Truth: Sojourner Truth's Knowing and Becoming Known." *Journal of American History* 81, no. 2 (September 1994): 461–92.

Parsons, Lynn Hudson. *The Birth of Modern Politics: Andrew Jackson, John Quincy Adams, and the Election of 1828*. New York: Oxford University Press, 2009.

Parker, Alison M. *Articulating Rights: Nineteenth-Century American Women on Race, Reform, and the State*. DeKalb: Northern Illinois University Press, 2010.

Parker, Alison M., and Stephanie Cole, eds. *Women and the Unstable State in Nineteenth-Century America*. College Station: Texas A&M University Press, 2000.

Penney, Sherry H., and James D. Livingston. *A Very Dangerous Woman: Martha Wright and Women's Rights*. Amherst: University of Massachusetts Press, 2004.

Phillips, Christopher. *The Rivers Ran Backward: The Civil War and the Remaking of the American Middle Border*. New York: Oxford University Press, 2016.

Pierson, Michael D. *Free Hearts and Free Homes: Gender and American Antislavery Politics*. Chapel Hill: University of North Carolina Press, 2003.

———. "'Guard the Foundation Well': Antebellum New York Democrats and the Defense of Patriarchy." *Gender and History* 7, no. 1 (April 1995): 25–40.

———. "'Prairies on Fire': The Organization of the 1856 Mass Republican Rally in Beloit, Wisconsin." *Civil War History* 48, no. 2 (June 2002): 101–22.

———. "'Slavery Cannot Be Covered Up with Broadcloth or a Bandanna': The Evolution of White Abolitionist Attacks on the 'Patriarchal Institution.'" *Journal of the Early Republic* 25, no. 3 (Fall 2005): 383–416.

Pingree, Allison. "America's 'United Siamese Brothers': Chang and Eng and Nineteenth-Century Ideologies of Democracy and Domesticity." In *Monster Theory: Reading Culture*, edited by Jeffrey Jerome Cohen, 92–114. Minneapolis: University of Minnesota Press, 1996.

Portnoy, Alisse. *Their Right to Speak: Women's Activism in the Indian and Slave Debates*. Cambridge, MA: Harvard University Press, 2005.

Powers, Ron. *Mark Twain: A Life*. New York: Free Press, 2005.

Quist, John W. *Restless Visionaries: The Social Roots of Antebellum Reform in Alabama and Michigan*. Baton Rouge: Louisiana State University Press, 1998.

Quist, John W., and Michael J. Birkner, eds. *James Buchanan and the Coming of the Civil War*. Gainesville: University Press of Florida, 2013.

Reinhardt, Mark. *Who Speaks for Margaret Garner? The True Story that Inspired Toni Morrison's Beloved*. Minneapolis: University of Minnesota Press, 2010.

Reiss, Benjamin. *The Showman and the Slave: Race, Death, and Memory in Barnum's America*. Cambridge, MA: Harvard University Press, 2001.

Robertson, Stacey M. *Hearts Beating for Liberty: Women Abolitionists in the Old Northwest*. Chapel Hill: University of North Carolina Press, 2010.

———. *Parker Pillsbury: Radical Abolitionist, Male Feminist*. Ithaca, NY: Cornell University Press, 2000.

Rockenbach, Stephen I. *War upon Our Border: Two Ohio Valley Communities Navigate the Civil War*. Charlottesville: University of Virginia Press, 2016.

Ross, Steven J. *Workers on the Edge: Work, Leisure, and Politics in Industrializing Cincinnati, 1788–1890*. New York: Columbia University Press, 1985.

Rothman, David J. *The Discovery of Asylum: Social Order and Disorder in the New Republic*. Boston: Little, Brown, 1971.

Rotundo, E. Anthony. *American Manhood: Transformations in Masculinity from the Revolution to the Modern Era*. New York: Basic Books, 1993.

———. "Learning about Manhood: Gender Ideals and the Middle-Class Family in Nineteenth-Century America." In *Manliness and Morality: Middle-Class Masculinity in Britain and America, 1800–1940*, edited by J. A. Mangan and James Walvin, 35–51. New York: St. Martin's, 1987.

Salafia, Matthew. *Slavery's Borderland: Freedom and Bondage along the Ohio River*. Philadelphia: University of Pennsylvania Press, 2013.

Salerno, Beth A. *Sister Societies: Women's Antislavery Organizations in Antebellum America*. DeKalb: Northern Illinois University Press, 2005.

Sanchez-Eppler, Karen. *Touching Liberty: Abolitionism, Feminism, and the Politics of the Body*. Berkeley: University of California Press, 1993.

Saxon, A. H. *P. T. Barnum: The Legend and the Man*. New York: Columbia University Press, 1989.

Scharnhorst, Gary. *The Life of Mark Twain: The Early Years, 1835–1871*. Columbia: University of Missouri Press, 2018.

Scull, Andrew. *Madness in Civilization: A Cultural History of Insanity from the Bible to Freud, from the Madhouse to Modern Medicine*. Princeton, NJ: Princeton University Press, 2015.

Sensbach, Jon F. *Rebecca's Revival: Creating Black Christianity in the Atlantic World*. Cambridge, MA: Harvard University Press, 2005.

Shade, William G. "Pennsylvania Politics in the Jacksonian Period: A Case Study, Northampton County, 1824–1844." *Pennsylvania History* 39, no. 3 (Summer 1972): 313–33.

Shire, Laurel Clark. *The Threshold of Manifest Destiny: Gender and National Expansion in Florida*. Philadelphia: University of Pennsylvania Press, 2016.

Silbey, Joel H. *The American Political Nation, 1838–1893*. Stanford, CA: Stanford University Press, 1991.

Simeone, James. *Democracy and Slavery in Frontier Illinois: The Bottomland Republic*. DeKalb: Northern Illinois University Press, 2000.

Smith, Adam I. P. *The Stormy Present: Conservatism and the Problem of Slavery in Northern Politics, 1846–1865*. Chapel Hill: University of North Carolina Press, 2017.

Smith-Rosenberg, Carroll. "Beauty, the Beast, and the Militant Woman: A Case Study in Sex Roles and Social Stress in Jacksonian America." *American Quarterly* 23, no. 4 (October 1971): 562–84.

Srebnick, Amy Gilman. *The Mysterious Death of Mary Rogers: Sex and Culture in Nineteenth-Century New York*. New York: Oxford University Press, 1995.

Stashower, Daniel. *The Beautiful Cigar Girl: Mary Rogers, Edgar Allen Poe, and the Invention of Murder*. New York: Dutton, 2006.

Taylor, Henry Louis, Jr., and Vicky Dula. "The Black Residential Experience and Community Formation in Antebellum Cincinnati." In *Race and the City: Work, Community, and Protest in Cincinnati, 1820–1970,* edited by Henry Louis Taylor Jr., 96–125. Urbana: University of Illinois Press, 1993.

Taylor, Nikki M. *Driven toward Madness: The Fugitive Slave Margaret Garner and Tragedy on the Ohio.* Athens: Ohio University Press, 2016.

———. *Frontiers of Freedom: Cincinnati's Black Community, 1802–1868.* Athens: Ohio University Press, 2005.

Tegtmeier, Kristen A. "The Ladies of Lawrence Are Arming! The Gendered Nature of Sectional Violence in Early Kansas." In *Antislavery Violence: Sectional, Racial, and Cultural Conflict in Antebellum America,* edited by John R. McKivigan and Stanley Harrold, 215–35. Knoxville: University of Tennessee Press, 1999.

Tetrault, Lisa. *The Myth of Seneca Falls: Memory and the Women's Suffrage Movement.* Chapel Hill: University of North Carolina Press, 2014.

Towers, Frank. *The Urban South and the Coming of the Civil War.* Baltimore: Johns Hopkins University Press, 2004.

Upton, Dell. "Inventing the Metropolis: Civilization and Urbanity in Antebellum New York." In *Art and the Empire City: New York, 1825–1861,* edited by Catherine Hoover Voorsanger and John K. Howat, 3–46. New Haven, CT: Yale University Press, 2000.

Van Broekhoven, Deborah Bingham. *The Devotion of These Women: Rhode Island in the Antislavery Network.* Amherst: University of Massachusetts Press, 2002.

———. "'Let Your Names Be Enrolled': Method and Ideology in Women's Antislavery Petitioning." In *The Abolitionist Sisterhood: Women's Political Culture in Antebellum America,* edited by Jean Fagan Yellin and John C. Van Horne, 179–99. Ithaca, NY: Cornell University Press, 1994.

Varon, Elizabeth R. *We Mean to Be Counted: White Women and Politics in Antebellum Virginia.* Chapel Hill: University of North Carolina Press, 1998.

Voss-Hubbard, Mark. *Beyond Party: Cultures of Antipartisanship in Northern Politics before the Civil War.* Baltimore: Johns Hopkins University Press, 2002.

Walters, Ronald G. *The Antislavery Appeal: American Abolitionism after 1830.* Baltimore: Johns Hopkins University Press, 1976.

———. "The Erotic South: Civilization and Sexuality in American Abolitionism." *American Quarterly* 25, no. 2 (May 1973): 177–201.

Warren, Wendy. *New England Bound: Slavery and Colonization in Early New England.* New York: Liveright, 2016.

Watts, Sarah. *Rough Rider in the White House: Theodore Roosevelt and the Politics of Desire.* Chicago: University of Chicago Press, 2003.

Weisenburger, Steven. *Modern Medea: A Family Story of Slavery and Child-Murder from the Old South.* New York: Hill and Wang, 1998.

Wellman, Judith. *The Road to Seneca Falls: Elizabeth Cady Stanton and the First Woman's Rights Convention.* Urbana: University of Illinois Press, 2004.

Wells, Jonathan Daniel. *Blind No More: African American Resistance, Free Soil Politics, and the Coming of the Civil War.* Athens: University of Georgia Press, 2021.

———. *The Kidnapping Club: Wall Street, Slavery, and Resistance on the Eve of the Civil War.* New York: Bold Type Books, 2020.

———. *Women Writers and Journalists in the Nineteenth-Century South.* New York: Cambridge University Press, 2011.

Woods, Michael E. *Arguing until Doomsday: Stephen Douglas, Jefferson Davis, and the Struggle for American Democracy.* Chapel Hill: University of North Carolina Press, 2020.

Wright, Daniel S. *The First of Causes to Our Sex: The Female Moral Reform Movement in the Antebellum Northeast, 1834–1848.* New York: Routledge, 2006.

Yanuck, Julius. "The Garner Fugitive Slave Case." *Mississippi Valley Historical Review* 40, no. 1 (June 1953): 47–66.

Yee, Shirley J. *Black Women Abolitionists: A Study in Activism, 1828–1860.* Knoxville: University of Tennessee Press, 1992.

Yellin, Jean Fagan, and John C. Van Horne, eds. *The Abolitionist Sisterhood: Women's Political Culture in Antebellum America.* Ithaca, NY: Cornell University Press, 1994.

Young, Kevin. *Bunk: The Rise of Hoaxes, Humbug, Plagiarists, Phonies, Post-Facts, and Fake News.* Minneapolis: Graywolf, 2018.

Zaeske, Susan. *Signatures of Citizenship: Petitioning, Antislavery, and Women's Political Identity.* Chapel Hill: University of North Carolina Press, 2003.

Zboray, Ronald J., and Mary Saracino Zboray. *Voices without Votes: Women and Politics in Antebellum New England.* Durham: University of New Hampshire Press, 2010.

INDEX

Note: Page numbers in *italics* refer to illustrations; those followed by "n" indicate endnotes.

abolitionists: Child, 28; gender ideology and, 68; men, critiques of, 92–93; sectionalism and, 110; Stone, 93; in Walnut Hills, 119; women's political involvement and, 100
academies, female, 114–15
advertising. *See* marketing and advertising
African Americans: in Cincinnati, 19, 95; feral African American girl episode (Cincinnati, 1856), 131–34. *See also* slavery
African Wild Woman of the Navidad, 101–5
Alabama Wild Woman, 105–7
Anderson, Erik, 124
animals and humans, boundaries between, 102–3
anthropology vs. sensationalism, 26–30, 33
arrests, 49–50
audiences, highbrow and lowbrow, 27–30
Ayers, Edward L., 96, 97
Aztec Children show, 28

Bacon's Mercantile College, 117, 156n19
Barnes, L. Diane, 96
Barnum, P. T.: Circassian Beauty exhibition, 21; Feejee Mermaid show, 100; Joice Heth show, 8, 10–11, 28, 32; hoax tradition and, 9–11; What Is It? show, 28
Beach, Moses Yale, *43*
Beach, Nancy Day, 42, *43*

benevolent organizations, 115–16
Bennett, James Gordon, 87
Blackman, George, 61, 124, 125
Bocock, Thomas, 98–99
Bond, Mrs., 82, 153n63
border communities and sectionalism, 96
Boylan, Anne, 99–100
Brooke, John L., 73
Buchanan, James, 79, 95, 109
Burgoyne, John, 47–54, 57, 62, 65–69, 91, 93, 117–18, 122, 127–28

Caddo Gazette, 13, 153n63
capture narrative: hoax tradition and, 15–16, 25–26; male mastery and, 4, 15, 19; masculine ideals and, 23–25; the promotional story, 14–19; race, whiteness, and, 19, 20–23; rape overtones in, 23; sexualization in, 18; violence against women and, 22
charitable intentions in display of people, 26–27, 32–33
charitable organizations and women's power, 115–16
Child, Lydia Maria, 28, 92
churches and women's power, 113–14
Cincinnati, OH: African Americans in, 19, 95; entertainment context in, 1–2; female academies in, 114–15; sectional differences and, 95–96; torchlight Republican parade (1856), 119–21; women's involvement in municipal government, 118
Cincinnati Columbian, 52–53, 65

Cincinnati Commercial: on capture narrative, 20; descriptions and physical appearance of Wild Woman, 30–31, 37, 128; on emotional range, 35–37; hoax doubts and, 25–26; initial story in, 3–4; on language, 35; Northcott interview, 20, 80–81; promotional story in, 11, 15–17, 26; on recovery, 35; Wild Woman first shown to editor at, 8

Cincinnati Daily Enquirer: on asylum, 90–91; on Burgoyne, 121; as Democratic, 81–82; on gossip and public opinion, 50–51; on *The Greek Slave,* 30; "I, I afraid" account, 148n20; on insanity trial, 48, 67–68; on physical appearance of Wild Woman, 31; on Walnut Hills women, 118–19, 157n34; on Walters's departure, 76; on Wild Woman in asylum, 84

Cincinnati Daily Gazette: on anti-Republican violence, 120; editorial, 12; on family of Wild Woman, 90; on insanity trial, 48, 52, 53–54, 61–62, 67; on language, 34; Northcott's ad in, 8–9; physical appearance not discussed in, 31–32; as Republican, 81, 87–88, 93; on "sadness," 38

Cincinnati Daily Times: favorable report and ad in, 11–12; on Glendale Female College, 114; on insanity trial, 52, 54–55, 67; jail report and interview, 64–66; on male feral Ohian, 131; on physical appearance of Wild Woman, 33–34; on Wild Woman as property of Northcott, 129–30

Cincinnati Female Seminary, 115

Circassians, 21

Clay, Henry, 99

clothing of the Wild Woman, 18, 41–44, 51–52

Comanche territory, 3, 16, 21–22

Cook, James, 15, 100

court case. *See* insanity trial

Cox, Hiram, 59–60, 62–63

Cox, Joseph, 52

cultural authority of women, 113, 121–22

cultural satire, 107–8

Dako, 27

Dall, Caroline Healey, 30

Dandridge, Alexander S., 55, 58–59

Dannenbaum, Jed, 118

DeFiore, Jane Crumpler, 99

Democratic Party, 79, 81–85, 94–95, 134

Dix, Dorothea, 64, 68, 144n71

Donnegan, J. T., 124

Douglas, Stephen, 83

eclectic medicine, 59

Elssler, Fanny, 32

emotion and wildness, 35–37

empowerment of women. *See* women's power and empowerment

Fairhead, James, 27–28

femininity: men's desires and projections about, 3, 18, 47, 56, 76; partisan beliefs on, 92, 120; standards of, 34; Wild Woman's return to, 68, 89

feralness: 1843 account of feral woman, 70–72; Alabama Wild Woman, 105–7; children, feral, 45; feral African American girl episode (Cincinnati, 1856), 131–34; hair and clothes as evidence of, 42; idea of feral people, 12–13; male feral Ohian (1856), 131; nationally known wild-woman stories, 13; regional patterns, 100–101; Wild Woman of the Navidad, 101–5; the Wild Woman's performance of, 33–38; wild women in American fiction, 71–75. *See also* human-zoo shows

Fillmore, Millard, 85

Ford, Bridget, 95

Foster, Hannah, 71

Frémont, Jessie Benton, 42–44, *43,* 92, 100

Fugitive Slave Law, 93, 104

Galon, Alice, 75–76

Garner, Margaret, 93

Garrisonianism, 119

gender and gender ideology: American ex-

pansionism and, 22–23; capture narrative and, 15, 19, 23–25; emotion and, 35–37; female entertainers and female bodies, 32; frontier women, gendered image of, 45–46; insanity trial and, 68; male gaze, 31; the powerless woman, 45–46; women as morally pure victims, 68, 109. *See also* masculinity; patriarchy; sex-tional politics; women's political activism; women's power and empowerment
gender fluidity, 104
Gilbert, W. S., 16
Glascock, Mr., 102
Glendale Female College, 114
The Greek Slave (Powers), 29, 29–30, 40, *41*, 45

hair of the Wild Woman, 41–44, 51–52
Hales, Jean Gould, 86
Hamilton, William, 57
Hawkes, Martha L., 115
hearing. *See* insanity trial
Hedrick, Joan, 119
Heth, Joice, 8, 10–11, 28, 32
Hicks, Rebecca Brodnax, 99
hoax tradition, 9–12, 15–16, 21, 25–26
Holland, Brenna, 70
human trafficking, 133
human-zoo shows, 2–3, 26–30, 69, 122. *See also* feralness

"Indians" (Native Americans), 20–23, 46, 59–60
insanity trial: about, 47–48; cultural aspects, 69–71; gossip story and public opinion on, 50–51; show closure and arrests, 48–49; testimony of Ann Walters, 61–66, 125; testimony of doctors, 56–61; undressing and examination by physicians, 53–56, 127; verdict, 66–69; *Wild Woman* novella and, 75–76; Wild Woman's appearance at, 51–53, 67–68; wild women in American fiction and, 72–75

Jackson, Andrew, 79
journalism, partisan. *See* political parties and gender ideologies

Kansas-Nebraska Act, 104
Kelley, Mary, 98, 114–15
Kent, Holly M., 42, 92–93
Know Nothing Party, 79–80, 85–86, 94, 117, 120, 157n22

Lampert, Sara E., 32, 126
Lane Seminary, 119
Langdon, O. M., 61, 91
language: "I, I afraid" account, 85–86, 87, 148n20; importance of, to Americans, 35; lack of, 34–35; reports of Wild Woman speaking, 34–35, 49, 64–65, 85–86, 123–24
leisure, highbrow vs. lowbrow, 27
Lincoln, Abraham, 83
Lincoln, Mary Todd, 127

Marcus, Alan I., 118
marketing and advertising: capture narrative as, 14–19; cultural satire and, 108; gender and, 32; hoax tradition and, 10–12, 25; Wild Woman of the Navidad fugitive slave ad, 104, 110
Marshall, Anne E., 95–96
masculinity: ideals of master and self-control, 23–25; male gaze, 31; male mastery, ideology of, 4, 15, 19, 23–24, 106, 130; reformist North and, 100
McHenry, John, 104
McIlhenny, John Joseph, 91
media attention, 11–12
mental health and illness: law on lunatics, 49; men and women, different reported causes for, 70; partisan beliefs on, 89; *Wild Woman* novella and, 75–76; women's sexuality and childbirth associated with, 56, 70. *See also* insanity trial
Menzies, Samuel G., 60
Mitchell, Mrs., 120

Monday, 27
Morrell, Benjamin, 8, 27–28, 32
Murphy, John A., 59

Native Americans, 20–23, 46, 59–60
Nelson, Annette, 32
A New-England Tale (Sedgwick), 72
Newman, Richard S., 100
Newton, Michael, 105, 128
Northcott, J. W. C.: blame placed on, 91; defense of displaying Wild Woman, 32–33, 88, 129; disappearance of, 52, 66, 76; education of Wild Woman and, 115; finances, 8; interview with *Cincinnati Commercial*, 20, 80–81; at jail, 64–65, 123–24; name, uncertainty about, 3; overview, 3; as owner of Wild Woman, 129–30, 133–34; plans for an eastern city, 48; as public face of the show, 8, 9; unknown age of, 13; venue changes by, 8–9; Walters testimony on, 64. *See also* capture narrative; Wild Woman of Cincinnati show; Williams, Joe
North-South politics. *See* sex-tional politics

parade by torchlight, Republican (1856), 119–21
Patch, Sam, 140n57
patriarchy: capture narrative and, 25; criticism of, 87, 93–94; Democrats and, 79, 83–84, 95; marriage, authority presumptions in, 126; model of men as masters of households, 23–24, 130; popular female entertainers and, 126; Republicans and, 87, 88, 93–94; sectionalism and, 110; Wild Woman of Alabama and, 106–7. *See also* gender and gender ideology; masculinity
Paul, Ann Eliza, 4, 82–83, 107, 124–27, 153n63
Phillips, Christopher, 95–96
phrenology, 55
political activism. *See* women's political activism
political parties and gender ideologies: the Democrats, 79, 81–85, 94–95; the Know Nothings, 79–80, 85–86, 94; partisan loyalties, 77; the Republicans, 79–80, 86–95; as sectional disagreements, 95; the Whigs, 79; the Wild Woman and the political press, 78–81. *See also* sex-tional politics
political power of women, 117–18
Porter, Isabella, 115
power and women. *See* women's power and empowerment
Powers, Hiram, 29, 29–30, 45
probate court. *See* insanity trial
puerperal mania, 59

Quist, John W., 98

race, 19–22, 101; Wild Woman of the Navidad and, 101. *See also* African Americans; Native Americans; whiteness
rape. *See* sexual assault and rape
Reilly, Mary M., 115
Reiss, Benjamin, 10
religion and women's power, 113–14
reproduction and mental health, 56, 70
Republican Party, 79–80, 86–95, 100, 117–21, 134–35
Rogers, Mary, 32, 147n13
"romance," 26
Ross, Steven J., 1, 24–25, 27
Rothman, David J., 69
Rowson, Susanna, 71
Rubin, Anne S., 96
Rush, Benjamin, 70

Salafia, Matthew, 96
Saturday Evening Post, 108
sectionalism. *See* sex-tional politics
Sedgwick, Catharine, 72
self-control ideal, 24
sensationalism vs. respectability and charity, 26–30, 33
sex-tional politics: Alabama Wild Woman and, 105–7; capitalism and, 97; Cincinnati

and sectional differences, 95–96; gender ideologies as North-South fault line, 98–100; regional media patterns, 100–101; slavery and, 96; Wild Woman of the Navidad and, 101–5

sexual assault and rape: capture narrative and, 23; by Indians, speculation of, 60; physician examinations compared to, 53–54; women's health and, 70

sexuality: capture narrative and, 18–19; women's, as destructive and disruptive, 71; women's mental health associated with, 56, 70

Seymour, Fred, 61

Shire, Laurel Clark, 22

Shreveport story, 82–83, 123–27, 153n63

slavery: abolitionism in Walnut Hills, 119; Barnum and, 10; Fugitive Slave Law, 93, 104; Garner case, 93; political parties and, 80; sectionalism and, 96; Wild Woman of the Navidad and, 103–5. *See also* abolitionists

Southern Ohio Lunatic Asylum, Dayton, 4, 68–69, 88–91, 147n8

South-North politics. *See* sex-tional politics

South Sea "Cannibal" exhibition (Morrell), 8, 27–28, 32

speaking and silence. *See* language

Stanton, Elizabeth Cady, 100

Sterrett, William, 124

Stevens, Mrs., 120

St. Martin, Alexis, 1

Stone, Lucy, 93

Stowe, Harriet Beecher, 72–75, 90, 92, 119

Sumner, Charles, 50

Taylor, Susie King, 11

temperance campaign, 118

Tourniaire, Madame, 1

trial. *See* insanity trial

Truth, Sojourner, 140n57

Twain, Mark, 16

Uncle Tom's Cabin (Stowe), 72–75, 119

Varon, Elizabeth R., 98

venues, 8

Voss-Hubbard, Mark, 86

Walnut Hills women, 48, 69, 70, 74, 117–21, 134, 157n34

Walters, Ann: about, 7; arrest of, 49; in court, 53; court verdict and donation fund for, 69; flight of, 76; in novella cover art, 39, 41; role of, 12–13; testimony of, 61–66, 125, 143n42. *See also* Wild Woman of Cincinnati show

Weekly Indiana State Sentinel, 14

Weld, Theodore, 119

Wells, Jonathan Daniel, 98, 99

Wesleyan Female College, 114

Whig Party, 79, 98

whiteness: Alabama Wild Woman and, 106; whiteness-in-danger theme, 21–22, 51; of the Wild Woman, 20–22

Wild Woman (the person): appearance at insanity trial, 51–53, 67–68; arrest of, 49; in asylum, 68–69, 88–91, 147n8; changes at end of exhibition, 37; emotional range of, 35–37; empowerment as actor, 122–27; empowerment if feral or mentally ill, 128–30; family, reported discovery of, 90; feral, mentally ill, or hoax, question of, 47–48, 122; hair and clothing of, 18, 41–44, 51–52; language, utterances, and speech, 34–35, 49, 64–65, 85–86, 123–24; in novella cover art, 41–44; physical descriptions of, 30–32, 37, 128; as the powerless woman, 45–46; as property, 129–30, 133–34; public opinion on, 50–51; recovery of, 35, 89–90, 91–92, 147n8, 149n30; residence of, 116–17; whiteness of, 20–22. *See also* insanity trial; Paul, Ann Eliza

Wild Woman of Cincinnati show: Barnum's Heth hoax, similarities with, 11; "clerk of the boat" correspondence, 14–15, 36; closure of, 48, 81; cultural satire on, 107–8;

Wild Woman of Cincinnati show (*continued*) entertainment context of, 1–2; feral performance, language, and emotional range in, 33–38; feral-woman stories and, 12–13; financial success of, 8–9; her appearance and behavior in, 30–32, 41–44; history of, 3; hoax tradition and, 9–12; as human-zoo show, 2–3; as national vs. sectional event, 97; opposition to, 48–49; popular appeal of, 20–26; the powerless woman, 45–46; sensationalism vs. charity and respectability in, 26–30, 32–33; Shreveport story on Williams and Paul hoax, 82–83, 123–27, 153n63; venues, 8; visual appeal of, 38–44. *See also* capture narrative; feralness

Wild Woman of the Navidad, 101–5

The Wild Woman; or, the Wrecked Heart (Galon), 38–44, *40, 44,* 75–76

Williams, Dr., 58, 69

Williams, Joe, 4, 82–83, 94, 107, 123–26, 153n63

women's political activism: in 1840s vs. 1850s, 98–99; hatred and violence in response to, 120; Know Nothing party and, 86, 120; Republican Party, identification with, 121; sectionalism and, 110; temperance campaign, 118; Walnut Hills women, 48, 69, 70, 74, 117–21, 134, 157n34; women's rights conventions, 116, 121

women's power and empowerment: academies and, 114–15; charitable organizations and, 115–16; churches and, 113–14; conservative thinkers and, 116–17; disempowerment of Wild Woman in trial and incarceration, 127; isolation of Wild Woman from sources of, 112–13; other feral Ohians and, 131–34; party politics and, 134–35; political power, 117–18; popular female entertainers and, 126; Walnut Hills women and, 117–21; Wild Woman as actor and, 122–27; Wild Woman as feral, traumatized, or hoax and, 122; Wild Woman feral or mentally ill and, 128–30

Wright, Marmaduke B., 55, 57–58, 69

Young, Kevin, 21, 51

Zboray, Mary Saracino, 98, 121

Zboray, Ronald, 98, 121

www.ingramcontent.com/pod-product-compliance
Lightning Source LLC
LaVergne TN
LVHW041206250326
834689LV00002BA/36